# Public Sector Leadership

Drawing its origins from the Human Relations movement of the early 20th century and from public leadership orientations emphasising human aspects, human-centred public leadership approaches leadership from a system's perspective. It explores societal institutions, organisations, and phenomena as an emergent system structure that manifests its existence through the multilateral and reciprocal interaction of its parts. Systems thinking and the need for systemic change suggest that one can only understand and improve a system by looking at how all the parts interact with each other, and how they are integrated. The systemic nature of public leadership refers to dynamic learning mechanisms as they relate to the contents of leadership development tools, which are derived mainly from the changing mode of the operating environment, from the leaders' own experience, from their own personalities, from a learning-by-doing approach to leadership development, and from the ways in which leaders learn and unlearn.

This book presents key concepts, approaches, origins, applications, and best practices to understand the evolution and nature of human-centred approach in public leadership. It introduces a new public leadership paradigm that is needed in a complex, internationally interconnected social, economic, cultural, and political environment. Based on scholarly public leadership research, in addition to the authors' professional experience as academics, managers, practitioners, and consultants, this volume offers guidance for decision-makers, public, business, and non-governmental sector leaders, managers, and practitioners on how to create a context and contents for human-centred leadership in the age of complex society and turbulent operating environment. It will be of value to researchers, academics, and students in the fields of leadership and public management.

**Petri Virtanen** is Professor of Administrative Science at the University of Vaasa, Finland, and the CEO of ITLA Children's Foundation.

**Marika Tammeaid** is Director of Development at ITLA Children's Foundation and a Solution-Focused coach, developer, and leadership trainer in Finland.

**Harri Jalonen** is Professor of Social and Health Management at the University of Vaasa, Finland.

## Routledge Studies in Leadership Research

20. **Researching Leadership-As-Practice**
    The Reappearing Act of Leadership
    *Vasilisa Takoeva*

21. **Adaptive Leadership in a Global Economy**
    Perspective for Application and Scholarship
    *Edited by Mohammed Raei and Harriette Thurber Rasmussen*

22. **Women Business Leaders**
    Identity, Resistance, and Alternative Forms of Knowledge in Saudi Arabia
    *Liela A. Jamjoom*

23. **Responsible Leadership in Corporate Governance**
    An Integrative Approach
    *Monique Cikaliuk, Ljiljana Eraković, Brad Jackson, Chris Noonan and Susan Watson*

24. **Leadership and China**
    Philosophy, Place and Practice
    *Edited by Ralph J Bathurst and Michelle Sitong Chen*

25. **Leadership and Narcissism in the Organization**
    *Mateusz Grzesiak*

26. **Public Sector Leadership**
    A Human-Centred Approach
    *Petri Virtanen, Marika Tammeaid and Harri Jalonen*

27. **Toxic Leadership**
    Research and Cases
    *Steven Walker and Daryl Watkins*

For more information about this series please visit: www.routledge.com/Routledge-Studies-in-Leadership-Research/book-series/RSLR

# Public Sector Leadership

## A Human-Centred Approach

**Petri Virtanen, Marika Tammeaid and Harri Jalonen**

Routledge
Taylor & Francis Group
NEW YORK AND LONDON

First published 2023
by Routledge
605 Third Avenue, New York, NY 10158

and by Routledge
4 Park Square, Milton Park, Abingdon, Oxon, OX14 4RN

*Routledge is an imprint of the Taylor & Francis Group, an informa business*



*Library of Congress Cataloging-in-Publication Data*
Names: Virtanen, Petri, author. | Tammeaid, Marika, author. | Jalonen, Harri, author.
Title: Public sector leadership : a human-centred approach / Petri Virtanen, Marika Tammeaid and Harri Jalonen.
Description: New York, NY : Routledge, 2023. | Series: Routledge studies in leadership research | Includes bibliographical references and index.
Identifiers: LCCN 2022026561 | ISBN 9781032071787 (hardback) | ISBN 9781032071848 (paperback) | ISBN 9781003205791 (ebook)
Subjects: LCSH: Leadership. | Public administration.
Classification: LCC HD57.7 .V57 2022 | DDC 658.4/092—dc23/eng/20220617
LC record available at https://lccn.loc.gov/2022026561

ISBN: 978-1-032-07178-7 (hbk)
ISBN: 978-1-032-07184-8 (pbk)
ISBN: 978-1-003-20579-1 (ebk)

DOI: 10.4324/9781003205791

Typeset in Bembo
by Apex CoVantage, LLC

# Contents

# Preface

William Foote Whyte, Professor of Industrial and Labour at Cornell University in the United States, published a book in 1959 with the title *Man and Organization—Three Problems in Human Relations* (Foote Whyte, 1959). In his book, Foote Whyte classified three fundamental problems that concerned industrial human relations at the time. The problems he took up in his analysis were *philosophical* (the connection between organisations and their environment), *theoretical* (the interface between theories about organisational life and organisational research), and finally *practical* (the use of research evidence to develop organisations and working life). William Foote Whyte was interested in how people behave in an organisational context and had already, a couple of years earlier, published a book on this theme, *The Organization Man* (Foote Whyte, 1956), which gained him a considerable reputation as a management guru of his time.

The research for Foote Whyte's 1956 book was sponsored by *Fortune* magazine and was grounded in field interviews with top executives in the United States. In his book, Foote Whyte concluded that emerging organisational man culture was about to foster an atmosphere in which employees chose to deny their own individuality for a sort of collectivism because they did not value individuality very highly. The organisation man culture eventually began to gradually vanish during the 1970s. Employees started to treat themselves, their colleagues, and fellow workers as individuals instead of conceiving of them as a collective. Parallel with this development, the 'company men'—corporate top executive legends and heroes—'stepped down' and the new cadre of business professional top executives inherited their positions.

The theme of this book—human-centredness as an approach integrated into public leadership—is also treated as a philosophical, theoretical, and practical question in the pages that follow. Human-centredness is inherently a philosophical construct since it discusses how human beings are treated in and by organisations. It also encompasses multiple theoretical dimensions that relate, for instance, to the functions of public authority. Furthermore, human-centredness is intuitively a very practical matter when we think about the spheres of organisational life: public organisations exist through the acts of humans and by people. Peter Drucker's (2017) seminal text and its title encapsulate elegantly this essential feature of organisations (*They're not employees, they're people*). In this regard, this book can be read as an antithesis to Frederick Taylor's scientific management, which approached human-centeredness and human values through top-down paternalistic view.

As we will go through in this book, a lot has happened in terms of human-centredness in public leadership over the past 75 years, since World War II. This evolution is however only one part of the story of this book. Our aim is to approach human-centredness by looking at what has happened in public leadership—i.e., leadership practised in public institutions and organisations during the period that covers roughly the timeframe running from the beginning of the 20th century up to the present day. Going back to Foote Whyte (1959), by the way: some 60 years ago, he was already grappling with the same ideas as us. In his book, he referred to the achievements of the Human Relations movement of the 1920s and 1930s and to the major multidisciplinary breakthroughs in gaining a comprehensive understanding of the motivational aspects of human beings, enabling him to plainly state that during the 1920s and early 1930s "researchers had discovered that man is a human being—even in industry" (Foote Whyte, 1959, p. 3). So, what then can we add to his historic insight? Shortly, we might add that this human-centred change had been ongoing since the beginning of the 20th century, but developments with respect to human-centred thinking were, as he surmised, still underway at the end of the 1950s.

The storyline of human-centredness in public leadership is, we will argue, rather long, but this does not mean that the progress of public leadership development has been a steady progression free from bouts of rapid acceleration and excruciating torpor. One issue which introduces turmoil into public leadership is the emergence of political populism, which has undoubtedly greatly affected the practice of public leadership globally in recent decades. Instabilities related to political populism have increased the pressure on top- and middle-level public officials, often compromising the traditional role of the civil service in contrast to those who are openly politically appointed as top civil service leaders (e.g., Moynihan & Roberts, 2021). Overall, this book parallels theme-wise significantly with the topical book by Bozeman and Crow (2021): their book explores public leadership that builds upon public values focused on the collective good and fundamental rights rather than profit, top-down authority, and the creation of distrust.

As echoed in this book's subtitle, we are engaged in an exploration of human-centredness in public leadership, not of public leadership *per se*. This entails that this book is about the leadership and management practices that take place in public institutions and organisations, and which consider the human dimension—we would argue—in a novel way. Instead of going into detail about the etymologies of these words, it is appropriate to note Stacey's (2010, p. 27) reference to the Greek, who have a word for leadership. *Archein* means to being, to lead, or to rule and *prattein,* to pass through.

Additionally, the corresponding Latin verbs are *agere* (to set in motion) and *gerere* (to bear). As far as the concept of the manager is concerned, it has French origins denoting one who handled horses (Stacey, 2010, p. 28).

The main argument or idea for this book is to present the key concepts, approaches, origins, applications, and best practices enabling us to best understand the evolution and nature of the human-centred approach in public leadership. The human-centred approach covers the principles and practices of a public leadership that involves the embedded and integrated human aspect. In this book, our intention is to scrutinise the special nature of the human-centred leadership model and its elementary role in providing common ground for need-triggered, trust-based, successfully led, co-created, and delivered public service. This book thus discusses the new public leadership paradigm that is increasingly required in our complex, internationally interconnected social, economic, cultural, and political environment. Drawing its origins back to the Human Relations movement of the early 20th century and from public leadership orientations emphasising human aspects, this book approaches leadership from a systems perspective. It explores societal institutions, organisations, and phenomena as an emergent system structure that manifests its existence through the multilateral and reciprocal interaction of its parts. Systems thinking and the need for systemic change suggest that one can only understand (and subsequently improve) a system by looking at how all the parts interact with each other and how they are integrated.

The systemic nature of public leadership refers to dynamic learning mechanisms as they relate to the contents of leadership development tools, which are derived mainly from the changing mode of the operating environment, from the leaders' own experience, from their own personalities, from a learning-by-doing approach to leadership development, and from the ways in which leaders learn and unlearn. Even though academic leadership scholarship derives its origins mainly from the United States—and we have extensively benefitted from this proliferating branch of research in our book—we hope that we address global public leadership challenges in our exploration acknowledging, of course, the diversity of existing administrative systems and their historical forerunners.

We heartfully thank our colleagues and friends at the University of Vaasa and Itla Children's Foundation for their comments, suggestions, and practical help. PhD student Jari Smedberg helped us in data collation for academic texts around the topic of artificial intelligence and public services. We owe special gratitude to Barry Bozeman (Arizona State University), Minna van Gerven (University of Tampere), and Darren Sinclair (University of Canberra), who kindly read the manuscript, provided constructive comments on our manuscript, and made explicit number of improvement ideas, which eventually improved the whole book.

Petri Virtanen, Marika Tammeaid, Harri Jalonen

## References

Bozeman, B., & Crow, M. M. (2021). *Public values leadership: Striving to achieve democratic ideals*. Johns Hopkins University Press. htpps://doi.org./10.1353/book.94852

Drucker, P. F. (2017). *The Peter F. Drucker reader*. Harvard Business Review Press.

Foote Whyte, W. (1956). *Organization man*. Simon & Schuster.

Foote Whyte, W. (1959). *Man and organization: Three problems in human relations in industry*. Richard D. Irwin, Inc.

Moynihan, D., & Roberts, A. (2021). Dysfunction by design: Trumpism as administrative doctrine. *Public Administration Review, 81*(1), 152–156. https://doi.org/10.1111/puar.13342

Stacey, R. D. (2010). *Complexity and organizational reality: Uncertainty and the need to rethink management after the collapse of investment capitalism*. Routledge.

# 1 Introduction

## 1.1 Why this book?

A recent report by the Centre for Public Impact blatantly criticises the status of current public services and how service- and policy-level learning occur—or do not as the case may be—in the running of public service delivery (CPI, 2021). According to the report, public service provision throughout the Western democracies shares several distinctive shortcomings lessening trustworthiness, value, quality, and impact in terms of public service delivery. The CPI-report's criticism is important in many ways, particularly from the perspective of how things have developed over time. The current problems of public service delivery have been foreseen for several decades—and importantly, these shortcomings and quality errors relate to the ways in which public services are led, managed, and delivered correlating closely with the idea of humanity that is embedded in service practices. According to the report (CPI, 2021, pp. 12–14):

> We have found that NPM (the New Public Management) is dehumanising: NPM is founded on Public Choice Theory, which believes that people are fundamentally selfish and cannot be trusted. Consequently, NPM believes that public servants must be forced to serve the public through the extrinsic motivation of reward and punishment—their performance must be "incentivised. . . . Because NPM is dehumanising, slow to learn, and fragmented, it is also massively wasteful. A public service that is managed using an NPM approach expends a huge number of resources in not helping people.

In what follows, we will explore this eloquent CPI-report's (2021) critique with a view to explaining, comprehensively, what the determinants and causes of it are, ultimately, to try to better understand how universal it is. Our lens in doing this relates to public leadership. Our aim is to view the human approach as a crucial factor in this kind of criticism. Doing so, we suggest, already helps to explain a lot about the situation. Human-centredness can be approached from an organisational point of view

DOI: 10.4324/9781003205791-1

(what happens in organisations) and from the perspective of service users (how service users and citizens are met and served in the context of accessing public services).

It is a genuine question to ask why human-centredness is such an important feature in the context of public leadership. What are the negative and positive consequences of human-centredness? What is the negative effect if human-centredness is not addressed as a vital ingredient in public leadership? Quick answer to this question is thus: without it, the legitimacy, value, and strength of leading public institutions diminish—and eventually eradicate and convert to faceless top-down bureaucracy. On the positive side, we see—if human-centredness is harnessed as the key element in public leadership—better performance in achieving societal goals in a way which strengthens democratic public values and stability in society. In this respect, Russian aggressive offensive on Ukraine (commenced in late February 2022) can be interpreted from the perspective of leadership morality—as a question of authoritative dictatorship versus human-centred leadership, which values people, democracy, and sovereignty.

Overall, this book is grounded on the idea that public leadership—and public service delivery for that matter—are slippery concepts in multiple senses. The concepts of public leadership, public and leadership, to start with, are difficult to define since their contents are value-loaded and culturally dependent. One might think, for example, that all kinds of leadership are to a certain extent public by nature because people in leadership positions are public persons regardless of the societal sector in which they are engaged. The word 'public' refers in this book to the public sector, public institutions, public organisations, and public administration—to institutional entities which are responsible for transferring public policies into action.

It should be noted that leadership means different things to different people. It is also an activity that can be conveyed through a variety of styles. In this book, leadership refers to the agency that operates in public organisations and is specifically about leading people. In practice, this definition focuses on the leaders that occupy leadership positions as delegates wielding the power vested in them. We do not however intend here to go into detail with respect to the differences between private and public sector leadership while nevertheless still acknowledging the nature and essence of leadership in the public domain. We find Morgan et al.'s (2019, pp. xv–xvi, 12–16, 46–54) comments about these differences useful when they argue that the uniqueness of public leadership is, first, grounded in legal missions, culture, history, and the values of public institutions and, second—consequently—about the shared collective societal purpose public leaders and managers have when they lead public institutions. This shared purpose is about building trust, legitimacy, and continuity related to public institutions and organisations.

Let us next turn to some common themes that induce confusion in trying to construct a comprehensive understanding of what public leadership is, both in theory and in practice. First, public leadership is often associated with public management issues and especially with paradigmatic public management approaches (which are termed public management systems in this book)—such as, for example, New Public Management (NPM) and New Public Governance (NPG)—discussed and made popular in public management textbooks over the past few decades. These approaches take a comprehensive view of how public sector institutions are orchestrated and organised for public service delivery and to fulfil their societal stability functions. Public leadership is only part of this story—which we think is a serious deficit in both NPM and NPG—making explicit what is the leadership practice in running government and other public organisations. Whereas NPM has traditionally put strong emphasis on the role of leadership, it has offered somewhat little about leadership principles, contents, and especially how human-centredness is addressed (see, e.g., Yeboah-Assiamah et al., 2019; Osborne & Gaebler, 1992). We feel the same story goes also for NPG: as a paradigm, the NPG had a lot to say about the context shift of public administration; while putting focus on governance networks, it did not touch upon public leadership's human-centredness issues that much, at the end of the day (see, e.g., Wallis & Gregory, 2009).

Second, a certain blurriness in respect of the public leadership concept is caused by the distinction between the various leadership models that have emerged across several societal sectors, leading to the perfectly reasonable question, is there anything distinctively public about public leadership at all when comparing it with leadership practice in other societal fields (e.g., in private businesses and in the non-governmental/third/voluntary sector)? Although considerable research evidence already exists concerning the similarities in leadership practice across the public and private sectors—for instance, Heres and Lasthuizen (2012) have argued that the principles of ethical leadership may be transferable across the public and private sectors—public leadership contains several distinctive features in these sectoral comparisons. Examples of these kinds of issues include the presence of politics and the role of public expenditure. Additional blurriness may also follow in making a distinction between leaders and managers, which are positions that overlap in the everyday life of organisations, as Mintzberg (2009, pp. 8–9) has noted.

Third, a possible conceptual misunderstanding comes into play when we consider the variety of existing administrative-political models globally and their evolution since the beginning of the 20th century. Echoing what Pollitt and Bouckaert (2000, pp. 25–28) have noted about the nature of public management reforms, the structure of any administrative-political system is always a three-dimensional balance between socioeconomic forces (global and national economic forces, socio-demographic changes, national policy making), political system (political ideologies, party political agendas, pressure from citizens), and the prevailing administrative system (the structure and functions of the administrative system, hierarchies, accountability mechanisms). Each of these forces help lay the ground for the practice of public leadership. Additional blurriness around public leadership practice and styles is made explicit in the textbooks and anthologies about public sector reforms, indicating how different and distinctive approaches can be adopted in analysing the reform process itself and the leadership practices within it (e.g., Van de Walle & Groeneweld, 2016; Bryer, 2021).

Fourth, the overall leadership of public institutions consists of two main groups: the political leadership and the civil service leadership. Political leadership is practised by front-line politicians—i.e., by presidents, ministers, members of the cabinet, members of the parliament, and other leading political persons put into positions of power through the mechanisms of representative democracy or through other means. Currently, the political-level leadership is, in many countries, moving in a populist direction in the hope of maximising electoral success—which, one way or another, exacerbates the functioning of traditionally neutral civil service structures through short-sighted and haphazard policy making. Strong, trustworthy, and effective civil service leadership can provide useful ballast against the dangers and excesses of political populism. Public leadership is stronger when it has a broad and institutionally shared legitimacy.

The main idea of this book then is to explore how the systemic nature of societal problems connects with the practice of public leadership, with the main argument being that there is strong connection between these entities. The systemic nature of societal problems profoundly shapes leadership orientations at all levels of governance (local, regional, national, and supranational) as well as public policy making (public policy, public administration, public organisations, and public services). Building upon the evolution of traditional public leadership theories, paradigms, and practice, the human-centred leadership approach constitutes an alternative model of leadership for the betterment of society. Human-centred leadership is based on human values (such as dignity and equity), dialogue, solving societal problems together, and seeing society as a systems-based network of phenomena and institutions.

One additional key feature in this book is the focus placed on leadership meta-skills and leadership development. As this book approaches leadership through a series of conceptual and theoretical lenses, it intends to remain a very practical guide to how leadership is practised in public institutions, in organisations, and through government reforms. In this process, the role of leadership meta-skills is important to meet the goals that public institutions have set and to highlight the scalable and generic role of public leadership within different sectors of the public administration. Meta-skills refer, for instance, to the ability to engage in critical thinking, putting learned issues in action, and learning to learn. Moreover, in so doing, we do not intend to neglect traditional approaches to the study contents of leadership—i.e., strategic leadership, process management, planning procedures—but rather, aim to underline the idea of bringing new skill sets 'to the table' to enable public institutions and organisations to work better in the context of complex societies and for the benefit and betterment of society.

Additionally, this book intends to balance the theoretical foundations of public leadership with the evolution of new understanding about the contents of human-centred leadership in the domain of public policies and public institutions (i.e., the shift towards shared leadership, self-management modes of leadership, meta-cognition), as well as government's role in society by coupling, analytically, leadership with learning, systemic change processes, and the value-generating delivery of public services (including accountability). This is to say that a considerable amount of research already exists about how to manage change processes in public administration and public services in accordance with the renowned change management theories (quite often grounding their rationale and logic with the seminal works of Kurt Lewin) and as structural institutional changes (e.g., Todnem & Macleod, 2009), but somewhat oddly all too often there is a lack of research focus on what would constitute the human dimensions and aspects as regards the implementation of these organisational changes.

In the context of this book, focusing on structural agency and top-down change models, it is also important to ask how public leadership functions in a way that takes into account the motivational aspects of employees, how to incorporate change leadership dimensions in change processes, how to re-think leadership skills requirements in implementing changes making explicit the human rationale of the changes, and especially how service users and citizens are involved in change processes as change initiators, planners, and implementing actors.

Consequently, the lack of the human side to change processes in public services underlines the idea that change processes—to be successful—should not be carried out with a top-down logic. This critique does not mean that the research tradition of managing change is on the wrong track or false, but rather that, at the very least, we can say it misses the critical point, in terms of understanding the human rationale in the context of organisational changes in public administration and public services.

Finally, this book conceives of complexity as the founding element of current and future public leadership theory and practice. Based on scholarly research about public leadership as well as our professional experience as academics, managers, practitioners, and consultants, our book hopefully offers practical guidance and a dash of wisdom to decision-makers, public, business, and non-governmental sector leaders, managers, and practitioners about how to create a context and curate content for human-centred leadership in a complex age where society constitutes a turbulent operating environment.

## 1.2 The societal and organisational context of public leadership

This book aims to explore the role of ongoing societal change, interrogating the boundaries and cross-sections between the nature of societal change and public leadership. This opening chapter explores this change—just to underline the pervasive nature of what is going on in our societies on a global scale. The world around us has changed in many ways, and this change is indisputably irreversible and circumambient. The digitalisation of services, digital platforms, accelerating technological progress, the increasing turbulence of the political climate and the rise of political populism and extremism, the proliferation of global pandemics, climate change, and how people have come to (re)consider their well-being are all examples of this change (e.g., Ansell et al., 2017). As the world has changed around public organisations and institutions, it has not left public organisations and institutions untouched.

How then does the multifaceted structure of this emerging societal arrangement connect with public leadership? Are public institutions and organisations adequately equipped to meet the challenges brought about by this complicated and complex society? Additionally, do we have enough information and know-how about the ways in which public organisations create and build their adaptivity and resilience to function as self-regulating, goal-directed systems able to cope with the demands of their operating environment? And finally, how can the practice of public leadership address these changes through the mechanisms offered by public policy instruments? Based on our earlier research (Virtanen & Tammeaid, 2020), we have concluded that in addressing societal change and increasing complexity, not only is there the issue of how ponderous public institutions and leadership can adapt to such multifaceted and multi-dimensional wicked problems; the very nature of governance mechanisms and public leadership practice must shift from a traditional hierarchical, state-centred top-down approach to one of networks, collaboration, and safety nets. This shift is an essential feature of the ongoing change in public administrations throughout the globe.

Over three decades, 'complexity' has influenced a range of work across the organisational studies literature. According to Mirvis (2006, pp. 65–66), complexity science is "a child of the late twentieth century, with roots in chaos theory, dynamical systems theory, fractal geometry, and other interdisciplinary logics". There is no scarcity of academic writings about the multifaceted nature and complexities of extant societies. Even a quick scan of the existing research literature helps us to understand that complexity thinking has assailed the bastions of the management and leadership disciplines. Complexity thinking has thus become something of a mainstream trend in management and leadership research and practice, leaving behind the self-referential academic silo it used to populate. From this perspective, Ralph Stacey remains an interesting academic figure since he has tried to combine diverse research topics while putting into context the complex nature of society itself, organisational realities, leadership in organisations, and finally organisational planning and anticipation in the age of growing uncertainty.

In fact, Stacey (2010) has opened the door to organisations in the age of complexity by presenting them as complex responsive processes in which human beings are engaged in many functional and conversational interactions and power relations. Stacey's primary question in his book is whether we should radically re-think the explanations and definitions our leaders, managers, and indeed all of us use in our ordinary organisational lives (Stacey, 2010, p. xi). In assessing public leadership in the current societal context, it is important to note that complex and complicated are not synonyms. Think, for instance, of current societal problems and the possibility to solve them through the means of public policies (e.g., Head & Alford, 2015). What is the nature (and content) of societal problems and challenges (i.e., social exclusion, obesity, climate change) and can they be addressed from the perspective of one public policy domain or from one public administration unit? Who takes responsibility for dealing with these over-arching policy dilemmas when no 'single' host organisation exists? The problem comes down to the question of how to involve conflicting interests and divergent perceptions among various actors (Head, 2022, p. 7).

Poli (2013, p. 142), then, has characterised the difference between complex and complicated elegantly. According to him,

> complicated problems originate from causes that can be individually distinguished; they can be addressed piece by piece; for each input to the system there is a proportionate output; the relevant systems can be controlled and the problems they present admit permanent solutions. On the other hand, complex problems and systems result from networks of multiple interacting causes that cannot be individually distinguished; must be addressed as entire systems, that is they cannot be addressed in a piecemeal way.

This means that the already complex political situation (in many countries) is organisationally exacerbated in the public sector by the increasingly wicked and intertwined nature of public policy issues, which demands civil service leadership and institutional renewal through the replacement of the traditional bureaucratic mindset with a more appropriate approach to public leadership.

It seems unavoidable then that the structures, divisions of labour, and service capacities of public administration will be challenged by rapid social change on a global scale and that this fundamental challenge has been exacerbated by the existence of (often ponderous) societal phenomena (such as social problems linked with e.g., social exclusion, minority issues, a variety of natural disasters and pandemics, emergent democracy related challenges, hazardous public policy making). Although it is fashionable to use and cultivate the 'change jargon', the context of public institutions and organisations has altered. An interesting question that emerges from this then is how this affects the leadership elements in the civil service and how these leadership cadres attempt to forge a level of cooperation with populist leaders while maintaining and developing the performance capability of public institutions in this febrile climate.

Moreover, it is reasonable to maintain that the current structures of public policies, institutions, and organisations are not sufficiently equipped with the essential cooperation structures that are relevant in bringing in functionable and impactful solutions to extant societal problems (from the perspective of service users) and to the performance and activities of public organisations (from the perspective of civil service staff). The reasons for this mismatch are plentiful. One possible solution is provided by Hamel and Zanini (2020, pp. 48–49), who claim that this is caused by long traditions of bureaucracy structures and a bureaucratic mindset, which has a long tail in the evolution of public institutions—and which is difficult to erase because it is familiar, systemic, self-replicating, and well defended.

## 1.3 Key concepts

We refer to certain key concepts throughout this book. These concepts relate to the rationale and arguments of this book (see Section 1.4), and they on the one hand describe the current stay of play in public leadership (for instance, the role of institutions in society) and are aspirational in nature on the other (for instance, understanding public leadership as a mechanism to strive public values). Explaining key concepts before revealing book's rationale is important because it gives the reader an idea for the starting point of the debate, rather than instantly focusing on a detailed way to adopted contextual frame.

First, public institutions, public organisations, and public administration are handled in the text partly independently and partly in a parallel manner. These concepts define the scope of society's public sphere. The concept of society's public sphere thus covers public institutions, organisations, and organisational entities that comprise public administration (e.g., Boin & Christensen, 2008; Goodin, 1996; Asaduzzaman & Virtanen, 2021).

According to Starbuck (2003, pp. 155–156), the usage of 'organisations' began in the latter half of the 19th century when people started to use 'organisation' as a general category of formally constituted medium-sized social systems. Public organisations, then, are vehicles in public policy making. They can be administrative by nature or part of public service delivery. Public organisations operate at different levels of governance—transnational, national, regional, and local depending on existing political-administrative systems. Public organisations are financed by public expenditure (i.e., taxes) and service payments and are accountable for their performance to service users and the public.

This book builds upon a public leadership definition that derives much of its origins from Van Wart (2017, pp. 26–27). It acknowledges public leadership's practical contents and gives guidance on what public leadership is within the context of public institutions and organisations. From this perspective, public leadership is a complex process consisting of various activities. It involves critical self-assessment of one's skills and capabilities and underlines the idea of skills development by approaching leadership from multiple and various contexts. Its prerequisites include skills such as fine-tuning with respect to the various leadership situations, and it is—by its very nature—anchored in goal attainment with predetermined policy and operational goals with respect to delivering outcomes that enhance societal development. We follow Van Wart's (2017) definition which builds, first, upon leadership skills and, second, on what leaders do. This kind of leadership definition is not of course exhaustive. We would like to add the following to understand how leadership is shaped. From the agency perspective, leadership is geared towards internal (organisational) activities (e.g., in organising the division of labour, teams, structures, decision-making, human resources, financial resources) and external activities (e.g., in focusing on analysing the operating environment, on cooperating with societal stakeholders, and on engaging with politicians).

In this book, the rationale for approaching public leadership from human-centred perspective encapsulates critique towards traditional approaches to public leadership that dominated the first half of the 20th century—e.g., the Great Man theory and the Trait theory (see Section 3.4.2 in this book)—that put heavy emphasis on the public leaders themselves, how they behaved, what their role in the society was, what constituted leaders' charisma, and so on. From this book's perspective, these traditional approaches were children of their time and looking at them now instantly lead at least us to recognise that these traditional approaches build upon wrong premises, especially with respect to *public* management. Putting public at the heart of public leadership constitutes the role of people, human values, and public values, which instantly put into the public leadership agenda how it enhances the idea of serving people and striving to achieve democratic ideals. Bozeman and Crow (2021, pp. 67–69) have recently defined this approach as *public values management*, which is not, interestingly, limited to cover only public administration and public services 'section' in society but reaching beyond cross-sectoral boundaries between public, private and non-governmental sectors within society, and thus also reflecting the ideals that are often linked with organisational responsibility.

Public leadership can also be constructed from additional and complementary perspectives. First, it can be judged and valued from a principles point of view. Public leadership contains values and can be made explicit through guiding principles. These principles are in essence the building of trust in public organisations. Second, it can be assessed as practice—i.e., how leaders do and what kinds of leadership mechanisms are put into practice in the carrying out of leadership tasks. We would like to describe this with the use of Argyris' (1993, 2005) note on 'theories-in-use'—i.e., what practical processes leaders develop for running their daily leadership function. Third, leadership is about using qualifications—personal, learned, unlearned—to 'succeed in being' a leader. Fourth, leading people always contains the use of authoritative power vested in leaders. Leaders have been assigned a mandate to use power—based on their leadership position, competence, and so on—the power dimension is always present in public-type institutions and organisations. Fifth, public leadership can be approached as a ratio of supply and demand. The supply side of leadership is about leaders providing their know-how and competence for the use of organisation to assist employees in achieving their performance goals for the benefit of society. Alternatively, the demand side of public leadership is about employee expectations and the management of these expectations. Sixth, public leadership is ideological, in the sense that it is always based on values—societal, organisational, collective, personal—but also on the very idea of man. The idea of man is about how leaders think about people—about people's motives, trustworthiness, loyalty, and so on. McGregor's (1960) seminal synthesis of organisational Y and X theories was an influential achievement in management theory, enabling us to better understand how people behave in organisations: According to McGregor (1960), management approaches could be roughly broken down into two 'theories'—the Theory X, which held a negative idea of employee motivations and Theory Y, which made positive assumptions about them. Approached from the X-theory, people are conceived as lazy, taking no responsibility for common goals, hence triggering a pervasive need to control the workforce, whereas the Y-theory approach values people *per se*. Seen in the light of Y-theory, work is a natural condition for people in their lives, self-guidance and trusting people to steer themselves is a prerequisite, and trusting people is a dominant condition in organisational cooperation, because people are seen as being collectively committed to the pursuit of collective actions in order to achieve common goals (Bennis & Schein, 1966; McGregor, 1960; Kleiner, 2008, pp. 36–37).

Parallel to the emergence of this human side to organisations, growing criticism emerged in the structural-functionalism school of sociology (one fundamental branch of science exploring organisations) over the disregard for human agency in the study of organisations. Homans (1973, pp. 50–51, 63–64), for example, has pointed out that when the theory of action—to give one example of a dominant sociological theory—was applied "to society, it appeared to have no actors and mighty little action". Homans further criticised that the actions of a human representing his/her personality reflect his/her actions with others—and this brings together the social system of human beings. The broader point Homans—who was one of the key figures of the Human Relations movement, as we will see in Chapter 2—suggested was that in understanding human agency, it is first necessary to understand social and organisational change.

Finally, leadership is about an exchange. This exchange can be transactional, reflecting the reciprocal engagement of leaders and employees through the mechanism of motivation, for example, via incentives. In this relationship, both 'sides' benefit because leaders produce positive organisational results while the employees' incentives are based on performance. Another form of exchange refers to transformational leadership, which is about cooperation between leaders and employees in putting strategies into action, to maximise goal attainment and to serve, in the best possible way, the public (Bass & Avolio, 1994). Summarising: leadership and managing can be approached from various perspectives to echo Mintzberg (2009, pp. 10–11)—of art (putting forward creative insights), of craft (based on experience and practical learning/unlearning), and of science (analysis based on systematic evidence from the real-world of organisations).

The roots of human-centredness in public leadership will be explored in detail in Chapter 2. The notion of human-centredness is based on human values and derives its origins from the perspective of organisation theory in the development of Taylorism and in particular the Human Relations movement at the beginning of the 20th century. In the context of this book, however, human-centred leadership ideology is not only about leading people but also relates to emphasising the role of people in organisations—as thinking, living, and emotionally conscious human beings. There is a strong belief that the adaptation of this leadership approach would improve the quality of work that takes place in public organisations, highlighting the presence of trust and self-direction. Additionally, human-centredness also refers to service users and citizens that are served by public institutions and organisations. We prefer not to call them clients or customers since it would lessen the role of citizenship in the use of public services. In a way, service users are (through their position as voters and taxpayers) more obviously owners of the services than clients who pay for them. This change of perspective triggers dramatic changes in the planning and implementation of public service delivery. For instance, in this new agenda, service providers and professionals are accountable for their actions not only bottom up within the bastions of public administration but also horizontally towards service users and citizens. Consequently, this shift brings about pervasive changes to traditional planning process in which service user participation has remained scarce or non-existent.

## 1.4 Rationale

The main rationale for this book is based on four interrelated arguments. We will discuss each, briefly, in turn next.

First, in this book, human-centredness concerns the overall constituency of public leadership—elected decision-makers, top civil servants, the middle management layers of public organisations and institutions, as well as service users. To understand the pervasive nature of human-centredness in public actions, there is a clear need to think broadly about society's public sphere. We are aware that there is the danger in conceiving this argument as a process-related issue—to create possibilities for co-design and participation—which means that our broad constituency comment needs to be clarified. If this is the case, let us argue further: the complexity of modern policy challenges demands that human-centredness is embedded in public leadership across all relevant institutions, governance levels, and policy-makers in a coordinated and consistent fashion—this demands, then, that the public leadership based on human-centredness encompasses following agencies: elected decision-makers, top civil servants, the middle management layers of public organisations and institutions, frontline service providers and workers, as well as service users. This way of thinking is congruent with the works of Dwight Waldo and others who have insisted that "nothing is more central in thinking about public administration than the nature and interrelations of politics and administration" (Waldo, 1987, p. 91).

Second, from the perspective of leadership, human-centred leadership practice in public institutions and organisations should be approached and credited—regardless of the level of leadership position—from the perspective of how public leaders lead people and not by what their effective administrative skills are. There is considerable research evidence to suggest that public leadership is most effective when it engenders 'buy-in' and support from relevant stakeholders than simply focusing on administrative efficiency and performance (e.g., Bourgon, 2007, 2017). This implies a capacity for consultation, engagement, deliberation, communication and, well, leadership, and it is these characteristics that are the focus of this book.

Third, public leadership human-centredness does not end with organisational boundaries. Human-centred thinking reaches beyond organisational boundaries and gets its vitality by considering the role and actions of public service users and citizens. Human-centredness can be approached by thinking in terms of open systems, which are not limited to single public organisations. Crossing organisational boundaries emphasises the existence of open networks that encompass the public and private spheres, and non-governmental sectors. Therefore, it is important to provide a nuanced role for public leadership in this context, one that does not rely on traditional top-down, hierarchical leadership but is able to build coalitions of broad support in such open networks and dialogue (e.g., Cullen-Lester et al., 2016; McGuire & Silvia, 2009).

Fourth, leadership meta-skills are essential in public organisations because they make administrative issues and topics easier to handle. Leadership skills are changing because of rapid societal change and because institutional and organisational structures have become increasingly complicated and complex. This new leadership impetus to take leadership to the next level while still counting on the bureaucratic strength of public organisations is still however in short supply. New horizons for public leadership are realised as public leadership meta-skills are identified, developed, and cooperatively enhanced as key leadership resources. Meta-skills are generic and transferable leadership skills and competencies that build upon learning and seeing public leadership as a cooperation forum (Virtanen & Tammeaid, 2020).

Finally, an issue that will not be specifically nor in detail covered in the upcoming chapters is to what extent public leadership focusing on human-centredness is something that is or should be 'led' by individuals or small, select group of individuals. In the context of this book, it can be both 'options' or only one of these. This means that leadership can be individual or—on the other hand—something that is shared and contributed by a collective. As a general note based on our earlier research (Virtanen & Tammeaid, 2020, pp. 87–90), however, we would like to emphasise the trend that has been taking place in both leadership theory and practice for quite some time: it concerns the shift in public leadership from traditional, conventional, and authoritative leadership model to collective self-steering by self-autonomous teams, which postulates the idea that teams have the power and responsibility over their work engagement and activities. This approach does not only bring about people-centricity to public leadership but also encapsulates the necessity of having diverse knowledge base for sorting out and handling emergent and intrinsically wicked problems that take place in the context of a complex society.

## 1.5 Plan for this book

This book progresses as follows.

After the introduction, the second chapter sets out the roots of human-centredness in public leadership. This chapter begins by analysing the role of human values in human agency, following the progression from human values to organisational development practice that has prevailed since the beginning of the 20th century. In this context, we discuss the principles of scientific management and in particular the Human Relations movement that gained importance at the beginning of this period in the United States—and later globally. It also focuses on how public institutions and organisations treat and serve their service users and citizens. This highlights the second important connection in respect of human-centredness in public leadership and deals with how service users are served. The second chapter not only makes explicit the human values in leadership (e.g., dignity, care, equity, and meaning) but also provides examples of best practices relating to the human-centred leadership approach from different levels of governance (public policy, public institution, and public service).

The third chapter outlines the contents of the human-centred approach to public leadership. Building upon humanistic traditions in leadership, this part of the book contains a short overview of public sector leadership theory and practice. From the perspective of service users and citizens, it is noteworthy here to acknowledge the accountability shift that follows from the adoption of the human-centred leadership approach—the shift from vertical to horizontal accountability models. Human-centred leadership includes a deep understanding of the organisational context, seeing leadership as a process (being relationally oriented), and based on humility as well as balancing the mental, physical, emotional, and spiritual aspects of being.

The fourth chapter frames the current societal context of public leadership pursued in public institutions and organisations. It is important to explore and understand the nature of societal problems which are often increasingly systemic. The need for a New Public Leadership rationale stems from the systemic nature of these societal problems and the themes addressed through public policies and public service delivery. Cross-organisational ways to cooperate, to build functional bridges across public institutions also covering other sectors' organisations (private businesses and non-governmental organisations), and to exercise joint cooperative sensemaking are increasingly important as government functions. The world outside public institutions and organisations has changed irrevocably; public institutions face complex societal problems and are ever more profoundly connected with media, political actors, citizens, service users, and populism than ever before. In public policy, the reductionistic approach designed to narrow definitions of societal problems and issues into 'governable pieces' not only is flawed but also makes no sense from a wider societal and sustainable development perspective. The solution to wicked societal problems cannot be solved in a single policy domain but only in collaboration with input from multiple policy sectors and cross-sectoral agencies.

The fifth chapter treats the contents of leadership meta-skills as an analytical and practical solution embedded in human-centred leadership practice. Grounded in up-to-date empirical research on Finnish government officials, leadership meta-skills are discussed in this section of the book in relation to the possibility of accelerating change, as well as creating suitable mechanisms to enhance cross-sectoral cooperation and placing the government's goals in a broader perspective. Public leadership meta-skills are transferable across governmentally and notably differ from what has been taken for granted as the core competences in leading public organisations. This chapter discusses in detail the origins and the evolution of leadership meta-skills by uncovering its four roots: socio-constructive and socio-cultural theories of knowledge creation and renewal, the co-creation view on systems changes, philosophy and the practice of reframing taken from the Solution-Focused approach, and the virtue ethics and strengths approach of positive psychology. The hindrances and support structures for harnessing meta-skills are also addressed in the frame of cross-sectoral public organising and leadership.

The sixth chapter presents a model showing how the human-centred leadership approach can be adopted in planning and in the implementation of government reforms. Learning and unlearning are important features embedded in government reforms because such reforms are not always successful. This chapter introduces new insights into attempts to alleviate the effects of government amnesia by advocating the idea of human-centred change leadership and exploring new possibilities and solutions for institutional learning at the level of government, public policy, public institutions, and public organisations. This chapter focuses, on the other hand, not on traditional public leadership orientations but rather on the leadership skills deemed relevant and necessary by leading people to better serve citizens in a human-centred way.

The seventh chapter investigates how public leadership can be developed by using systemic approaches at the level of public leaders, public organisations, and government collectives. At the individual level, it is essential to make explicit the motivation to learn and unlearn. If you do not have this motivation, then the time and money investment in leadership training are, essentially, wasted. Teaching and learning public leadership change-makers are reflected in this chapter from the point of view of training institutions and everyday leadership practice in public organisations. The six public sector leadership meta-skills presented in Chapter 5 constitute the background material for this exercise. Adopting these meta-skills is discussed particularly in the light of transformative and collaborative adult learning as enablers of human-centred leadership reform. Overall, the organisation of leadership development and training faces overwhelming challenges due to the systemic nature of societal problems—leadership challenges are, to a major extent, cooperation challenges, which means that traditional leadership training models no longer suffice. Leadership development thus increasingly becomes something that you accomplish together in dialogue with other people by solving common societal, institutional, and organisational problems.

The eighth chapter of the book draws together the main rationales of the ideas presented in the book and looks at the challenges to human-centred public leadership and the government response. The concluding chapter summarises the essence of the human-centred approach to public leadership by encapsulating leadership dynamics as a mechanism (leadership styles), context (contingency factors), and outcome (performance goals indicating leadership success). Approached from the organisational and service user perspective, this chapter discusses public leadership human-centredness as a theoretical construct, as a practice and as principles.

Each chapter includes a list of the referenced literature.

## References

Ansell, C. K., Trondal, J., & Ogard, M. (Eds.). (2017). *Governance in turbulent times.* Oxford University Press.

Argyris, C. (1993). *Knowledge for action: A guide to overcoming barriers to organizational change.* Jossey Bass.

Argyris, C. (2005). Double-loop learning in organizations: A theory of action perspective. In K. G. Smith & M. A. Hitt (Eds.), *Great minds in management: The process of theory development* (pp. 261–279). Oxford University Press.

Asaduzzaman, M., & Virtanen, P. (2021). Strong, transparent public institutions and meta-governance. In W. Leal Filho, A. M. Azul, L. Brandli, A. Lange Salvia, P. G. Özuyar, & T. Wall (Eds.), *Peace, justice and strong institutions. Encyclopedia of the UN sustainable development goals*. Springer. https://doi.org/10.1007/978-3-319-71066-2_125-1

Bass, B., & Avolio, B. (1994). *Improving organizational effectiveness through transformational leadership*. Sage.

Bennis, W. G., & Schein, E. H. (Eds.). (1966). *Essays of Douglas McGregor*. MIT Press.

Boin, A., & Christensen, T. (2008). The development of public institutions: Reconsidering the role of leadership. *Administration & Society*, *40*(3), 271–297. https://doi.org/10.1177/0095399707313700

Bourgon, J. (2007). Responsive, responsible and respected government: Towards a new public administration theory. *International Review of Administrative Sciences*, *73*(1), 7–26. https://doi.org/10.1177/0020852307075686

Bourgon, J. (2017). *The new synthesis of public administration: Fieldbook*. Dansk Psykologisk Forlag A/S.

Bozeman, B., & Crow, M. M. (2021). *Public values leadership: Striving to achieve democratic ideals*. Johns Hopkins University Press. htpps://doi.org./10.1353/book.94852

Bryer, T. A. (Ed.). (2021). *Handbook of theories of public administration and management*. Edward Elgar Publishing. https://doi.org/10.4337/9781789908251

CPI. (2021). *Human learning systems: Public service for the real world* (Multiple authors). Center for Public Impact. www.centreforpublicimpact.org/assets/documents/hls-real-world.pdf

Cullen-Lester, K. L., Woehler, M. L., & Willburn, P. (2016). Network-based leadership development: A guiding framework and resources for management educators. *Journal of Management Education*, *40*(3), 321–358. https://doi.org/10.1177/1052562915624124

Goodin, R. E. (Ed.). (1996). *The theory of institutional design*. Cambridge University Press.

Hamel, G., & Zanini, M. (2020). *Humanocracy: Creating organizations as amazing as the people inside them*. Harvard Business Review Press.

Head, B. W. (2022). *Wicked problems in public policy: Understanding and responding to complex challenges*. Palgrave Macmillan.

Head, B. W., & Alford, J. (2015). Wicked problems: Implications for public policy and management. *Administration & Society*, *47*(6), 711–739. https://doi.org/10.1177/0095399713481601

Heres, L., & Lasthuizen, K. (2012). What's the difference? Ethical leadership in public, hybrid and private sector organizations. *Journal of Change Management*, *12*(4), 441–466. https://doi.org./10.1080/14697017.2012.728768

Homans, G. C. (1973). Bringing men back in. In A. Ryan (Ed.), *The philosophy of social explanation* (pp. 50–64). Oxford University Press (Originally published in *American Sociological Review* as an article in 1964).

Kleiner, A. (2008). *The age of the heretics: A history of the radical thinkers who reinvented corporate management*. Jossey-Bass.

McGregor, D. (1960). *The human side of enterprise*. McGraw-Hill.

McGuire, M., & Silvia, C. (2009). Does leadership in networks matter? Examining the effect of leadership behaviors on managers' perceptions of network effectiveness. *Public Performance & Management Review*, *33*(1), 34–62. https://doi.org/10.2753/PMR1530-9576330102

Mintzberg, H. (2009). *Managing*. Berrett-Koehler Publishers, Inc.

Mirvis, P. H. (2006). Revolutions in OD. In J. W. Gallos (Ed.), *Organization development* (pp. 39–88). Jossey-Bass.

Morgan, D. F., Ingle, M. D., & Shinn, G. W. (2019). *New public leadership: Making a difference where we sit*. Routledge.

Osborne, D., & Gaebler, T. (1992). *Reinventing government*. Addison-Westley.

Poli, R. (2013). A note on the difference between complicated and complex social systems. *CADMUS Promoting Leadership in Thought That Leads into Action*, *2*(1), 142–147. www.cadmusjournal.org/files/pdfreprints/vol2issue1/reprint-cj-v2-i1-complex-vs-complicated-systems-rpoli.pdf

Pollitt, C., & Bouckaert, G. (2000). *Public management reform: A comparative analysis*. Oxford University Press.

Stacey, R. D. (2010). *Complexity and organizational reality: Uncertainty and the need to rethink management after the collapse of investment capitalism*. Routledge.

Starbuck, W. H. (2003). The origins of organization theory. In H. Tsoukas & C. Knudsen (Eds.), *The Oxford handbook of organization theory* (pp. 143–182). Oxford University Press.

Todnem, R., & Macleod, C. (Eds.). (2009). *Managing organizational change in public services: International issues, challenges and cases*. Routledge.

Van de Walle, S., & Groeneweld, S. (Eds.). (2016). *Theory and practice of public sector reform*. Routledge.

Van Wart, M. (2017). *Leadership in public organizations: An introduction*. Routledge.

Virtanen, P., & Tammeaid, M. (2020). *Developing public sector leadership: New rationale, practice and tools*. Springer.

Waldo, D. (1987). Politics and administration: On thinking about a complex relationship. In R. C. Chandler (Ed.), *A centennial history of the American administrative state* (pp. 89–112). Free Press.

Wallis, J., & Gregory, R. (2009). Leadership, accountability and public value: Resolving a problem in "New Governance"? *International Journal of Public Administration*, *32*(3–4), 250–273. https://doi.org/10.1080/01900690902732608

Yeboah-Assiamah, E., Asamoah, K., & Adams, S. (2019). Transdisciplinary public leadership theory: Between the extremes of "traditional public administration" and "new public management". *Journal of Public Affairs*, *19*(1), e1887. https://doi.org/10.1002/pa.1887

# 2 The roots of human-centredness in public leadership

## 2.1 Human values

A cursory glance at the existing literature on public administration and public service motivation, encompassing the notion that public action and the motivation to be employed in public sector fundamentally concern human values, especially those that are societally acknowledged and justified (e.g., Perry, 2000; Perry & Hondeghem, 2008; Perry & Wise, 1990; Maddock, 2012; Page, 2016). Building upon these discussions over public service motivations, it is easy, perhaps, to agree that it is part of the human condition to consider what is valuable in life and why should we be thankful for these offerings. Values and morality are not, however, the same thing. Morality refers to intentional human action based on values (what human beings consider as valuable things in life). Moral actions can be evaluated as good or bad, right, or wrong. Respect for people, dignity, forgiveness, and thankfulness are among those things that human beings value and respect regardless of their background. In this sense, values are lighthouses for human beings. They guide us through the storms and calm waters of everyday life, consciously or unconsciously. These human value sets are not however uniform but rather are plentiful, multifaceted, and culturally relative. Overall, human values are individually and collectively important because of their potential to guide value which entails self-direction, autonomy, and trust for success in life.

Furthermore, human values can be categorised by emphasising their content differences. The World Values Survey (2021), for instance, makes a distinction between traditional and secular-rational values on the one hand and survival and self-expression values on the other: *traditional values, for instance*, emphasise, the importance of religion, parent-child ties, and traditional family values. *Secular-rational values* extol the opposite preferences, putting less emphasis on religion, traditional family values, and authority and putting forward several alternative guidelines for people to follow. *Survival values* underline the role of economic, physical, and social security. Finally, *self-expression values*, for example, prioritise environmental protection, tolerance of others, especially gender (and minority) equality and demands for participation in decision-making in economic and political life.

DOI: 10.4324/9781003205791-2

From the perspective of the World Values Survey, it is apparent that strong cultural, geographical, and wealth correlations exist in relation to how countries across the globe score in terms of values: according to the World Values Survey, societies with high scores in secular-rational and self-expression values include the Nordic countries (Sweden, Norway, Iceland, Denmark, and Finland), Japan, the Benelux-countries, Germany, France, Switzerland, and a considerable number of English-speaking countries. Finally, values are culturally related. As the pioneering work of Hofstede (1991) suggests, culture is mental programming, about learning (not inheriting), always decisively a collective phenomenon, and people carry different levels of culture with them—consisting of transnational, regional, gender, generation, social class, and organisational levels of cultural embeddedness. This same also holds true for values.

## 2.2 Organisation as a value frame

Public leadership, especially as it relates to the delivery of public services and encountering service users and citizens, is inherently about values. Morgan et al. (2019, pp. 100–102, 107–110), for instance, specify three distinct spheres for public service ethics, avoiding 'wrong-doing', doing 'good', and finally 'personal ethics' (making explicit the value frame of public leaders). The problem with these ethics 'labels' and consequent 'rule of thumb' ('know the architectonic structure of legal authority', 'know what is prohibited', 'know the moral legacy of your country's administration structures' etc.) is that they oversimplify the essence and content of morality and ethics in public institutions. A further problem is that they address the morality aspect in a one-dimensional fashion, towards either the employees or the service users/citizens but not towards both agency groups simultaneously.

The organisational value dimension also suffers from additional oversimplifications. The first concerns how organisational values are created in the first place—are they constructed in top management workshops and made scalable top-down to all organisational compartments? Or are they value proposals made explicit by senior managers and delivered to their employees? Second, there is the concern that relates to the deployment of organisational values in everyday life practice—how they are 'lived' through the processes and put in practice. The third oversimplification deals with the nature of organisational values *per se*—how organisational values are constructed in terms of their content and how they can be made to function at all levels of any given organisation. In what follows, we will briefly discuss this third value oversimplification a little further from a moral reasoning point of view.

One fundamental problem concerning values *per se* and thus organisational values relates to what Bauman (1993) terms the distinctive feature of ethics and morality in the age of postmodernity. Although his argument was made three decades ago, it remains valid precisely because of the multifaceted and complex nature of modern society: according to Bauman (1993, pp. 11, 31–32), current moral phenomena (to be tackled with ethics) "are not regular, repetitive, monotonous, and predictable in a way that would allow them to be represented as rule guided". That means that ethical codes do not easily suffice in an organisational world where e.g., conflict situations are emergent by nature and thus not easily predicted—which means that while moral issues are constantly dealt by with human beings, they cannot be dealt with using specific ethical codes since the issues of morality tend to bypass set criteria.

To develop Bauman's reasoning over current moral phenomena further, McKeever and Ridge (2006, pp. 6–14) produced an important definition by speaking of moral principle as something which can be conceived of as value in an organisational context. Moral principles guide action—if they are suitable for action in a specific context/frame. On closer inspection, different kinds of moral principles clearly exist. First, we can think of moral principles as standards which, in McKeever's and Ridge's terminology, are as necessary truths referring also to Kant's categorical imperative. Second, there are useful directional guides for a moral agent in situations when standards do not suffice (in practice they rather seldom work). A well-functioning guide is an oversimplification ('work hard, it pays off'). Third, action-guiding standards, in essence, proper standards for most of the people, most of the time, and in most situations. Fourth, there are algorithmic decision-making procedures which are pretty, if not all, mechanical ('if X happens, do Y'). And finally, we have 'moral truth-makers', which refer to moral truths made true by generalisations.

Issues for further scrutiny are raised, for example, by presenting the following questions from the perspective of human-centredness in public organisations:

- What are moral standards and action-guiding standards in the context of public administration? This is an interesting question which has probably been discussed in all public organisations. Or at least there are certain prevailing moral standards which have gained unconscious recognition ('to protect and to serve', 'we aim at creating value for service users', 'client-centredness is our core value' etc.).
- Is there a role for moral guides in public organisations? Or should there be a role for them? This is a difficult question to tackle since there have been significant changes in organisational cultures in public administration globally, nationally, regionally, and even locally, and quite often these changes are due to different existing leadership styles and cultures.
- How can public organisations make use of algorithmic decision-making procedures and moral truth-makers? Most likely this is not possible in practice (i.e., professional and organisational quality standards can never cover all ethical decision-making sequences) but in theory it is possible.

It is essential to think about the contextual dependence of organisational moral principles and their relation to organisational culture. As organisational culture is conservative by nature, it takes time to change it. This also applies to organisational moral principles. They are embedded in organisational practice, in a good or a bad way or something in-between. From a leadership point of view, it is crucial to understand how leaders behave because this is reflected in how organisational 'citizens' behave towards others and in the context of the relationships they have with their service users. Overall, it is important to collectively construct a moral vision through participatory processes because this makes explicit the organisation's moral code and improves the explanatory depth related to moral principles. Participation increases joint commitment to the moral code and practice.

It would be naive, however, to think that everyone, all the time, rigidly follows their own personal value codes, never mind those relating to external organisational values: human errors and failures caused by the systemic nature of organisations and society do not leave public policies or public organisations untouched. In addressing organisational 'bad behaviour', one must bear in mind the fundamental distinction between morality and natural evil (e.g., McCord Adams & Adams, 1990). Morality refers to intentional human actions that can be evaluated as good or bad, right or wrong. Natural evil, then, concerns disasters, damage and accidents that are beyond human control and occur independently of human activity. The dark side of organisations is brought about when you look at and judge organisations by looking at them as forums of administrative evil—which is a concept that appeared in academic discussions in the late 1990s, introduced by Adams and Balfour in their book *Unmasking Administrative Evil* (1998, fifth edition Balfour et al., 2020) and which took its inspiration from the work of Bauman (1989), especially from his treatise on the Holocaust and from Arendt (1958, 1963) on her account on the banality of evil.

In the context of public administration and public organisations, administrative evil refers to actions by civil servants and government employees when they do what they are expected to do to fulfil their organisational roles and responsibilities without minding or recognising that they are engaging in, or contributing to, evil (Virtanen et al., 2022). Administrative evil and the complex nature of organisations—which is a feature of this book—are interconnected conceptually through the idea of emergence. Bella (2006), for instance, maintains that evil practices arise in the absence of intentionally bad or harmful decisions or actions: this means that evil simply takes place when 'ordinary people' take actions they consider proper and necessary, as Arendt (1963) has pointed out with reference especially to Nazi-leader Adolf Eichmann, who insisted that he was only following orders from his superiors when re-settling the Jewish population during the 1930s and later on by sending them to Nazi-regime concentration camps. Conceptually, the emergence of evil is based on systemic triggers and developments and arises out of complexity, typically marked by unpredictability, uncertainty, and feedback loops.

## 2.3 The origins of organisational human-centredness

Starting from the late 18th century, industrialisation began to heavily impact how human beings were viewed, namely, as workers and subsequently as the users of products made possible by factory assembly lines and, eventually, as citizens. Industrialisation affected how and where people lived their lives, how they succeeded during their life-course, and how the whole society changed. This change concerned all parts of society—not only setting up factory-type production lines but also the growth of population, urbanisation, and the prevalence of health- and well-being-related problems.

What was also new was in fact the interconnectedness and path-dependence of societal phenomena, particularly social problems. From a US perspective, Wilensky and Lebeaux (1958, pp. 49–51) reported—in a book that intended to grasp the nature of industrialisation in the United States and its aftermath in the making of the US welfare system and public service mechanism—in the late 1950s that many of the problems that underdeveloped areas in the United States faced after the World War II were the very same as those that the United States had suffered in the decades after the Civil War (1861–1865).

As noted previously, the human-centred approach to organisations and institutions is not new. Roethlisberger (1946), for instance, one of the key figures in the Human Relations movement of the 1920s and 1930s, called for more human understanding in his research about how foremen behave in industrial organisation. For Roethlisberger (1946, p. 39), this human understanding "arises from the dynamic interaction of many social forces" that are present in work environments. Roethlisberger was interested in understanding the feelings of modern foreman, surrounded by many people, and having constant interactions of many kinds.

It is important here to note that the idea of leadership itself involves leading people who are already engaged in a variety of relationships with each other. Human-centredness often features among the works of the most seminal management thinkers of the past century. Take, for instance, Mary Parker Follett (1868–1933), a social worker originally by training, political scientist and management consultant, a pioneer in leadership by profession, who was profoundly interested in the individual in the group and society. According to Moss Kanter (1995, pp. xvi, xviii), "Follett sent one principal message: relationships matter. Underpinning all her work is the importance of relationships, not just transactions, in organisations". According to Moss Kanter, Parker Follett had "a philosophy of relationships stemming from a belief in human goodness and cooperative spirit". Parker Follett was important also—from the perspective of human-centred public leadership—because of her use of the concept of integration. As integration refers to the combination of parts into a whole, for Parker Follett integration was distinctively a social process which was to be approached with new specific concepts (e.g., points of view, interests, or ways of knowing) in order, consequently, to understand the new dimension of human activity (i.e., the human integration) (Parker Follett, 1924; see also Morse, 2010, pp. 232–233).

In the context of this book, human-centredness is about understanding how people think, how they work, what motivates them, how they behave, and how they engage in cooperation with each other in the context of public institutions, administration, and organisations. In contrast to other works based on leadership research, particularly with those focusing on private corporations and businesses, this book reaches beyond these organisational boundaries and brings to the public administration 'stage', service users, and citizens, those who public administrators are there to serve. This connection underlines the role of employees as public servants in public administration while, traditionally, in the business management literature, human-centredness is generally approached from a rather narrow perspective covering only the employee side in its analysis.

This is, of course, not to say that business management books specialising in private businesses do not address the customers' and service users' roles from the point of leadership and service design. There is plenty of evidence for that, but it is nevertheless clear that the role of public administrators and service users/citizens is of fundamental importance, given the accountability function of these public organisations. In the approach adopted here, this notion of horizontal accountability, stemming from service user satisfaction and service need fulfilment, is viewed as fundamentally important because it highlights the role of public leadership and of public administration more generally in society. Public administrators are responsible for service users because they organise services for the common good and with common resources collected through taxes and service payments.

Against this background, we will next look briefly at the origins' of human-centredness and concentrate on the organisational perspective and try to address questions such as why human-centredness has been addressed, by whom, and for what purpose. As such, we begin by returning to the beginning of the 20th century. Frederick W. Taylor (1856–1915), the father of what is today known as *Scientific Management*, was an American mechanical engineer, efficiency expert and later, management consultant.

Taylor's seminal work was published in 1911 in two volumes with the title *The Principles of Scientific Management*. The publication of these papers by the Journal of Accountancy in a two-part series, May and July of 1911 (Taylor, 1911a, 1911b), laid down the foundations to scientifically scrutinise work to increase worker performance and thus organisational efficiency (Giannantonio & Hurley-Hanson, 2011). Moreover, as Hindle (2008, pp. 310–311) reminds us, Taylor's publications about principles were, at the time, the first management bestsellers and their influence spread quickly beyond the

United States: Taylor's papers were, for instance, instantly translated into French and Henri Fayol reportedly admired them, some versions of Taylor's publications also reached Russia, where Lenin himself was interested in the ideas put forward by Taylor and exhorted Russian workers to follow his ideas and scientific reasoning in understanding the nature of work and the quest for improved efficiency. The influence of Taylorism was subsequently seen in the Soviet economy's approach to industrial planning at the first half of the 20th century.

Taylor then was one of the vanguard figures in leadership during the early decades of industrialisation in the United States between 1890 and 1920. But he was not the only one. US universities also jumped in to help supply factories with new leadership competencies and managers: The Wharton School at the University of Pennsylvania was founded in 1881, Harvard Business School in 1908, and Stanford's Graduate School of Business in 1925 (Hamel & Zanini, 2020, p. 287). Kleiner (2008, pp. 8–9) notes that Taylor's influence on organisations was long-lasting, among other contemporary management thinkers of the first part of the 20th century—e.g., that of F. Donaldson Brown of the DuPont Corporation and Alfred Sloan of GM. By the mid-1950s then, practically every large company had emulated their formulas, structures, and strictures.

Judged from the present day's perspective however, the novelty and ground-breaking tone of Taylor's ideas have all but vanished. Our knowledge concerning human motivation and practice has proliferated across a variety of scientific disciplines while the command-and-control aspects of leadership so dear to Taylor have lost their grandiosity. Even though the principles of scientific management lived on, new approaches to management and its understanding of human beings began already to proliferate in the late 1910s and particularly from the 1920s onwards. According to Mirvis (2006, pp. 60–61), after World War II, the leading management thinkers finally recognised the limits of Taylorism and started to seek a new understanding and rationale for organisational human agency. On the socioeconomic front, recovery from the great depression of the early 1930s and the devastation of World War II unified the United States in a hitherto unforeseen manner with these developments subsequently being reflected in the emerging organisational scenery.

Organisational leadership was also reinvented. New approaches to leadership grasped the motivational aspects related to work in factory-type facilities and to a broadened understanding of what determinants impact better performance and thus create greater satisfaction and well-being at work. Wilensky and Lebeaux (1958, pp. 42–43) note that this was an important societal point industrialisation brought about in the United States: the US response to the human problems of industrialism "represents a constantly moving compromise between the values of security and humanitarianism . . . ., on the one hand, and individual initiative and self-reliance in the competitive order on the other".

## 2.4 The way to Hawthorne and beyond

Interest in the study of work organisations proliferated at the beginning of the 20th century. Research focused on topics that related to human motivation. The intervention logic of this research was brought about by the need to uncover the determinants for human motivation that would enable the development of working conditions such that they would create the conditions in factories to maximise efforts to improve efficiency. The groundbreaking research that took place at the Hawthorne (Chicago) Works of the Western Electric since the latter half of the 1920s changed the way in which the motivation of people was viewed as a decisive factor in enhancing productivity. The Hawthorne studies have been broadly reported already during the research process (e.g., Mayo, 1933) and repeatedly and increasingly thereafter. One interesting description of the Hawthorne research process is provided by Homans (1946), who himself was one of the progenitors of the new research methodology to understand human motivations related to work and who actively participated at the time in Hawthorne research along with other key researchers (e.g., Elton Mayo, Chester Barnard, and Fritz J. Roethlisberger). Homans (1946) did not only report how motivational aspects were research-wise approached but also made explicit new approaches in respect of how workplace innovations can be put into practice and how, for instance, change resistance can be handled and dealt with in factory-type facilities.

From a contemporary perspective, Donkin (2010, pp. 164–165) reported on the business story of Western Electric, holding the view that already during the 1910s, through Taylorism and scientific management, it was understood that the nature of the working environment (at the time, in factory-type facilities) correlated with the well-being, mood, and morale of employees in the factory workforce. Hawthorne was the industrial site of Western Electric during the 1910s and 1920s—a small industrial metropolis, where around 30,000 men and women worked on assembly lines making telephone equipment (Donkin, 2010, pp. 166–167). At the time, Hawthorne was an experiment to find out how work could be organised in a way that motivates people—while also, interestingly, assembling and bringing together contemporary and upcoming management and quality movement gurus, such as Joseph Juran (1904–2008), W. Edwards Deming (1900–1993), Elton Mayo (1880–1949), and Fritz Jules Roethlisberger (1898–1974).

As a pervasive and penetrating company idea, human-centredness in Western Electric was embedded in the company's organisational culture (e.g., Donkin, 2010, pp. 167–168, 170–171): Western Electric did not want to overlook topics and issues that related to the well-being of its workers, bearing in mind, of course, that well-being and other motivational aspects were seen as the determinants of better worker outputs (the company ran, for instance, an evening school for its workers called the Hawthorne University). From today's perspective, the Human Relations movement is most often remembered through the intellectual research capacity and achievements of Elton Mayo.

Mayo was invited by Western Electric in the mid-1920s to Hawthorne to organise further experiments in the quest to further motivate Western Electric's workers. Mayo arrived at Hawthorne not only by kind invitation but buoyed by a large grant from the Rockefeller Foundation. Australian in origin, Mayo first joined Pennsylvania's Wharton School at the beginning of the 1920s and then moved to Harvard after he had already begun work at Hawthorne. In 1926, he was nominated by Harvard Business School to be Professor of Industrial Research (Hindle, 2008, pp. 271–272). At the time, affiliated with Harvard, Mayo and his current and upcoming colleagues (e.g., Fritz J. Roethlisberger, Chester Barnard, and George C. Homans) were convinced that offering workers new responsibilities, trusting in them, offering them new work-related benefits (lunches for example) in various experiences carried out in Hawthorne, significantly increased their productivity. Until now, it remains somewhat unclear what was Mayo's role as the initiator of Hawthorne's insights about work motivation and approach to humanism—Kyle (2006), for instance, has advocated the view that Boston businessman and devoted Taylorist Henry S. Dennison preceded Mayo in considering humans not only as egoistic utilitarian 'animals' but also as humans with high-level psycho-social needs and strive for social relationships in work-related contexts.

The Harvard research group was also interested in the formal and informal organisational structures at Western Electric and how they affected the way of working. Additionally, what was also interesting here was that workers' opinions were also heard in providing channels and opportunities for feedback in a new way, giving them the opportunity to tell their superiors how they felt about various issues related to their work. These findings were based on the worker consultation programme during which roughly 20,000 employees of Western Electric were interviewed by Mayo and his colleagues' research teams. It seems evident that the Hawthorne studies represented something of a backlash against Taylorism which, by then, had seen its heyday in management thinking.

Life was not however easy for Mayo and his contemporary colleagues at the time as they tried to convince industrial tycoons of the multifaceted benefits that would follow when workers' opinions, feelings, and emotions were discussed in relation to improving the performance and productivity of the organisation or company. Scientific management principles were—at the beginning of the 1930s—still considered by some to be like commandments in tablets of stone, to use the wording of Donkin (2010, p. 173). Mayo, moreover, increasingly ran into trouble, accused of a lack of objectivity in organising the experiments such that they would support his opinions. Clearly, scepticism towards his work and ideas remained strong.

The Hawthorne studies were not completed without disagreement between the key researchers. Donkin (2010, pp. 174–175), for instance, reports on the existence of contrasting views between Mayo and his researcher colleagues Roethlisberger and William Dickson (originally a Western Electric engineer at Hawthorne): Mayo "had his own theories about management-worker relations and he used his interpretations of the Hawthorne experiments to reinforce and consolidate his preconceived views". Though, because of the experiments carried out in Hawthorne during the 1920s and early 1930s, new understandings of the importance of human relations at work had secured a foothold in the corporate bodies of the United States and which soon scaled up from Hawthorne to become a global phenomenon.

In summary, the roots of human-centredness in the overall leadership practice, approached from the organisational point of view, are multiple and derive their origins from multiple thematic sources stretching back to the early 20th century. First, work-related human agency has been addressed in management thinking since the heyday of scientific management, as originated by F.W. Taylor and his contemporaries It then proliferated after the Human Relations movement's influential research findings at Western Electric in the 1920s and 1930s. The Human Relations movement´s importance especially during the 1920s and 1930s was however fundamental—under the influence of E. Mayo and F.J. Roethlisberger—which meant a change in human-centredness focus related to organisations (and factories in particular): the Human Relations movement brought human motivation to the centre of our understanding of organisational efficiency and performance. Second, human-centredness has taken different forms in the evolution of general management theories, paradigms, and practices over the past century. Human-centredness is not a specific domain nor an approach in any of the prevailing schools of thought that have addressed the role of leadership in organisations. Public sector institutions did not remain isolated bastions in the proliferation of human-centred management thinking based on a better understanding of human motivation. As wisdom increased around the role of motivation in improving organisational performance, public institutions and organisations started, after World War II, to rapidly adopt this new approach. Organisational human-centredness also gained considerable impetus from the evolution of Organisation Development (OD), from late 1940s onwards and under the influence of the National Training Laboratories (NTL) in the United States and the Tavistock Institute in the United Kingdom. Based on and influenced by industrial and organisational psychology, organisational behaviour, human agency, and teambuilding, OD laid new ground for understanding various approaches to organisational change including, for example, the T-group and the total systems approach to change (e.g., Warner Burke, 2006). From the human-centred perspective, action research embedded in OD had a commitment to democratic change, while this democratic ethos, as a utopian aspiration underlined the possibility for people to work collaboratively and to define collectively the challenges they encountered (e.g., Benne, 1964; see also Mirvis, 2006, pp. 57–58, 77–78). Third, the domain of human-centredness was enlarged to cover organisations' employees beyond organisational boundaries quite late in the day. The scope of human-centredness in organisational studies was broadened further in the domain of public administration since the 1980s and 1990s with a new public service ideology that emphasised the idea of shifting the focus from the carrying out of administrative tasks and duties to serving the service users, citizens, service delivery mechanisms, service quality and design (and re-design), quality protocols, improved accountability, and customer satisfaction. We will explore this development phase in the next section of this book.

## 2.5 From the service user perspective to human-centred public service leadership

Human-centredness in public leadership emerged also from other perspectives in the context of public administration. This broad perspective relates to citizens and to the ways in which service users were treated and served by public service professionals. This section of the book approaches this other dimension of human-centredness beyond or outside the organisational perspective. This dimension relates to how service users are treated and served through the various public service delivery mechanisms. Our approach considers three distinctive, though overlapping, themes in public service delivery—first, public service based on service-dominant logic, the importance of which has increasingly grown in public service delivery over the past decade. Second, public service quality initiatives implemented in most of the OECD countries since the 1980s. And thirdly, public service design ideology based on service user involvement through co-creation and co-production practice.

### *2.5.1 Service science and service-dominant logic in public service delivery*

Public services are distinctive elements of the public sector. They are the contact point where public intentions breach the realm of the private citizens as public service users. Therefore, it is essential to look at how service science approaches have developed since the late 20th century (e.g., Normann, 1995). Since the 1990s, the dominant public management theories—notably the New Public Management (NPM) and the New Public Governance (NPG)—have emphasised the quest for savings in public expenditure, better productivity, improved quality, more efficient government operations, the introduction of market orientation especially in service delivery, and better implementation of public policies. This has called for novel service integration approaches and more solid mechanisms in relation to public service production and implementation. This development has taken place in the context of service science, service management, and more broadly from the perspective of service-dominant logic.

Originally, based on contributions by Vargo and Lusch (2004; see also Lusch & Vargo, 2014), service-dominant logic approaches value creation from a holistic point of view, illustrating how actors and resources are integrated through joint service systems agendas and mechanisms. This reframing of public service delivery as a joint value-creation process through the cooperation of service providers, cooperating bodies, and service users not only improves the effectiveness of and goal attainment of publicly initiated public services but also brings about a fundamental shift as traditional (and mechanistic) public service implementation is transformed into a value-creating entity, which promotes a rethinking of the goods versus services perspective (e.g., Trischler & Scott, 2016). Over the past decade (i.e., since the beginning of the 2010s) or so, as reported for instance by Westrup (2018), there have been numerous examples of the acceptance of service-dominant logic in the field of public service delivery research (e.g., Osborne, 2018; Osborne et al., 2014; Petrescu, 2019; Hodgkinson et al., 2017). The essential point of the service-dominant logic is, from the human-centredness point, that it aims at value creation for the service users and more specifically with service users, which means that service users are interconnected to service delivery through a variety of co-creation mechanisms and types. Overall, during the 2010s, several seminal contributions on service-dominant-logic adaptations in public services have been published which have also critically assessed the problems of that adaptation process (e.g., Osborne, 2010, 2018, 2020).

### *2.5.2 Quality assessment and development in public services*

Public service definitions are numerous because public service quality can be addressed from so many perspectives, for multiple reasons and from multiple rationales. Øvretveit (2005, p. 539), for instance, defines the service user of public services as "a person receiving benefit from the service. . . . The person may make use of a direct service (e.g., library, social welfare) or be an indirect user (e.g., public health education)". Further, Øvretveit (ibid.) approaches public service quality from both the service user and organisational perspectives: public service quality is about "meeting the need of the most in need of the service, within higher level requirements, available resources and the lowest cost".

Industrial quality programmes started on both sides of the Atlantic Ocean long before World War II and particularly from the late 1940s onwards. World War II did however represent a considerable turning point in terms of industrial production performance (*War Factories*), quality management as well as project, programme, and process management practices, and this was also reflected in the newly emerging post-war public sector and welfare organisations. The conventional assessment was that the result of World War ll was, ultimately, dependent on the number of tanks, artillery, ships, and aircraft deployed. For that reason, Winston Churchill and his allies placed a lot of their political capital on the Lend-Lease programme, which facilitated the supply of armaments from the United States in the early years of the war (Simms & Laderman, 2021). The development of nuclear weapons in the Manhattan project brought about not only the end of the bloody war but also new ways to embed quality controls into planning and the assembly line. Ironically, many of the most prominent war-time quality engineers became world-famous in the world of quality management after the war. Concerning the service industry, attention to commercial (service business) quality is relatively recent, dating back to the latter half of the 20th century. The involvement of state, government, and public authorities in public administration and public service delivery has—in principle—had a long history, dating basically back centuries. This long history has not necessarily, however, meant that public authorities have had serious concerns about how citizens have been served through the collected taxes and collated 'service payments'. The main concern through the centuries thus related to the use of public expenditure and to the need to make public administrations and services as efficient as possible. The service quality approach—e.g., through Citizen's Charters that proliferated first in the UK from the beginning of the 1990s and then throughout most of the OECD countries—was adopted in public services globally and extensively in the developed countries from the late 1980s onwards. Noteworthy here is the rationale that emerged in the public service quality movement three decades ago, precipitating a fundamental shift between the traditional view of public service, which had addressed service as a theory and practice from the perspective of professional autonomy and agency (i.e., how different professions in public administration and welfare professions in the context of the welfare state carried out their professional tasks). This traditional quality practice was based on professional education/training and the regulation of professional activities by law. The rationale behind the shift that took place in the late 1980s reflected increasing concern for public service quality: this shift was brought about by concerns that followed on from the emergence of consumeristic service ideology, the use of a variety of quality tools and protocols, and the freedom for service users to choose the type of services they required (See, e.g., Øvretveit, 2005, pp. 540–541).

As an overall development trend, it should be noted that the economic (because of the growth of public expenditure), social (service user satisfaction for services), and environmental (growing concerns for hazardous environmental public policies including shocks related to quality-related disasters, e.g., the Chernobyl nuclear power plant accident in 1986 in Ukraine) imperatives for quality improvement increased considerably during the 1980s and 1990s (Beckford, 1998, pp. 5–6). This 'reality check awakening' resulted in growing concern over the poor quality of public services which, in turn, led to numerous modernisation projects, programmes, and initiatives in transnational, national-, regional-, and local-level governance designed to address how public service delivery was organised and managed and how service shortcomings could be improved. For, instance the European Commission launched several quality initiatives and protocols for EU Member States during the latter half of the 1990s.

From the perspective of the 2020s, approaches to public service quality have undoubtedly matured since the shift from profession-based quality to a more service-user-focused understanding of public service quality and value-creation through service ecosystems for the benefit of the service users and society (e.g., Cluley et al., 2021; Petrescu, 2019; Schmidt, 2008). This process has been aided by the extensive use of customer or user approaches, legal approaches and regulations, organisational quality assessments, a variety of quality accreditations, standards-based approaches to quality management and the deployment of comprehensive organisational development (OD) initiatives, projects, programmes, and protocols. Although the focus on service users has gained ground in the domain of public services in recent decades, numerous sources of critique have remained in response to the adoption of these public service quality ideologies. One might, for instance, take issue with ideas promoting the application of quality tools and design in public services when these applied tools originate from the manufacturing industry. Moreover, an important question here remains how to include paternalistic approaches in service quality (deciding for and not with the service user—e.g., child custody issues, or committing a person to involuntary medical treatment). Consequently, it is worth problematising how controversial it is to provide good service when the outcomes of public services are difficult to measure or if there are no public resources to be allocated to alleviate the effects, for example, of social exclusion or child maltreatment. And finally, as we know that societal problems are wicked by nature, because of their systemic emergence (Head & Alford, 2015)—how it is possible to get professionals to work together in cooperation to improve service quality and needs-based goal attainment?

### *2.5.3 Co-creation for creating value*

According to the seminal analysis of Payne et al. (2008), co-creation consists of three interrelated phases through which service users are engaged to take part in service design: the encounter phase (inviting citizens, consumers, and service users to take part in co-creation and setting the agenda for joint collaborative working); the joint value-creation phase, in which people from various agencies work together according to a set of agreed principles); the supplier value-creation phase, during which the supplier/provider of services organises its service delivery and further development agendas and portfolios within the service-system in the agreed manner (see, also Magno & Cassia, 2015). The process phase construction presented by Payne et al. works well across different business sectors, as well as in the non-governmental and public sectors. Seen from the perspective of public services, there are certain drivers that make the adaptation of Payne et al.'s phase structure relevant. According to Osborne (2010) and Virtanen et al. (2018), these mechanisms include the nature of public policies (the emergence of austerity measures) and societal problems, the trend towards service personalisation, increasing pressures for service integration (deriving their origins from efficiency/effectiveness rationales, the expansion of public debate for the greater horizontal accountability of public actions, and societal pressure for more participatory public policies and public service delivery).

The use of public services comes with different service user roles. You can be regarded as a customer who uses services and perhaps also pays for this service. At the beginning of the 2010s, the notion of public service users gained increased attention because this meant that service users were now entitled to take part and/or participate in service production, in the designing and re-designing of public services and service delivery mechanisms. Fledderus et al. (2015, pp. 146–147) eviscerate the reasons behind service user engagement promotion in public service sector: first, this relates to the quality of services which are difficult to assess, given the often intangible nature of those services (think, for instance, of social work consultancy services between social worker and client); second, because services cannot be produced as homogenously as physical products can; thirdly, due to the fact public services are difficult to separate into production and consumption elements because this process occurs through the interaction between service provider staff and service users.

Co-creation ideology entails that citizens and service users are more than just the co-creators of services. According to Voorberg et al. (2017, pp. 178–179), in co-creation initiatives citizens are regarded as partners "who have specific resources and competences which are valuable for (re)designing public service delivery". Voorberg et al. further advocate the view—which is important from the human-centred leadership point view—that co-creation is important because it embeds the idea of mutual learning for the benefit of society. This agenda postulates that mutual learning is a social process which is based on mutual trust and effort. This mutual process of learning is also connected to the innovativeness of public services. Some scholars (e.g., Bason, 2010) hold the view that this is a democratic and legitimate way in which to improve the effectiveness of public services and a prerequisite for sustainable innovations.

Taken together, then, the strengthened service dimension in public service delivery has come from different sources and through multiple mechanisms. This development has changed the service ideology of public service as well as dramatically altering how citizens and services users are treated. Service co-creation brings about not only the idea of working together as civil service representatives for the people but also that of contributing to public service re-design and re-calibration with the people. Moreover, ongoing change in the media and communication environment has accelerated this process—the Internet, platform economy, and social media have emerged as powerful societal forces in shaping the role of public service users. Service dominant logic and the public service quality initiatives and mechanisms that enhance participation in service development are both prerequisites for service re-design and mechanisms promoting human-centredness in the everyday lives of those in the public authorities providing services to those in need.

## 2.6 Synthesis—human-centred public leadership in the service of society

The human-centred approach to public leadership is based on human values—on things that people see as valuable societal principles. In practice, human-centredness comes together from the understanding that combines organisational (employee) and service user perspectives to reframe the context for public leadership. Bringing together these two dimensions entails thinking about the connection between these 'variants' of the human approach.

One answer to this question is provided by the notion of service mentality, which is an essential ingredient in what has, since the 1970s, been termed servant leadership. This approach to leadership—originally referenced and conceptually codified in the writings of Robert K. Greenleaf (e.g., Greenleaf, 1977), who claimed that leadership is based on wisdom and service mentality. For him, wisdom can be achieved through the intentional process in which the leader deploys the use of personal experience, reflects on their personal experiences, creates possibilities for insights and learning, and makes changes actionable (Frick, 2018, pp. 13–19). Additionally, servant leadership specifically addresses the idea of service although placing emphasis on organisational citizens—i.e., employees. Irving (2018, p. 27) has summarised this service-bound mindset in servant leadership as follows:

> Servant leaders lead out of the conviction that service of people is not merely a means to a great end, but is inherently valuable in and of itself. . . . The leader´s capacity to transcend self-interest in service of others is vital for servant leadership practice.

Finally, the combination of the dimensions of human-centredness in public leadership builds upon research evidence which makes explicit the connection between these two entities—the organisational and service user perspectives. What we know from previous research is that strengthening of public service staff motivation, by nurturing stronger ties connecting organisational values, employee values, and goals and through the practice of tailored human resource management approaches, is a reliable and efficient mechanism to enhance employee performance and consequently organisational goal attainment (e.g., Christensen et al., 2017; De Simone et al., 2016). From the service user perspective, growing amount of research evidence suggests that engaging service users in service development and service design increases service users' positive views of public services, legitimating them and thus improving public accountability, trustworthiness, and the overall position of the service user to be accepted and recognised as a value creator in the service systems framework (Trischler & Scott, 2016; Virtanen et al., 2018).

## References


Adams, G. B., & Balfour, D. L. (1998). *Unmasking administrative evil*. Sage.

Arendt, H. (1958). *The human condition*. University of Chicago Press.

Arendt, H. (1963). *Eichmann in Jerusalem: A report on the banality of evil*. Viking Press.

Balfour, D. L., Adams, G. B., & Nickels, A. E. (2020). *Unmasking administrative evil* (5th ed.). Routledge.

Bason, C. (2010). *Leading public sector innovation: Co-creating for a better society*. Policy Press.

Bauman, Z. (1989). *Modernity and the Holocaust*. Chicago University Press.

Bauman, Z. (1993). *Postmodern ethics*. Blackwell.

Beckford, J. (1998). *Quality: A critical introduction*. Routledge.

Bella, D. A. (2006). Emergence and evil. *Emergence: Complexity & Organization, 8*(2), 102–115. https://doi/10.emerg/10.17357.8beaf7902c1f6b13392ceba575e69af0

Benne, K. (1964). History of the t-group in the laboratory setting. In L. Bradford, J. Gibb, & K. Benne (Eds.), *T-group theory and laboratory method: Innovation in re-education* (pp. 80–135). Wiley.

Christensen, R. K., Paarlberg, L., & Perry, J. L. (2017). Public service motivation research: Lessons for practice. *Public Administration Review*, 77(4), 529–542. https://doi.org/10.1111/puar.12796

Cluley, V., Parker, S., & Radnor, Z. (2021). New development: Expanding public service value to include dis/value. *Public Money & Management, 41*(8), 656–659. https://doi.org/10.1080/09540962.2020.1737392

De Simone, S., Cicotto, G., Pinna, R., & Giustiniano, L. (2016). Engaging public servants. *Management Decision, 54*(7), 1569–1594. https://doi.org/10.1108/MD-02-2016-0072

Donkin, R. (2010). *The history of work*. Palgrave Macmillan.

Fledderus, J., Brandsen, T., & Honingh, M. (2015). User co-production of public service delivery: An uncertainty approach. *Public Policy and Administration, 30*(2), 145–164. https://doi.org/10.1177/0952076715572362

Frick, D. M. (2018). Wisdom as a pillar for servant leadership. In D. van Dierendonck & K. Patterson (Eds.), *Practising servant leadership: Developments in implementation* (pp. 11–24). Palgrave Macmillan.

Giannantonio, C. M., & Hurley-Hanson, A. E. (2011). Frederick Winslow Taylor: Reflections on the relevance of the principles of scientific management 100 years later. *Journal of Business and Management, 17*(1), 7–10. https://digitalcommons.chapman.edu/cgi/viewcontent.cgi?article=1037&context=business_articles

Greenleaf, R. K. (1977). *Servant leadership: A journey into the nature of legitimate power and greatness*. Paulist Press.

Hamel, G., & Zanini, M. (2020). *Humanocracy: Creating organizations as amazing as the people inside them*. Harvard Business Review Press.

Head, B. W., & Alford, J. (2015). Wicked problems: Implications for public policy and management. *Administration & Society, 47*(6), 711–739. https://doi.org/10.1177/0095399713481601

Hindle, T. (2008). *Guide to management ideas and gurus*. Profile Books.

Hodgkinson, I., Hannibal, C., Keating, B., Buxton, R., & Bateman, N. (2017). Toward a public service management: Past, present, and future directions. *Journal of Service Management, 28*(5), 998–1023. https://doi.org/10.1108/JOSM-01-2017-0020

Hofstede, G. (1991). *Cultures and organisations: Software of the mind. Intercultural cooperation and its importance for survival*. McGraw-Hill.

Homans, G. C. (1946). The Western electric researchers. In S. Dean Hoslett (Ed.), *Human factors in management* (pp. 210–241). Harper & Brothers.

Irving, J. A. (2018). Leader purposefulness and servant leadership. In D. van Dierendonck & K. Patterson (Eds.), *Practising servant leadership: Developments in implementation* (pp. 25–42). Palgrave Macmillan.

Kleiner, A. (2008). *The age of the heretics: A history of the radical thinkers who reinvented corporate management*. Jossey-Bass.

Kyle, B. (2006). Henry S. Dennison, Elton Mayo, and human relations historiography. *Management & Organizational History, 1*(2), 177–199. https://doi.org/10.1177/1744935906064095

Lusch, R. F., & Vargo, S. L. (2014). *Service-dominant logic: Premises, perspectives, possibilities*. Cambridge University Press.

Maddock, S. (2012). Public leadership: Motivated by values not bonuses. *The International Journal of Leadership in Public Services, 8*(3), 112–120. https://doi.org/10.1108/17479881211279986

Magno, F., & Cassia, F. (2015). Public administrators' engagement in services co-creation: Factors that foster and hinder organisational learning about citizens. *Total Quality Management & Business Excellence, 26*(11–12), 1161–1172.

Mayo, E. (1933). *The human problems of an industrial civilization*. The Macmillan Company.

McCord Adams, M., & Adams, R. (Eds.). (1990). *The problem of evil*. Oxford University Press.

McKeever, S., & Ridge, M. (2006). *Principled ethics: Generalism as a regulative rule*. Clarendon Press.

Mirvis, P. H. (2006). Revolutions in OD. In J. W. Gallos (Ed.), *Organization development* (pp. 39–88). Jossey-Bass.

Morgan, D. F., Ingle, M. D., & Shinn, G. W. (2019). *New public leadership: Making a difference where we sit*. Routledge.

Morse, R. (2010). Integrative public leadership: Catalyzing collaboration to create public value. *Leadership Quarterly, 21*(2), 231–245. https://doi.org/10.1016/j.leaqua.2010.01.004

Moss Kanter, R. (1995). Preface. In P. Graham (Ed.), *Mary Parker Follett: Prophet of management* (pp. xiii–xix). Harvard Business School Press.

Normann, R. (1995). *Service management: Strategy and leadership in service business*. Wiley.

Osborne, S. P. (2010). *The new public governance? Emerging perspectives on the theory and practice of public governance*. Routledge.

Osborne, S. P. (2018). From public service-dominant logic to public service logic: Are public service organizations capable of co-production and value co-creation? *Public Management Review, 20*(2), 225–231. https://doi.org/10.1080/14719037.2017.1350461

Osborne, S. P. (2020). *Public service logic: Creating value for public service users, citizens, and society through public service delivery*. Routledge.

Osborne, S. P., Radnor, Z., Kinder, T., & Vidal, I. (2014). Sustainable public service organisations: A public service-dominant approach. *Society and Economy, 36*(3), 313–338. https://doi.org/10.1556/SocEc.36.2014.3.1

Øvretveit, J. (2005). Public service quality improvement. In E. Ferlie, L. Lynn, & C. Pollitt (Eds.), *The Oxford handbook of public management* (pp. 537–562). Oxford University Press.

Page, M. (2016). Public leadership. *International Journal of Public Leadership, 12*(2), 112–128. https://doi.org/10.1108/IJPL-12-2015-0030

Parker Follett, M. (1924). *Creative experience*. Longmans, Green.

Payne, A. F., Storbacka, K., & Frow, P. (2008). Managing the co-creation of value. *Journal of the Academy of Marketing Science, 36*(1), 83–96. https://doi.org/10.1007/s11747-007-0070-0

Perry, J. L. (2000). Bringing society in: Toward a theory of public service motivation. *Journal of Public Administration Research and Theory, 10*(2), 471–488. https://doi.org/10.1093/oxfordjournals.jpart.a024277

Perry, J. L., & Hondeghem, A. (2008). *Motivation in public management: The call of public service*. Oxford University Press.

Perry, J. L., & Wise, L. R. (1990). The motivational bases of public service. *Public Administration Review, 50*(3), 367–373. https://doi.org/10.2307/976618

Petrescu, M. (2019). From marketing to public value: Towards a theory of public service ecosystems. *Public Management Review, 21*(11), 1733–1752. https://doi.org/10.1080/14719037.2019.1619811

Roethlisberger, F. J. (1946). The foreman: Master and victim of double talk. In S. Dean Hoslett (Ed.), *Human factors in management* (pp. 39–59). Harper & Brothers.

Schmidt, V. A. (2008). Discursive institutionalism: The explanatory power of ideas and discourse. *Annual Review of Political Science, 11*, 303–326. https://doi.org/10.1146/annurev.polisci.11.060606.135342

Simms, B., & Laderman, C. (2021). *Hitler's American gamble: Pearl Harbor and the German march to global war*. Allen Lane.

Taylor, F. W. (1911a). Scientific management: Principles and methods. *Journal of Accountancy, 12*, 117–124.

Taylor, F. W. (1911b). Scientific management: Principles and methods, part II. *Journal of Accountancy, 12*, 181–188.

Trischler, J., & Scott, D. R. (2016). Designing public services: The usefulness of three service design methods for identifying user experiences. *Public Management Review, 18*(5), 718–739. https://doi.org/10.1080/14719037.2015.1028017

Vargo, S. L., & Lusch, R. F. (2004). Evolving to a new dominant logic for marketing. *Journal of Marketing, 68*(1), 1–17. https://doi.org/10.1509/jmkg.68.1.1.24036

Virtanen, P., Lehtonen, T., & Raisio, H. (2022). Reaching out into the dark side of organization: The banality of administrative evil in the light of two case examples. *Scandinavian Journal of Public Administration, 26*(2), 3–21, June 2022 on-line. Ahead of print.

Virtanen, P., Stenvall, J., Kinder, T., & Hatem, O. (2018). Do accountabilities change when public organisations transform to service systems: A new conceptual approach. *Financial Accountability & Management, 34*(2), 166–180. https://doi.org/10.1111/faam.12149

Voorberg, W., Bekkers, V., Timeus, K., Tonurist, P., & Tummers, L. (2017). Changing public service delivery: Learning in co-creation. *Policy and Society, 36*(2), 178–194. https://doi.org/10.1080/14494035.2017.1323711

Warner Burke, W. (2006). Where did OD come from? In J. W. Gallos (Ed.), *Organization development* (pp. 13–38). Jossey-Bass.

Westrup, U. (2018). The potential of service-dominant logic as a tool for developing public sector services. *International Journal of Quality and Service Sciences, 10*(1), 36–48. https://doi.org/10.1108/IJQSS-02-2016-0013

Wilensky, H. L., & Lebeaux, C. N. (1958). *Industrial society and social welfare: The impact of industrialization on the supply and organization of social welfare services in the United States.* Russell Sage Foundation.

World Values Survey. (2021). Retrieved June 6, 2021, from www.worldvaluessurvey.org/WVSContents.jsp

# 3 The evolution of public management systems and public leadership

## 3.1 The logic of intentional acts

Social institutions are a distinctive feature of humanity. The diversity of social institutions is immense. Searle (2010, pp. 91–92), for instance, makes a distinction between governmental institutions (e.g., legislature, executive, military, fiscal), special-purpose institutions (e.g., hospitals, schools, universities, trade unions, churches), economic institutions (e.g., business enterprises and conglomerates, real estate companies, banks, insurance companies), general-purpose structural institutions (e.g., money, private property, marriage), sport institutions (e.g., national leagues, sports clubs), and unstructured informal uncodified institutions (e.g., friendship, love, family). As such, it is fair to suggest that we are all constantly engaged with multiple social institutions in our daily lives.

The question of power is always present in social institutions. Searle (2010, pp. 145–147) specifies power in human social and institutional reality as deontic power, which he describes as the diversity of institutional power agendas with such entities as obligations, authorisations, permissions, and requirements. From the perspective of human-centred public leadership, there are also other powers which are not power-over type power factors but more the power-with kind of power modes that are based on persuasion and the ability to set common agendas, dignity, and mutual trust, and respect for others. This collective empowering power enables cooperation. Furthermore, according to De Vries (2016, p. 25), "government comes into existence through the organisation of individuals or groups with common interests who try to further those interests by creating a government". Reaching common interests and going beyond contradictory views do not happen without intentional action, and intentional actions do not occur without the human relationships that constitute the basis for human cooperation.

Traditional bureaucracy theory and practice, however, is built upon a strict division of labour between organisational units and agency. This does not leave cooperation out but underscores the practice of carrying out work tasks separately. Those who have worked for public institutions and

DOI: 10.4324/9781003205791-3

used public services will likely agree that this still reflects the current reality of public administration. The barriers to giving power 'away' to the people however remain high. The paradox here of course is that the rewards accrued by trusting people, both employees and service users as well as citizens more generally, would raise the legitimacy and trustworthiness of public services. This shift is gaining ground, little by little. The central claim of this book is that the doing-things-together mentality is evolving paradigmatically in public administration and public service. This entails focusing on human relationships when scrutinising the opportunities to renew public leadership and to develop it in a more human-centred direction. Theoretically, the doing things together mentality implies the reciprocal nature of human relationships. From a collective point of view, human communities, both formal and informal, are about the relationships and mechanisms that enhance communication (e.g., language) and intentionality. Human society is also equipped with distinctive institutional structures that, according to Searle (2010, p. 200) "create and distribute deontic power relationships by assigning status functions, and with those status functions differing social roles, in the society".

Cooperation is anchored in human relationships. Sennett (2013, p. ix), for example, has strongly advocated the view that humans are characteristically responsive towards each other. This entails cooperation which is, according to Sennett (2013, pp. 5–6), an exchange that assumes that it is beneficial for everybody involved. Cooperation based on human relationships is the essential core of organisational life. Every modern state, one way or another, favours cooperation; doing things together is a useful state of action because it is difficult to achieve something by yourself. This entails structures that make this possible and the dismantling of organisational hindrances that inhibit joint practices and collective mind work. One known problem here is the isolation of organisational units—a symptom that categorises individuals in organisations into detached silos which inhibit the scaling of expertise, innovativeness, and the proliferation of organisations' collective mind (e.g., Tett, 2015).

Collective intentionality refers to collective action. This has been a very distinctive feature of human beings and human civilisations more generally throughout the course of history. On this point, as Hamel and Zanini (2020, p. 157) note, "as human beings, we´re programmed for community". This means that intentional and intimate collaboration is central to human life. From the perspective of collectives, human beings feel safe in collective action when the mission of the collective is worth caring for, communication is open, you feel safe, you have the right and the capacity to self-determine, when you are eager to experience new working methods, when the accountability function is based on peer-to-peer relationships, and you experience mutual respect and familiar respect.

Cooperation and mutual learning are different sides of the same coin. Human-centredness can be explored from both dimensions, and they constitute one key element of human civilisation. Searle (2010, pp. 43–46) connects this with collective intentionality, which has become a permanent issue in analytical philosophy. According to him, collective intentionality has a logical structure distinctive to human beings; it is based on the capacity of human beings to act according to the principles of collective intentions which become explicit in cooperative planning and implementation. It is thus essential to recognise the scope and level of mutual intentionality among those involved in a given situation or enterprise (see Searle, 2010, pp. 56–57):

- Intentionality can refer, first, to collective prior intentions which are based on previous engagements, trust for mutual commitment, and joint activities. The deployment of collective prior intentions brings about the promise of mutual planning among the parties involved but also the management of expectations. This argument is valid in the two-dimensional understanding of human-centredness in public leadership—from the perspective of people-centred organisation (relationships between organisational citizens) and from the perspective of how service users are involved in service-design and their role in horizontal accountability.
- Second, intentionality is embedded in collective intentions-in-action grounded in ongoing cooperation practice, which requires common understanding of e.g., the division of labour, joint understanding about putting in place commonly agreed agendas, and agreements about how to solve emerging problems and misunderstandings once they arise). In public services, this requires leadership models that enhance employees' self-direction according to organisational values, raising awareness of the opportunities for service users to take part in the co-designing processes and dynamics, thorough competencies for co-working in teams consisting of public service professionals and service users, as well as a readiness to trust people to make their own decisions about how to proceed during joint co-creation practice.
- Thirdly, there is the overall notion of collective recognition, which is grounded on weaker forms of collective intentionality and is expressed as, for example, explicit attitudes on working together for common goals. This meta-level bridge of commitment is difficult to pinpoint, never mind speaking about it as a change driver. In collective recognition, the use of language and the choice of semantics is essential, because they form the basic structure for mutual trust. Interestingly, and importantly from the perspective of human-centredness in public leadership, human understanding about the dynamics, contents, and use of language has proliferated over the past century. During the 20th century, the logic and philosophy of language have been two of the areas in philosophy in which indisputable progress has been made (e.g., Stanley, 2010; Searle, 2010).

Pulling these ideas together then, we can say that humanity is about mutual learning. In the scope of human-centred public leadership, learning is always common, done together, about humans, acknowledging the systemic nature of everyday life and its determinants. The learning framework for public leadership thus concerns humans as well as learning from others and it takes place in systemic society.

## 3.2 Leadership styles inspired by humanism

Understanding of organisational culture and work-related motivation gradually increased from the 1950s onwards. Echoing Kleiner (2008, pp. 12–13), the 1950s brought about a watershed between the 'numbers culture' productivity paradigm that had prevailed since the beginning of the 20th century and the paradigm that approached humans and organisations differently, with a more in-depth nuanced understanding of how humans act and behave and explanation of what motivates them.

From today's perspective, it might sound odd, but during the 1950s understandings of humans in the organisational context changed dramatically over time though the change was incremental in nature. People were no longer viewed as being inherently lazy and thus in need of control, though such views faded only gradually. Rather, people were thought to be good at heart, which made them trustworthy. Moreover, these new understandings in relation to work-related motivation brought about a new impetus for quality improvement in relation to work, which was no longer viewed as an unnecessary evil but seen, rather, as a necessary virtue. The quality of work was also seen as beneficial for employers. It was now understood that when the quality of work is at good level and employees feel motivated in their work tasks, money will also follow. As we have argued earlier, leadership is about being with and for humans. As this is the case, leadership research has focused on how people are led and treated in organisations. Different schools of thought on leadership, not to speak of the leadership trends emanating from the popular business leadership literature and leader biographies in bookstores at airports, take a somewhat different approach to defining the human-centric essentials in their *corpus*.

Servant leadership, for example, which we discussed earlier in Chapter 2, started to gain ground in the 1970s, introducing an essentially new idea around the issue of leading people. From theoretical perspective, servant leadership was about serving people, predominantly organisational citizens, i.e., employees and not service users, customers, or clients. It was considered to take place when the leader makes the best use of their leadership competence, reflecting personal experience, which in turn creates opportunities for insights and learning and makes necessary organisational and operational changes actionable (e.g., Dierendonck & Patterson, 2018; Irving, 2018).

Another example of a leadership strand that underlines the aspect of humanistic ideas, ideals, and values is provided by humanistic management, which, according to Melé (2003), approached leadership from the perspective of the human condition and orientated itself towards the development of human virtue. Humanistic leadership is one prominent example of the leadership trend that has also gained considerable academic attention (e.g., Melé, 2016) and has carried the ethos of the Human Relations movement throughout the 20th century by addressing the idea of genuine humanism that is embedded in leading people. Humanistic leadership—originating from Lilienthal's (1967) book *Management: A Humanistic Art*—approach human beings from a holistic and comprehensive perspective addressing human dignity, the common good, and human development more generally. What is noteworthy, however, in the case of the humanistic management tradition, is the focus on people-centred organisation. Humanistic management presupposes that human and business ethics should not contradict but be complementary and parallel. Humanistic leadership treats the notion of the organisation in a very specific way. López et al. (2018), for instance, stress that organisation is a human accomplishment that responds to the social nature of the human being. Organisations thus build upon the social nature of man and are a necessity for human existence as we know it. Humanistic leadership and management then, focus on human agency as a prerequisite to understanding what the leadership rationale is. According to Melé (2016, pp. 35–36), the main idea behind humanistic management is in fact that it is oriented "not only to obtaining results through people, but also, and above all, toward people themselves, showing care for their flourishing and well-being" This echoes both Taylorism (during the 1910s and 1920s) and the Human Relations movement (of the 1920s and 1930s).

The essential difference between humanistic management (originating in the 1970s and popularised during the last decades of the 20th century) and the management ideologies of the beginning of the 20th century is the idea of how leaders are supposed to act and behave in their everyday leadership practice. In humanistic management, leaders must deal with the uniqueness of each employee and the singularity of every leadership situation which means—to echo the original book title by Lilienthal (1967)—that the leader's approach to leading people is more like being an artist than a follower of a learned set of guidelines. Both Taylorism and the Human Relationship movement included the idea—although they were very different in terms of understanding the role and nature of human motivation—that the leader should follow the formal leadership protocols in controlling and motivating employees. The distinctive difference between the Humanistic leadership tradition and the idea behind the human-centred approach in public leadership advocated in this book is the rationale around what are the organisational boundaries for leading people in a humanistic way. While the Humanistic management focuses on employees and organisational agency, human-centredness in public leadership works only if service users and citizens are involved in the humanistic leadership 'algorithm'.

One of the latest arrivals to speak in favour of understanding human motivation and the role of humanity at work is the (business) book called *Humanocracy*, which was published by Hamel and Zanini in 2020. Hamel and Zanini's point of departure is the critique of bureaucracy which, according to the authors, hinders organisations from flourishing and makes them less innovative. Hamel and Zanini do not speak at all about public organisations but instead provide a long list of topics which, they claim, hinder organisations' success, crush creativity, and stifle initiative. Critical building blocks out of this organisational dilemma require new ideas and a new blueprint or roadmap to a better future. They place significant focus on motivational aspects, new strategic models to leverage the experience of organisations that have become mired in bureaucratic dilemmas, new mindsets for employees and leadership to escape industrial age thinking about progress, mobilisation for organisational change, and embedding the principles of humanocracy (e.g., ownership over work, market orientation, openness, and the willingness to experiment). Placing the blame on bureaucracy, Hamel and Zanini (2020, pp. 20–21) define humanocracy as follows:

> We need to put human beings, not structures, processes, or methods, at the centre of our organisations. Instead of a management model that seeks to maximise control for the sake of organisational efficiency, we need one that seeks to maximise contribution for the sake of impact. . . . In bureaucracy, human beings are instruments, employed by an organisation to create products and services.

Hamel and Zanini lead us then to think about the case for humanocracy in public administration, particularly from the perspective of public leadership. Bearing in mind the stability function public administration has in our societies, it would be unwise and even flawed to think that all public employees are rebellious, against the rules, seeking constant innovations, and searching for creativity in all their actions. It would be encouraging to think that all public employees and public leaders are bolstered with new competencies enabling them to better serve society, that they are eager to cooperate, willing to go beyond organisational siloes, capable of the rapid deployment of common (based on taxes) resources for the betterment of society, and ready to serve the people who are engaged with public services as service users. Furthermore, the value of bureaucracy depends on how we define and conceive of bureaucracy as a concept. If it is understood as Hamel and Zanini (2020) are suggesting, then perhaps very few would disagree with their views. But if we take this concept as a major paradigm detailing how public institutions have been orchestrated to serve society since the late 19th century, then the door is open for confronting views. Meier and Hill (2005), for instance, have advocated the view that bureaucracy as a management doctrine in public administration not only will survive in the current century but will flourish. Grounding their argument on the writings of Max

Weber, Meier and Hill (2005) think that the bureaucratic division of labour, clearly defined hierarchies, and the occupation of tasks based on expertise is still the best way to understand and organise the public administration.

In summary, it is easy to agree with both views and the arguments behind them. The main point perhaps emerging from these discussions is that bureaucracy should strive to keep up with the emergent challenges provided by our complex and multifaceted societies and encourage public employees to find better solutions to promote cooperation and work for the benefit of service users and citizens. Moreover, it is fair to say that public sector entities and public policy planning and service delivery have changed considerably from the era of the 1990s during which the New Public Management (NPM) and especially strong anti-bureaucratic management approaches—the Westminster model (the UK, Australia, New Zealand, Canada) and the US model of the 1980s and 1990s—advocated strongly that public sector organisations should move towards business sector type management methods and dynamics. This 1990s-era emphasis still exists, of course, but has been challenged by new ideas around the public sector's role in society (e.g., Mazzucato, 2021), including new approaches such as those offered by service-dominant logic (e.g., Osborne, 2018) supporting public service delivery and the strengthened role of public organisations caused by global pandemics (especially COVID-19; e.g., Dzhurova, 2020). The COVID-19 pandemic is seen as a game changer for public administration and leadership, creating pressure to develop "new organizational vocabulary, mindset and set of routines" (Ansell et al., 2021, p. 954).

From the perspective of public leadership and this book's view on human-centredness, there are however several limitations to all three leadership approaches discussed here—servant leadership, humanistic leadership, and the leadership humanocracy approach. The limitations concern how they define the scope of the humanistic view, regardless of the motivation for emphasising humanistic ideas and especially concerning the point that in these leadership traditions humanity and humanism end at organisational boundaries. They all are concerned with organisational citizens—employees—which is essential of course but does not suffice in the public domain in which societal betterment remains a key feature. This then is the reason why it is important to understand the logic, rationale, functions, and aim of public institutions and organisations.

## 3.3 The diversity of public management and political-administrative systems

### *3.3.1 Public management systems*

Since the beginning of the 20th century, the traditional bureaucratic public management model has been effective in building upon certain core principles. These include the differentiation of politics and administration, rule obedience, expertise, a hierarchical approach to organisation, civil service competence building, and a strict division of labour. Leadership is organised and practised top-down in traditional bureaucratic organisation, and the operational context for the bureaucratic model was a closed society, which entailed limited interest for cross-departmental, cross-organisational, and cross-sectoral cooperation with other organisational units. In this context, citizens and service users are conceived as subordinate to the system. Known functional problems in the traditional bureaucratic model have been addressed in relation to elasticity, adaptability, and innovativeness deficits as well as the non-existence of leadership as a civil service profession.

The first signs of New Public Management (NPM) as a public management model appeared during the 1980s. Hood (1995), for example, notes that changes in public sector accounting in many OECD countries were fundamental to the rise of the new management doctrine as well as its associated doctrines of public accountability and organised best practices which, in turn, proliferated globally during the 1990s (Hood, 1991). Furthermore, in the United States, a book by Osborne and Gaebler (1992) entitled *Reinventing Government* heavily criticised government 'business' by arguing that the US government's problems in respect of government and public service delivery were rooted in the bureaucratic operations model with its origins in the 1930s and 1940s. According to the authors, by the 1990s the operating environment of the public sector had changed dramatically, which had led to the need for radical change across public organisations in relation to cost-effectiveness and accountability, result-based steering in running public policies, putting forward private business examples as templates for public authorities, and finally embedding the entrepreneurial approach in the minds of public sector leaders. From the perspective of human-centredness in public leadership, the new public management was, ultimately, a model which applied as a closed system focused, to a certain extent, on employees but hardly at all on service users and citizens from the perspective of integrating them into public service design. Instead, New Public Management brought about significant differentiation to policy making with its broad critique of the public sector for being overly bureaucratic and inefficient. This resulted in a shift from an input/output activity model to one focused on outcomes and effectiveness and to a desire for better leadership enabling all this to be put into practice. Criticism of the New Public Management model rose significantly after the turn of the millennium with new topics such as the role of management consultants, the suitability of the model from the perspective of developing e-government, the overemphasised emergence of the 'audit society', the paralysis by analysis phenomenon, and the lack of management and resilience mechanisms (e.g., Power, 1997; Hood, 2004; Hood & Dixon, 2016; Lapsley, 2009).

The New Public Management doctrine started to lose its explanatory power and mainstream strength as a public management trend already by the end of the 1990s. The emergence of New Public Governance (NPG) came then to be seen as a potential solution to the deficits of New Public Management. The New Public Governance approached public management from an alternative view, compared to that of New Public Management (e.g., Klijn & Koppenjan, 2016). New Public Governance attempted to deal with the growing complexities facing globalised networked society, shifting the focus of management from organisations to organisational networks and governing *per se*. New Public Governance—operating in the context of open systems and cooperation—turned the focus of attention then to cross-sectoral issues and governance networks and subsequently to the context of meta-governance, i.e., the governance of governing and thus related to coordination of one or more governance modes by deploying different mechanisms and strategies to overcome government failures (Gjaltema et al., 2019).

From the perspective of functional cooperation between organisations from different societal sectors, New Public Governance complemented well the emergence of service science and particularly notions of service-dominant logic as well as the logic of service ecosystems. According to Osborne (2006), New Public Governance introduced a wide range of approaches to governance, which can be uncovered within the existing public leadership and management literature and scholarship—such as introducing new theoretical insights into institutional relationships within society, defining governance as the machinery of 'self-organising inter-organisational networks' related strongly to the domain of service delivery, and using governance as a way to explore the workings of public policy communities and interest networks. From the human-centred approach in public leadership perspective adopted in this book, New Public Governance represented an important new phase in the attempt to situate service users in the context of public service delivery. Torfing and Triantafillou (2013), for example, have emphasised the fact that New Public Governance not only shifted the public leadership focus from single organisations to governing and governance issues but also shifted public service delivery towards more co-production and co-creation cooperation between service providers and service users. New Public Governance then introduced new meaning and motivation to the new participatory, interactive, and less direct forms of governance currently emerging in many liberal democracies (see also, Sorrentino et al., 2018).

### *3.3.2 Present-day public management system*

The contemporary public management system across the globe—and regardless of the administrative-political traditions between countries—is not a pure model representing the ideas of the traditional bureaucratic, New Public Management (NPM) or New Public Governance (NPG) models, but a blend of each, blending sedimented elements of all three—i.e., these three systems were not really Weberian 'ideal types' but sedimented on top of each other because management paradigms in the Khunian sense (as with the social sciences in general) are never wholly replaced because they are supported as belief systems, not as pure scientific facts. To rephrase the wording used by Bouckaert and Halligan (2008, pp. 36–40, 55–58, 76, 177), the present-day public management system—at least in the Western world and in the OECD countries—has determinants that can be traced back to Pre-Weberian, Weberian, and Neo-Weberian models of political-administrative systems of public administration.

First, the Pre-Weberian model existed until the 1980s and was made explicit as monolithic 'Weberian grand ministries', top-down leadership, law-based, input-driven, tax collecting, organisational systems that focused on procedure and due process, in/out kind of performance measurement and thus rather intuitive goal-attainment and accountability protocols. Second, the traditional Weberian model, then, can be seen as a close cousin of the pre-Weberian model, now based on single loop learning, aiming to understand the possibilities for resource-allocations but still fixated with registration and 'old-school' use of strategic resource deployment, aiming to reach all relevant standards for operational procedures and efficiency. The Weberian model prevailed in most OECD countries during the 1980s and included classical bureaucracy with administrative processes that focus on fixed administrative processes distant in particular from external pressure from the operational environment, media, and all relevant societal stakeholders and partners.

Thirdly, the Neo-Weberian model that came into effect during the 1990s under the influence of New Public Management (NPM) and later through the emergence of New Public Governance (NPG) is still based on public law that covers administrative laws and regulations. In the Neo-Weberian model, public law is still the main embodiment of public institutions and organisations. Although the Neo-Weberian model is fundamentally a State of Law (*Rechtsstaat*), its civil servants are not just bureaucrats in the context of the law but also increasingly belong to the managerial profession. Consequently, this shift brings with it a new focus on performance, effectiveness and—perhaps most importantly—customers and service users. The Neo-Weberian model of public management emphasises the rights of the citizens and particularly human rights and increasingly addresses the rights and duties of service users, which entails a new status for services in the gradual adaptation of the game of offer and demand in public service delivery.

In summary, the countries with traditional public administration traditions, at least in Europe, have shifted from the Weberian to the Neo-Weberian model over the past couple of decades, given the influence of New Public Management (NPM) and, subsequently, New Public Governance (NPG) and their modernisation drive. In this process, the interaction between civil service professionals is highlighted because of the demand for more customer-tailored service integration. Consequently, a considerable variety of new service delivery models have been introduced and put into practice—i.e., contracting out, ly-owned industries and service companies owned and operated by public institutions, fashionable public-private partnerships, and the extensive deployment of a variety of market-type mechanisms (MTMs). The shift towards this neo-Weberian model also includes a significant focus on managing performance better with a deliberate re-focusing of administrative effort from efficiency to effectiveness.

## 3.4 The evolution of public sector leadership theory and practice

### *3.4.1 Public management and public leadership*

The evolution of public management systems makes explicit the changing role of service users and citizens. Over the past century, a remarkable shift has taken place with citizens now conceived of as service users in the context of public service delivery with the relationship between service providers and users viewed as an essentially cooperative one. By the end of the 20th century, public service users were no longer simply viewed the subordinate followers of different regime types and public management systems but rather as active agents taking part in societal development. To understand how the idea of people-oriented organisations has evolved within the various public leadership styles, we will focus next on the evolution of public leadership after World War II.

Much has been written about public leadership over the past few decades, but this body of work has been dwarfed by writings on public management and public administration. This work has been published as academic textbooks, journal papers, and semi-academic book-format publications. In what follows, we will identify some of the milestones in the development of public leadership theory, its contents, and main trajectories. This is essential to understand the evolution of public leadership in theory and in practice. Conceptually, it is important to note that public management and public leadership here refer to two different dimensions of governing the public sector, but also that they are far from synonyms.

In the context of this book, public management is an overall umbrella concept that refers to the practice of how public sector institutions and organisations are organised to serve society. The historical traditions of public management traditions go back centuries. Lynn (2005), for instance, states that the origins of the field of public management can be traced to the practice of 17th- and 18th-century cameralism and German *Statswissenschaften* and—if going even further back in the course of history—in early appearances of bureaucratic practices and public administrations in Confucian China and the medieval Orient. Public leadership, then, focuses on how public institutions and organisations are led. Obviously, it is perfectly reasonable to argue that it is questionable whether public leadership has ever had a distinct nature in comparison to general leadership theory, and it is not clear whether public leadership has features that are applicable only to the domain of public administration.

Some highly specific characteristics of public leadership are clearly central to the practice of leadership in the government sector, such as the role of political decision-making, the use of public funds, the need for transparency on public expenditure, the opportunity to use (paternalistically) public power, and the ideal of serving citizens and the electorate. Overall, however, it seems that public leadership theory development has followed the general evolution of leadership theory and practice. As such, public leadership thinking follows in lockstep with leadership theory in general—i.e., the principles and approaches that take place in other sectors of society, primarily in the private sector.

### *3.4.2 Public leadership—conventional theoretical trajectories*

Van Wart (2017) distinguishes five thematically and time-wise overlapping epochs of public leadership from the perspective of theory and research over a period of roughly 150 years. The value of Van Wart's typology is its distinctive focus on the public leadership topic within the predominant public management paradigms and models (i.e., such as New Public Management and New Public Governance). In reading Van Wart's typology, it is important to bear in mind that his ideas are grounded on developments that took place in the United States though they are generally scalable to other countries regardless of the nature of different political-administrative models and at the very least to most of the Western countries.

Van Wart's typology of public leadership 'epochs' are discussed and commented on briefly in the general literature (Van Wart, 2003, pp. 218–220, 2013a, 2013b, 2017, pp. 14–15; cf. Denis et al., 2005, pp. 447–449; Orazi et al., 2013). In this book, we do not intend to go into great detail with regard to these Van Wart's leadership 'paradigms' for various reasons: first, they are overlapping and, second, there are somewhat different typologies available in the evolution of public leadership over the past century (e.g., Morgan et al., 2019, pp. 18–23, who discuss trait-based and individual-centred theories, group-centred theories, contingency theories, and organisational and institutionally centred theories). In what follows, then, this book investigates the main epochs of the evolution of public leadership because it helps to pinpoint the idea of organisational human-centredness, which clearly emerged to prominence in the latter half of the 20th century.

The Great Man theory prevailed at the end of the 19th century, underlining the role of uniquely talented and insightful individuals who made possible societal change. As the name suggests, the great majority of these great leaders were men, which means that leadership positions at the time were strongly determined by gender. According to the Great Man theory, great men were born leaders, with no learning in leadership practice required.

Great leaders by birth had the gift of leadership brilliance imprinted in their DNA. Great Man theory has generally declined in support but has survived at the extremities of political ideology up to this day. North Korean leaders, for example, are still described in terms of their tremendous talents and competencies which renders them superhuman—at least according to political propaganda. From a human-centredness point of view, other humans are, in practice, non-existent beyond their duty to serve, in the context of leadership as understood by these Great men. Human-centredness comes into the picture only from the paternalistic perspective ('I do what is best for you') or with a philanthropic flavour ('I exist and have the will to help you').

The Trait theory (or the subversions of it) was the dominant paradigm in the public leadership scene during the first half of the 20th century. As the title suggests, trait theory emphasised the recognition of importance of individual leadership talents, skills, and properties. In practice, this meant that certain individual traits shape your habitus as a leader. According to trait theory then, a prominent leader can be recognised through the traits that relate to a leader's personality and individual personality traits. Trait theory was at its zenith during the era of the scientific measurement of leadership and work development and in the context of adopting scientific principles in management (put forward by F.W. Taylor) and partly also during the 1920s and 1930s under the influence of the Human Relations movement.

Contingency theory was the dominant leadership theory in terms of leadership practice and in the domain of public administration from World War II until the end of the 1980s. This theory considered situational factors and leadership contexts crucial in determining the nature and role of leadership. Contingency theory shifted the focus of leadership from the leader's skills and competencies towards a general understanding of the behavioural aspects of leaders (i.e., how they behaved in carrying out leadership practice), which resembled the breakthrough experiences of the Human Relations movement of the 1920s and 1930s.

Transformational theory prevailed paradigmatically until the late 1970s/early 1980s. It shifted the focus of leadership towards making public sector strategies actionable and—overall—emphasised the idea of organisational change. Kurt Lewin's role in organisational change management theory has been pivotal, and this must also be acknowledged in writing about human-centredness in public leadership. According to Burnes (2006, p. 134), for example, "few social scientists have received the level of praise and admiration that has been heaped" upon Lewin. From the perspective of change management, Kurt Lewin's role was highly influential already in the late 1930s, having left his homeland, Germany, in 1933 because of the political takeover by the Nazi party and having settled at the University of Iowa in the United States, Lewin's ideas about change management focused on the acts of humans—how people behave in change situations and what generic processual phases took place in organisational changes: Lewin became famous through his anecdotal notes, such as "you cannot know an institution until you try to change it" (Kleiner, 2008, p. 22).

Known for his work on field theory, group dynamics, action research methodology, and the stepwise approach to change theory (Burnes, 2006, pp. 137–143), Kurt Lewin passed away in 1957 at the age of only 56. By the time of his passing, he had already made a seminal contribution in the fields of social psychology and applied organisation research undertaking pioneering work on these scientific themes (e.g., Lewin, 1935, 1936; see also Cummings et al., 2016; Wheeler, 2008; Kleiner, 2008, pp. 21–22). Although sometimes criticised for advocating a top-down management-driven approach to change (Burnes, 2006, pp. 153–154), Lewin's subversive thought about change management was, first, to involve all relevant stakeholders and participants to take part in change processes (i.e., through their full commitment) and, second, to create internal and external pressure for organisational change, rather than try to influence the organisational citizen's behaviour directly.

When approaching organisational change like this, organisational change itself converts to a system which enables and hastens the change process—and alternatively, if the organisational change system maintains satisfaction with the current status quo, then change itself is inhibited. Under these intellectual (and practical) circumstances, the role of organisational culture was now understood as a powerful mechanism to influence organisational performance and goal attainment.

Moreover, it is important to acknowledge that the servant theory of leadership existed parallel to transformational leadership theory from the late 1970s onwards. As a public leadership model, the conceptual construct of servant leadership underlined public leaders' ethical responsibilities to followers, taxpayers, and citizens. The public leadership's and leaders' role more generally was to serve the service users of public services and citizens (see also Bourgon, 2017).

Finally, over, approximately, the past three decades (i.e., since the early 1990s) we have seen a growing tendency to treat public leadership theory and practice as an era of multifaceted theories emphasising a variety of leadership approaches in the domain of public administration. The development trajectory of public management and leadership was now increasingly based on the New Public Management system model topped with a blend of leadership styles and mechanisms with the aim of contributing to the development of society and the well-being of service users and citizens. From the 1990s, once the public leadership theories, as adapted by Van Wart (2017), began to wither, there was a growing tendency to develop public leadership professionally at least in most of the OECD countries. Since the 1990s, multiple theoretical, conceptual, and practical leadership approaches have been developed and adapted in public organisations to grasp the nature and content of public leadership in an increasingly fast-changing operating environment.

### *3.4.3 Diversifying landscape of public leadership*

From the 1990s onwards, the diverse field of public leadership has called for the development of holistic and sophisticated frameworks for public leadership to reflect the ongoing turbulent societal changes and other emergent societal phenomena, including, for instance, digitalisation and the general sweep of technological progress. Denis et al. (2005, pp. 449–452), for example, have identified two contrasting dimensions in public leadership theory and practice that have prevailed since the 1980s. On the one hand, we have the entrepreneurial view of leadership, which emerged in the aftermath of the emergence of New Public Management (NPM) and which extensively highlighted the value-for-money perspective in public service delivery, as well as encouraging public authorities to embrace innovativeness and service quality in their strategies and organisational practice. While on the other, we have the stewardship view of leadership, which evolved during the peak years of New Public Management (NPM), advocating the modernisation of public institutions and organisations, as well as the introduction of a new entrepreneurial brand for bureaucratic quality.

Stewardship leadership included this idea—in a somewhat conservative and non-progressive manner—as the guardians of public goods and values, thus reflecting what was previously outlined in conjunction with the servant theory of public leadership. Additionally, ever since the turn of the millennium, additional approaches to public leadership have covered network perspectives to leadership and a value-creating perspective in leading public institutions thus referring to the principles of service science and particularly service-dominant logic in public service delivery (Denis et al., 2005, pp. 452–457).

It should also be underlined here that it is perhaps rather erroneous to argue that leadership theory is generic by nature. There are some general characteristics in leadership regardless of the societal sector in which it is practised, but evidently there are also some very distinctive features related to the leading of public institutions and organisations in public administration. Pollitt (2003, pp. 19–22), for instance, has underlined the specifications of public leadership by reminding us about the public administration's environmental factors (e.g., the presence of formal legal codes and regulations); organisational transactions (e.g., the production of 'public goods' instead of commercial products); and organisational roles, structures, and processes (e.g., the existence of political powers in organisations due to the task of public policy goal attainment).

Among current public administration scholars, Van Der Wal's contributions are noteworthy because he has published extensively about the specific nature of public leadership, public values in contrast to business values, and new public leadership requirements for the 2020s, as well as the public administration's role in promoting resilience in order to cope with global disasters such as the COVID-19 pandemic (see, e.g., Van der Wal, 2017, 2020; Van der Wal et al., 2015; Virtanen & Tammeaid, 2020).

## 3.5 'Human-centred' reflections in public service delivery

For several reasons, the importance of public service delivery rapidly ascended the political agenda from the1990s onwards. This occurred, in part, due to the emergence of various legitimacy problems and particularly to the financial constraints on public administrations across the globe. The legitimacy challenge was reflected, as noted previously, in the promotion of public service quality awards, competitions, best practice showcases, and the publication/deployment of service charters (e.g., Cheung, 2005; Clark, 2000; Thomassen et al., 2012).

In a US context, seminal contributions by Denhardt and Denhardt (2015a, 2015b) and Guy and Rubin (2015) addressed the role of public service and service providers and professionals as a service and serving citizens based on societal values in contrast to being an implementation mechanism of administrative action. The book entitled *The New Public Service: Serving, Not Steering* by Denhardt and Denhardt (2015b), for instance, advocated for the creation of a framework for the reaffirmation of democratic values, citizenship, and service in the public interest—and aimed to put these principles into practice through a well-designed public service delivery model. This model was based on core principles such as conceiving service users as citizens, not as customers, aiming to seek the public interest in carrying out service delivery, and—important from the perspective of human-centredness—valuing people and their actions, not just meeting the productivity and efficiency targets. What prompted this adjustment in the conception of public services over time? In what follows we will focus on five issues that have emerged onto the agendas of politics, public policy, and public administration across most of the OECD countries.

First, the explicit notion that public services have a comprehensive moral purpose. To attain this goal, *public services* ought to constitute morally, operationally, and functionally a healthy approach to meeting the challenges faced in helping people to gain and maintain their autonomy, freedom, and well-being (e.g., Center for Public Impact, 2021, pp. 28–29, 76–80).

Second, the emergence of service dimension thinking entailed a radical shift around the ways in which service users and citizens were served. The paternalistic 'power-over' way of looking at service users has been gradually replaced with a service mentality that concentrates on dignity and respect for people. Public service has thus become 'shorthand' for those useful and people-helping activities that fully empower human beings helping them to cope with life's unexpected problems. This shift welcomes the diversity of people, enhances individual and collective capabilities for improved resilience, and supports people through the development of strong human relationships and trust. The service mentality issue does not mean that public services are no longer without radical contradictions, far from it. There are at least two potential issues embedded in the service mentality theme that call for further scrutiny. Think for instance of the motivation for and commitment of the social worker in youth services in helping young people when their line manager tells them that the social worker unit is under threat because of the need for budget cuts. And think about the situation in which the given social worker is forced to *take* a young person into custody against their will. Yes, these are contact points for contradictions and the solution in these situations is, regardless of the decision the social worker or their superiors must take, to engage in social work with dignity and respect for the young people in question.

Third, public service delivery relates strongly to public leadership. In understanding public services' role as a forum for public leadership, we first must look for the feature elements of local level service systems which are, by definition, an integrated web of diverse public services. This requires the deployment of integrated leadership (Morse, 2010), which approaches leadership by seeking cooperation and alliances beyond organisational boundaries and thus through cross-sectoral dynamics and coordination. Kinder et al. (2021) label this as relational leadership that takes place in collaborative networks at local levels of governance. According to them (Kinder et al., 2021, pp. 20–21), public leadership in local public service ecosystems synthesises approaches taken from social learning, logic-of-practice, trust, and services-as-a-system, which makes it challenging to test empirically because of the systemic nature of the service ecosystem. Public service-related leadership thus takes its shape in relationships that enable collective learning and, in a way, follow the learning-by-doing-together principle. From the perspective of public service teams, this leadership mode is seen as complementary to that which takes place at the team level close to service users. At the boundaries with service users, the most prominent leadership design relates rather to self-direction than to top-down leadership authority,

Fourth, public service is today increasingly based on co-creation and experimentation, rather than being grounded on a 'public authority knows best' mentality. Co-working with public service delivery among service professionals also covers service users. This brings about the idea of increased service adaptation by involving service users in the design processes of publicly funded services. Experimentation mechanisms are a welcome arrival in public service delivery since experimentation potentially brings new ways to improve public services: experiments are essential to ensure the usefulness of new service models. The underpinning logic of experimentation is simple at the outset—as Jensen (2020) has recently advocated—but the possibility for demonstrating causal effects (and the use of relevant and appropriate research techniques, the use of randomised control trials for instance) for the development of public policy purposes is far from simple. Lember et al. (2019, pp. 7–8, 11–12) have recently argued that this calls for diversity of interaction between service professionals and service users since "interaction between citizens and professionals is a key precondition for any co-production or co-creation relationship to emerge and evolve" and the role of technology should not be neglected in this process. The role of technology is manifold because of multiple channels and varieties of technology, which can be communicative (allowing communication between partners), processual (allowing selection of specific target groups and nudging), actuation (increasing human-to-machine connection and learning), and sensing (allowing interaction and making personalisation of services possible) technologies. There is also an emerging evidence base that even hard-to-reach people can be engaged in the co-creation of public services through digital means. For example, Jalonen et al. (2021) have illustrated how social media discussions of socially withdrawn youths can be used as a stimulus to enrich the knowledge base in terms of the co-creation of public services.

Fifth, public service is increasingly about societal learning again, for a variety of reasons, but mostly based on the proliferation of participation mechanisms, deliberative politics and related public policy making, and the extensive role of the free flow of information (through social media in particular). As a general note, concerning organisational learning in public organisations, in this book we follow pretty much what Moynihan and Landuyt (2009) said, stating that organisational learning is dynamically attributed to both cultural and structural factors in public organisations. This means that organisational learning is derived from the intersubjective meaning experienced by organisational actors (leaders, managers, and staff members) and is reflected largely in tacit knowledge rather than explicitly considered decisions and in the context of the organisation's culture (Moynihan & Landuyt, 2009, pp. 1098–1100). The combination of cultural and structural logic related to learning becomes important when we think of attempts to study and understand the maturity of organisational learning. To accomplish this thought process, it is not useful to look only at the dimensions of organisational culture but also to the structural procedures (in public organisations) that create opportunities for individual and collective learning (training, consultation, HR practices, competence development etc.).

In the context of public service cooperative learning, Lowe et al. (2020) speak of human learning systems, with which they refer to a focus on human agency (what happens in relationships between human beings), collective generative learning (see Senge, 1990, 2020), and the systems perspective. Lowe et al.'s point is made in conjunction with the conclusions of Moynihan and Landuyt (2009), who emphasised the role of learning forums in the organisational learning process. Senge's distinction between adaptive and generative learning is also insightful in this context, because adaptive learning is always reactive (and passive, in many cases), whereas generative learning builds upon innovativeness and the scalability of good ideas and promising practices and thus creating opportunities for organisational learning. This learning provokes the following questions: how does learning fit into public service leadership and how is it brought alive and maintained in cooperation with service users? Furthermore, additional reasoning concerns what learning means and for whom, for what, and with whom and how learning motivation abounds across the diversity of stakeholders. Additionally, how creating learning mindsets engages with enabling positive human relationships and public service goal attainment. And finally, how learning combines with experimentation.

## 3.6 Human-centredness and multiple accountabilities

### *3.6.1 Accountability matters*

Well-functioning government, proper public service delivery, goal attainment, and performance measurement provide much of the legitimacy for public administration. Accountability is a central issue in considering the use of public finances for the benefit of citizens and for the betterment of society. It is easy to agree with Schillemans (2011, pp. 389–390), who criticises the certain blurriness of 'accountability' as a concept and as a practice: accountability has, for instance, been used as a synonym for many political ambitions, goals, and values such as transparency, equity, democracy, efficiency, responsiveness, responsibility, and integrity. Blurriness around the notion of accountability as a concept and as a practice relates, as Weber (1999) notes, to the fact that all accountability variations are socially constructed, often featuring informal interactions as opposed to formal reporting and responsibility governances.

The core of the accountability notion related to public agency is, given and accepting the conceptual blurriness and loose concept deployment, the goal attainment of public actions *vis-á-vis* publicly agreed performance goals. From this perspective, the approach towards accountability is somewhat clearer: according to Boven's (2005, p. 182) seminal text, public accountability "is the hallmark of modern democratic governance. It refers to a process through which people and institutions in power are held responsible and accountable in public for their actions and expenditures".

In this book, we maintain that varieties of vertical accountability—referring to the top-down goal-attainment agenda and bottom-up accountability reporting agenda—are trademarks for any public organisation system that operates in a 'closed' society framework, focusing on individual organisations. The human aspect belongs to this vertical version of accountability, but with limited range and volume. In vertical accountability, the human aspect is created by top-down/bottom-up hierarchies with public institutions and organisations. The vertical accountability model is not, however, by any means totally outdated. On the contrary, it has relevant processual scope consisting of distinct process phases, such as *information circulation* (by accountable organisations/agency), *debate* (in conjunction with principal and the agent), and finally *consequences* declaration, which may comprise praise or sanctions (tightened regulations, fines, discharge of management, or even the termination of the organisation) (Schillemans, 2011).

The shortcomings and practical problems related to verifying accountability through traditional performance monitoring and metrics are well-known. The main reason for these problems includes the complex nature of society, which is constructed by means of various social and institutional networks and interdependences. In this societal context, evaluating and assessing effectiveness becomes not quite impossible but certainly intellectually difficult. Much of the current criticism is not, however, new. March (1978), for instance, provocatively criticised rationalistic performance management ideologies as early as the late 1970s for being blind and short-sighted to failing to properly conceive of the social mechanisms incorporated in the dynamics of accountability and performance monitoring/reporting.

### *3.6.2 Two versions of horizontal accountability*

With traditional vertical accountability challenged, should we try to find alternative solutions to tackle these shortcomings and failed intentions, looking instead perhaps at a human-centred focus in the dynamics of accountability? We think that this presents a potentially fruitful approach to addressing accountability in a way that not only advocates the idea of human-centredness in public leadership but which also addresses the idea of developing society to enhance democratic improvement and the creation of well-being at the societal level.

The idea of horizontal accountability contrasts with the practice of vertical accountability and is extremely important in adopting a human-centred approach to leading public organisations. Schillemans (2011), for instance, has written extensively on horizontal accountability, which differs from traditional forms of accountability in public administration, where a superior usually demands accountability from a subordinate. Schillemans' analysis of horizontal accountability with data from the Netherlands is one attempt to understand and conceptualise the horizontal version of accountability. Conceptually, we term it *horizontal accountability for decentralised government organisations with limited scope for human-centredness*. It concerns defining horizontal accountability in the context of a decentralised government system in which principal–agent relationships are far from clear, thus creating problems relating to democratic control deficits because ministers and parliament are formally constrained in demanding accountability from semiautonomous agencies. The human aspect is embedded in this setting of horizontal accountability because it takes place through socially constructed relationships. Countries, of course, have different mechanisms to deal with decentralised semiautonomous organisations. For instance, in Finland, government agencies are under the political control of the Ministries (and Ministers, for that matter) and report directly to their line Ministries on their performance, whereas in Sweden, government agencies are constitutionally accountable to the government, not the Ministries. Another horizontal accountability model concerns public service delivery and especially the functions, performance, and outcomes of service (eco)systems. This model of horizontal accountability treats the idea of being accountable for an issue and phenomenon that takes place in an open society in a web of institutions, organisations, and service providers that operates at all levels of governance, from the national and regional to the local levels of service delivery. In this book, we call this version of horizontal accountability, *horizontal accountability for public service systems with an expanded scope for human-centredness*.

This alternative view of horizontal accountability stems from various thematic roots. First, it resonates with the idea of service-dominant logic and the emergence of service ecosystems within the broad context of seeing public services not as organisations but as service systems. Second, this version of horizontal accountability can be seen as a manifestation against New Public Management, which gained traction as part of a neoliberal ideological approach to hollow out the state, to reduce state spending, often disguised as modernisation, quality programmes, and as the scaling and dissemination of best practices. The main idea of this version of horizontal accountability rests upon the idea of seeing accountability as horizontal and reciprocal information flows between service providers and service users and in the creation of spaces and opportunities for service users to be given a 'voice' in service delivery and service design. This also introduces new in-depth dimensions for service users (and for human-centred accountability) to be involved in accountability processes and to forward their arguments about the value-creation they have generated in using the services. This shift constitutes a significant change from traditional accountability modes, which have remained structural and stagnant by nature. In this new accountability setting, social media naturally play a significant role (good news moves fast and bad news even faster), as well as the concepts of comprehensiveness and reciprocity. Accountability is in this new version understood not only as the information flow between agents concerning the value and content of service deployment but also as values, empathy, dignity, and user-experience, which now forms a multi-layered understanding of accountability (e.g., Virtanen et al., 2018, pp. 166–167, 171).

## 3.7 The dissolution of public office as a physical space—the European and Nordic context

In the context of working life, the role of teleworking/remote working has increased significantly over the past couple of decades—even prior to the COVID-19 pandemic and covering most societal sectors. Felstead and Henseke (2017) have, for instance, suggested that the increase in remote working represents a global trend, relating to the detachment of work from place. It also seems that remote working, reflecting the idea 'flexible working', i.e., addressing work arrangements that allow flexibility on how long, where, when, and what times employees work, is associated with high organisational commitment, job satisfaction, and the promotion of well-being at work. The downside of remote working is however increased work-related stress, work intensification, and a greater inability to draw a clear definition between work and spare/free time.

In the vocabulary of the European Foundation for the Improvement of Living and Working Conditions (Eurofound), which publishes the European Work Conditions Survey (the so-called EWCS survey), telework and ICT-based mobile work are "any type of work arrangement where workers work remotely, away from an employer's premises or fixed location, using digital technologies such as networks, laptops, mobile phones, and the internet" (Eurofound, 2020b, pp. 5–6). According to the Eurofound definition, telework refers to regular home-based work (e.g., employees who frequently use ICT to work from home), highly mobile ways to engage in working life (i.e., employees who frequently use ICT to work and have a high level of mobility), occasional work activity (i.e., employees who occasionally use ICT to work from locations other than their employer's premises), and finally to the work by the self-employed (i.e., self-employed workers who occasionally or frequently use ICT to work from locations other than their own premises). The latest survey (data collation in 2015) was published in early 2016 and the data collation was based on 44,000 interviews in 28 EU Member States.

According to the EWCS 2015 synthesis report (Eurofound, 2020b), 19% of workers in the European Union Member States had telework/ICT-related arrangements at work (i.e., working 'out-of-office'). Across the European Union, this kind of arrangement was most widespread in the Nordic countries (e.g., 38%, 33%, and 24% of the workforce in Denmark, Sweden, and Finland. Other European Union countries with relatively high shares of these kinds of work arrangements were the Netherlands (31%), Luxembourg (29%), the UK (27%), France (26%), and Estonia (25%). The sectors with the highest proportions of workers with these kinds of arrangements were information and communication (57% of workers), professional and scientific activities (53%), financial services (43%), real estate (43%) and, interestingly and from the perspective of this book, public administration (30%). Furthermore, the COVID-19 crisis caused rapid changes in working out-of-office practices over a very short period in Europe.

After the outbreak of the COVID-19 pandemic in spring 2020, teleworking became the customary mode of working for many employees. A Eurofound (reported in Eurofound, 2020a) e-survey showed that in July 2020, nearly half (48%) of the respondents classified as 'employees' worked at home at least periodically, and over a third (34%) of the workforce reported worked exclusively and permanently from home during the latter half of 2020. An essential marker for working from home was education level in 2020: according to Eurofound (2020a), three-quarters of employees with tertiary qualifications (74%) worked from home while only 14% of those with a secondary education did so. Another noteworthy divide in terms of homeworking was brought about by sector, with a higher incidence in most service sectors (notably education, financial services, and public administration) and a lower incidence in 'frontline' sectors (such as health, transport, and agriculture).

Even though working from home was already a growing trend before the COVID-19 pandemic, the pandemic dramatically changed attitudes to remote working. Since the spring of 2020, working from home became a key policy instrument used by governments across the world as a means of minimising the spread of the pandemic (see, e.g., Reuschke & Felstead, 2020). The pandemic skewed somewhat further the differentiation of jobs though it brought about an overall transformation (see Exhibit 2 on the case of Finland) towards working from home. Jobs in financial, professional, and technical services were more easily adjusted to remote working than those in low-skilled, high-service, and labour-intensive sectors. Furthermore, certain characteristics in relation to labour force status saw workers treated unevenly; men, the better educated, the higher paid, and those in higher skilled jobs were more likely to have the ability to work from home if they chose to do so (See also Galanti et al., 2021).

The Nordic countries stand out when reflecting on out-of-office working in public administration during the COVID-19 pandemic. Virtanen and Yli-Viikari (2021), for instance, have stressed that one explanation for shifting the public workforce to 'out-of-office' mode relates to the digitalisation of public services and government actions prior to the COVID-19 pandemic. The case of Finland, for instance, suggests that the digitalisation of central government operations and work processes (including a solid digital data infrastructure) has been a high priority across the Finnish ministries and government agencies for over a decade before the pandemic, thus making possible implementation of the digital leap to remote working by public administration organisations easy and quick during the late spring and summer of 2020.

The detachment of 'work' from 'place' in public administration potentially delivers several considerable impacts in relation to the human-centred approach to public leadership. One such impact relates to the narrative of change in respect of public authority, where the traditional bureaucratic office as an office for authoritative power is diluted since the functions of public offices are changing as well as their physical format. As the leadership-related, supervising-related, and expert-related work is distinguished from the bureaucratic work mode that used to be so distinctive of the public authority mode, the traditionally distinctive features and gestures of authoritative power (the location of public offices, the sizes and contents of office rooms, the ways of working) are themselves also transformed. The change may not however be that radical after all, since public administration expertise rests upon collaboration and working together in networks, which means that collaboration among public authorities across organisational boundaries has already been a distinctive feature of public administration and public services for some time. Networks of public administration experts at different levels of seniority have existed for several years.

Remote working brings about issues related to human-centred dimensions in public leadership that cover both leading people (employees) and creating participatory forums for service users. Speculatively speaking, the detachment of work from the office environment may bring about multidimensional, often partly counterproductive, effects on recruitment processes for public administration. Intuitively speaking, it may be that there are experts who value the idea of remote working (or working in a way that is not office-dependent), and there are people who would like to continue the 'office-way-of-working' in the future. From the perspective of recruiting the best possible experts for public administration, remote working is most likely to be an asset from the employers' perspective. Remote working brings in an additional flavour to professional transformation as well as to how leadership takes place in remote working conditions and how public leaders develop and maintain psychological contracts with employees grounded in mutual trust. One interesting issue in organising future public virtual/physical workplaces relates however to the emergence of co-working spaces and learning labs, in which collaboration can take place among experts from different fields/sectors of the public administration. From the perspective of public service users, remote working of course creates quite a different context from traditional office work. Apparently, 'street-level' professionals still work to a certain extent from their offices—social workers meeting their clients, doctors and nurses working in hospitals, teachers teaching in classrooms—and encounter service users face to face, but it is also obvious that public service delivery is—after the COVID-19 pandemic—better equipped to offer more of a multi-channel service delivery approach than it used to be. The digitalisation of public services is, nevertheless, a global phenomenon (see Section 3.8).

## 3.8 The accelerating rise of digital algorithmic bureaucracy

### *3.8.1 Technology as a context for democratic governance—policy agendas and the globally unequal division of development resources*

Bearing in mind that technology is an important factor in safeguarding democratic governance, increasingly affecting the public leadership and human-centredness embedded in it (e.g., Fung, 2015; Luna-Reyes, 2017; Bullock et al., 2020). From the human-centredness perspective, approached from the service user point of view, certain factors in public service delivery are more important than others. Clearly, however, service culture (how people are encountered face to face and virtually) sets the framework for how the service user is treated when they use services. On the other hand, the availability of public services is made available for service users through various channels, namely, physical offices or virtual services based on digitalisation, smart technologies, blockchain solutions, cognitive computing systems, artificial intelligence, and the emergence of smart city ideas.

Approached from the public policy perspective, agenda setting related to the deployment of artificial intelligence has strengthened in parallel with the onset of technological progress and the proliferation of digital initiatives, applications, and experiments. For example, 42 countries signed up to the OECD principles on artificial intelligence in 2019, to agree on their commitment to ensure that artificial intelligence systems are designed in such a way that is safe, fair, and trustworthy. Furthermore, under the umbrella of the OECD, in 2020, altogether 14 governments, along with the European Union, joined together to create the Global Partnership on Artificial Intelligence (GPAI), an initiative supporting the responsible development and use of artificial intelligence and digitally organised public services.

The latest Government AI readiness index was published in 2020 (Shearer et al., 2020). The report focused on the question of how ready governments are to implement artificial intelligence in the delivery of public services to their citizens. The index is composed of three 'pillars', namely, government, the technology sector, and data and infrastructure. As far as the government pillar is concerned, the index focuses on the level of strategy—i.e., the government's vision as it relates to AI in public services, whether it incorporates ethical considerations, the government's digital capacity, and the adaptability of government (public) organisations. The technology-related index criteria relate to the supply of AI tools from the technology sector (size, innovation capacity, human capital), whereas data and the infrastructure dimension consists of the tools that need to be built with operatives trained to a high-quality standard using representative data and requiring the appropriate infrastructure to be delivered to and used by citizens, focusing especially on infrastructure, data availability, and data representativeness.

According to the 2020 AI readiness report, the United States was No. 1 in 2022, followed by a cluster of European countries, such as the UK, Finland, Germany, and Sweden. Overall, North America and Western Europe were the top regions globally illustrating the unequal division of resources (financial and competence-based) and thus an overwhelming challenge to meet the UN's Sustainable Development Goals. The lowest-scoring regions globally on average were Sub-Saharan Africa, Latin America and the Caribbean, and South and Central Asia. The AI Government Readiness Index 2020 report concluded that for most of the world's governments, the use of artificial intelligence in public services is still in its infancy and thus that understanding readiness is crucial (Shearer et al., 2020, pp. 4–8).

### *3.8.2 The proliferation of digital public service practice and research*

Simultaneously with the proliferation of digitally delivered public services, the amount of research on digital public services has diversified and multiplied particularly over the past couple of decades. This research 'explosion' is something of a newcomer as a topic in the public services literature bearing in mind that artificial intelligence already appeared in public decision-making in the aftermath of World War II. Concerning this research 'explosion', De Sousa et al. (2019) for example note in their recently published systematic review, a growing trend of interest in artificial intelligence and digitally delivered services in the domain of public administration and public services during the period 2000–2018, with India and the United States as the most active countries in this regard. In their review, most of the studies explored represented public services, economic affairs, and environmental protection.

In addition to the analysis by De Sousa et al. (2019), it is reasonable to note that a considerable number of studies related to artificial intelligence and digital public services have also been published in Latin America (especially in Brazil), Australia, and—at an accelerating rate—in China. Detailed scrutiny reveals, however, that the full deployment of artificial intelligence is still far from maturity although plans for digital government and data ecosystem planning are already well underway (e.g., Van Noordt & Misuraca, 2020). It seems evident though that the digitalisation process in respect of public services and public administration is continuing at a steady pace to the extent that Vogl et al. (2020) have suggested a new way of conceptualising public administration in the context of digitalisation, smart technologies, and artificial intelligence. Vogl et al. (2020, p. 955) predict that algorithmic bureaucracy (Criado & Gil-Garcia's (2019) equivalent term is smart government) calls attention "to the need to study the imbrication of computational algorithms with traditional public sector organizing", and this process obliges new understanding of collaboration, the operational context, collective intelligence, service user and employee feedback, and equality of outcomes.

There are two complementary (and overlapping) ways to approach smart technologies and artificial intelligence in public administration and specifically as they relate to public services. Smart technology and artificial intelligence are, first and foremost, a public service, which means that citizens can make use of the data-systems that are put in place by public authorities (in housing, in road traffic, in using/looking for service facilities in the context of everyday life) (see, e.g., López-De-Ipiña et al., 2016; Luciano, 2020). A complementary way to understand the essence of smart technologies and artificial intelligence is then, second, to conceive of them as elements of public service which address the idea of improving and maintaining public services with the help of digitalisation. Smart technology and artificial intelligence as an element of public service can take place either in the digitalisation of existing services with the help of smart technologies, often leading to a situation where service organisations deliver the 'wrong things in the right way', or the reorganisation of current public services first followed using digitalisation to provide service users with the best possible service value.

### *3.8.3 Smart technologies affecting human-centredness in public leadership*

Smart technologies constitute something of a paradox from the perspective of human-centredness in public leadership. On the one hand, algorithmic bureaucracy can lead to increased efficiency and productivity, service availability, and cost-effectiveness. Digital innovations, smart technologies, and artificial intelligence may, on the other hand, also result in multiple forms of harm and wrongdoing: data biases, surveillance, and control can lead to the reinforcement of inequality, discrimination and the criminalisation of citizens, minorities, particularly those from the most vulnerable groups of people. Consequently, this may lead, in the worst case, to oppression and the persecution of people, a considerable lack of transparency in decision-making in the public administration, and the deterioration of accountability in public institutions and public organisations. This, in turn, entails varieties of injustice, a lack of societal trust and the decay of legitimation related to societal institutions. Finally, this process can also lead to violations of privacy and fundamental human rights abuses. In the most pessimistic scenarios, algorithm-driven content curation poses a threat to both our privacy and the functioning of democracy (e.g., Zuboff, 2019).

Smart technologies have indisputable consequences for public administration, public services, and public leadership. These effects relate to public employment (some routine tasks will continue to be automated and handled automatically and new competence requirements related to technology abound). New competence requirements cannot be met by traditional training programmes, projects, and courses but by creating a learning culture that nurtures public institutions and organisations. Attitudes of senior managers in public organisations are not necessarily technology-driven due to the competence gaps. Technology progress often hastens cross-sectoral collaboration because of the role and contents of organisational data and data maintenance. Data follows societal phenomena rather than traditional organisational boundaries. This will, in most cases, affect how public organisations and their operational processes are organised, orchestrated, and led. One interesting consequence is the role and domain for automated, grounded in algorithms, decision-making in public organisations, and related machine-to-human and machine-to-machine learning modes and dynamics. Finally, there is the question of accountability (discussed in Section 3.6), which connects with smart technologies and artificial intelligence through, for instance, how accountability data is collated automatically, making sense of the experiences of service users when they have engaged with public service delivery. These dynamic transfers the contents of work in public organisations from traditional public-administration-based siloed bureaucracy towards a more nuanced collaboration and interdisciplinary working mode, from experience-based leader-driven decision-making to data-driven decision-making at the front line (of public service delivery) and public institutions from rigid and risk-averse to agile, experimental, and adaptable service systems. This development underlines the idea that smart technologies and artificial intelligence are here, first, not for private benefit but instead for the public good and, second, that digital transformation is not about technology but is rather a far more pervasive organisational, service-oriented, and leadership-related change (see, e.g., Fountaine et al., 2021).

## 3.9 Human-centred public leadership as a science: the emergence of new research 'hot-spots' and divergent research methodologies

### *3.9.1 State-of-the-art and research-related 'hot spots'*

Public leadership is a subject of science. Science, then, is about "the development of systematic knowledge through research", as Mintzberg (2009, pp. 10–11) asserts. How then has human-centredness been addressed in the research literature on public leadership? The answer is perhaps however rather equivocal. Plenty of research has been carried out on public leadership reflecting the overall development of leadership as a science. Moreover, there is no scarcity of research about public management systems and public leadership. There is however much less research evidence on human-centredness studies focusing on the creation of people-centred organisations in public institutions and public organisations though the past couple of decades have seen the emergence of a co-creation dynamic in public service delivery, which has been extensively addressed in public administration scholarship of which the book by Junginger (2017) provides a prominent example.

From the perspective of this book, however, scientific gaps clearly remain, which inhibit human-centredness in public leadership from reaching its full potential. As a general note, we would like to address the importance of approaching public leadership through multidisciplinary research, which would raise awareness about the systemic nature of leadership and the difficulties of getting to grip with it by using single methodology solutions. Second, public leadership is a theoretical and empirical construct that is evolving constantly, thus calling for meta-analyses about how research evidence has been put into practice. This notion comes close to intervention study ideology, which refers here to analytical judgements about how research has been deployed in the development of public organisations and public service delivery.

There are a number of highly interesting thematic focus areas for research from the perspective of human-centredness in public leadership. For instance, these new thematic areas include the following 'hot spots' for research:

First, the topic of collaboration and mutual learning among top civil servants and the practice of integrative leadership in the everyday life of public managers and people in executive leadership positions in public organisations at different levels of government is very important: integrative leadership, according to Morse (2010, pp. 231–232), relates to "a process of developing partnerships across organizational, sectoral and/or jurisdictional boundaries that create public value". Furthermore, it is also essential to look for trajectories of integrative thinking from the perspectives of politics (political leaders) and public policies and civil service leadership in public organisations.

Second, top civil service career development dynamics have remained somewhat underutilised as a research theme. This research topic focuses on how the elements of rotation (within government and between government and other sectors of society (e.g., the practice in Singapore, the Netherlands, and Canada), cross-learning, unlearning, and competence building can be implemented in a way that enhances motivation for public leaders and thus strengthens their abilities for goal attainment and meeting performance objectives. Third, the orchestrating and maintenance of organisational communication and the creation of people-oriented organisations merits more theoretical, conceptual, and empirical research. Language matters as does how values are conceived within organisations. The creation of public organisations' vision of public values also represents an important phase in the process of creating the conditions for service user participation. This is a preliminary step for joint value-creation for the betterment of society. Fourth, self-steering in people-oriented organisations and the emergence of autonomous teams in the context of public service delivery do not happen by themselves and do not mean that public services are not managed and led. This remains an important theme from the human-centred leadership perspective. The transformation from bureaucratic units of civil servants to (semi-)autonomous teams of public service professionals is a dynamic process constituting a profound change in organisation culture. Research should be calibrated to these topics to gain a better understanding of how the self-steering of public organisations enhances the human-centred focus in public administration. Fifth, the management of emergent cross-cutting societal phenomena that do not fall into the categories of public policies and public organisations is a crucial theme around how service users' needs are pinpointed. It is known, of course, that these phenomena exist, but what is less known is how they are pinpointed, dealt with, and the key adaptation mechanisms in public organisations and public service delivery, enabling us to better handle these societal challenges. Interestingly, such phenomena, for example, social exclusion, homelessness, obesity, and mental health-related problems, challenge the existing structures around public policies and public services at all levels of governance (local, regional, national, transnational, and global), and thus there is a need to tackle and deal with them by means of different governance and public leadership models and varieties, including also relevant meta-governance structures. Our assumption is that this also calls for new meta-cognition structures and dynamics in public leadership and formal and informal solutions for shared leadership. Breslin et al.

(2017, pp. 160–161) have labelled this as research of societal intersectionality which enables

> a critical analytic lens for expanding our knowledge of leadership in public organizations as well as highlighting barriers to leadership opportunities. By emphasizing multiple and simultaneous dimensions of social inequality—most commonly gender, race, class, and sexuality—intersectionality reveals the unique experiences of individuals who occupy multiple marginalized social categories.

Taken from the perspective of human-centredness, this approach focuses on both dimensions of the human, namely, that of people-centred organisations and that of involving service users and citizens to be an integral part of service design, service delivery, and accountability judgement.

The research hot-spots call for new methodologies to explore in detail human-centredness in public leadership. The rationale for this upgraded public leadership methodology stems from research methodologies that gained popularity roughly 50 years ago, when researchers first became interested in what leaders do when they lead people. Mintzberg (1990), for instance, echoing his seminal book, *The Nature of Managerial Work* published in 1973 (Mintzberg, 1973), argued 30 years ago that ignorance of the nature of managerial work is manifest in various ways in modern organisations: folklore and facts about managerial work contradict, for example, the assumption that the manager is a reflexive systematic planner of activities able to customise themselves with research evidence, suggesting that managers work at an unrelenting pace and that their actions are characterised by brevity, variety, and all sorts of discontinuity (see also Mintzberg, 2009).

### *3.9.2 Translational leadership research*

The bottom-line is that understanding the contents and role of leadership, as Mintzberg (1973) has suggested, is essential. Mintzberg was right with his critical approach and arguments. We think that this kind of rationale is a prerequisite for seeing how human-centredness can be better integrated into the study of public leadership. To advocate human-centredness in public institutions and organisations, a further elaboration of Mintzberg's seminal work is essential and relates to the question of how public leaders think at their work and then how they act accordingly. This question is grounded on two research methodology variants that are necessary to consider when focusing research on public leaders' human-centredness. We will discuss each in turn.

First, public leadership always comes with a logic. It can be formal, informal, explicit, implicit, reasonable, or dumb—or something between these entities. If we follow the wording of Bourdieu (1990), the logic of public leadership can be traced by analysing leadership practices as they take place in running public administration, that is, how public leaders organise their work, what is the logic in putting together single job tasks in the organisational context, how leadership practices evolve and develop over time, how leadership actions are considered, valued, evaluated, learned, and unlearned. Actions and activities of leadership reflect the logic of leadership practice. This means that if we do not understand leadership practices and in particular the logic embedded in them, we cannot understand leadership and leadership functions. Leadership practice constitutes what leaders do. This introduces the idea that leaders should think deeply about their own assumptions and beliefs and find a link to how they correlate with their actions. To put this into the context of organisational learning (e.g., Argyris, 1993; Argyris & Schon, 1978), this kind of understanding of leaders' and managers' work practices facilitates double loop learning in leading public policies, organisations, and ecosystems.

There are numerous theoretical and conceptual approaches to leadership from which to choose when exploring leadership practice. As the level of attention given to positive psychology and salutogenetic understanding of people is constantly rising, these theoretical underpinnings are worth experimenting with in relation to research on public leadership. According to Van Woerkom et al. (2021, p. 221), this calls for a change of research perspective on organisations and leadership:

> More and more scholars and practitioners have become convinced that health and well-being in organizations should not only be explored from a pathogenic perspective focusing on risk factors and diseases, but also from a salutogenic perspective, focusing on resources for the positive promotion of health and well-being.

Exploring human resources from the perspective offered by positive psychology will strengthen and deepen the human-centredness focus related to the leadership of public institutions and organisations. This conceptual, theoretical, and methodological turn in the exploration of public leadership could shed new light on public leadership, as well as on its role as an adaptation mechanism and as a conveyor of resilience.

Second, it is possible to enrich the research on public leadership by incorporating translational elements to research agendas, settings, data collation and analysis, and research output dissemination. In broad terms, translational research refers to the application of basic or theoretical discoveries to the development of practical applications. From the perspective of human-centred public leadership, the essential elements of translational research on leadership incorporate three distinctive features: a research agenda that stems from leadership practice, involving all relevant stakeholders and beneficiaries in all research phases starting from creating the research agenda, data collation and ending up with the interpretation of research findings, and, finally, translating research findings back to leadership practice in a way that facilitates organisational development and public service design.

This definition can be complemented with lessons learned from other disciplines that are present and constitute the scholastic field of leadership. In the field of medicine, for example, translational research relates to the encouragement and promotion of multidisciplinary collaboration, to incorporating the diversity of stakeholders and patients to take part in research, to engaging a variety of communities to determine their needs for health innovation—and, finally, with scaling and supporting the adoption of best medical and health practices. The key ideas from this definition are high-class theoretical, conceptual, and empirical research involving all relevant stakeholders and beneficiaries and translating research for the benefit of the design and re-design of public institutions, organisations, and service delivery.

The window of opportunity is now open for research on human-centredness embedded in public leadership. Learning experiences from translational research methodology adopted in the field of medicine and health research (e.g., Waldman, 2006) welcome, first, the involvement of service users in research and service delivery for improved innovativeness and, second, translating research into leadership practice in public organisations. According to Savory (2010) for instance, translational research can be focused on innovation technologies, new product development, computer software, the re-design of public services, or the development of information systems.

## 3.10 Synthesis—public leadership as a human-centred system

The evolution of public leadership and public management systems has been a lengthy one. A scan of the relevant research literature provides some insight into how human-centred thinking has emerged into leadership ideology as it relates to public administration. As a general note, it should be emphasised here that the evolution of public sector leadership styles since the beginning of the 20th century has moved, in parallel, with the development of general leadership theories, trends, and paradigms.

From the public sector perspective, the 1990s were something of a turning point in this development with the emergence of New Public Management as a public sector management theory/paradigm topped with the dissolution of autonomous public leadership theories, which were then replaced by the creation of public leadership as a profession and a profession incorporating a blend of leadership theories, concepts, and practices. A general shift towards neo-Weberian government models in which the rule of law is important as well as the basic constitution of public actions has emerged in parallel with the idea of public leaders as the representatives of a leadership profession. Oddly enough, though, to conceive of public leadership as a profession is rather novel as a theme in organisational development even within the context of public administration itself. Today, public leadership is very much about the meta-level determinants that create the conditions for human-centredness to be strengthened. These include trust, cooperation, the exchange of ideas, giving voice, and doing things together.

Public services—i.e., the borderline between the state/public domain and the citizens as a constituency has been moderated heavily in the major OECD countries since the emergence of New Public Management as a central public management system since the beginning of the 1990s. This has generated numerous upheavals in respect of service user involvement and participation possibilities, performance metrics, and horizontal accountability mechanisms. Horizontal accountability understood as a co-working forum between public service providers and service users brings about a significant change to more traditional accountability processes that have remained top-down, structural, and stagnant.

In contrast, perhaps contrary to expectations, the COVID-19 pandemic has not been such a dramatic factor in promoting an increase in remote working in the public administration sector. At least in the Nordic countries, the increasing trend towards remote working has been evident for several years prior to the COVID-19 pandemic. In Section 3.7, we saw that the case of Finland suggested that the gradual increase in remote working is broadly related to most societal sectors, including the public administration. It is evident that the detachment of work from place will eventually influence the human-centredness of public leadership. It will, for instance, bring about new contents and contexts in terms of how to lead people in 'remote-mode'. From the perspective of service users, the dissolution of public office facilities will likely change how people feel about public offices when such places change format to something very different. The new co-working places used by public employees do not possess the same role as traditional public service facilities used to. Scholarship around public leadership has proliferated, particularly in recent decades. To enhance the development of human-centredness in the context of public organisations and public services, more practice-oriented translational research is however required. This would enhance the functional links between leadership theory and leadership practice. It is evident that this would also benefit public leaders in their everyday work.

## References

Ansell, C., Sørensen, E., & Torfing, J. (2021). The COVID-19 pandemic as a game changer for public administration and leadership? The need for robust governance responses to turbulent problems. *Public Management Review*, *23*(7), 949–960. https://doi.org/10.1080/14719037.2020.1820272

Argyris, C. (1993). *Knowledge for action: A guide to overcoming barriers to organizational change*. Jossey-Bass.

Argyris, C., & Schon, D. (1978). *Organizational learning: A theory of action perspective*. Addison-Wesley Publishing Co.

Bouckaert, G., & Halligan, J. (2008). *Managing performance: International comparisons*. Routledge.

Bourdieu, P. (1990). *The logic of practice*. Polity Press.

Bourgon, J. (2017). *The new synthesis of public administration: Fieldbook*. Dansk Psykologisk Forlag A/S.

Bovens, M. (2005). Public accountability. In E. Ferlie, L. Lynn, & C. Pollitt (Eds.), *The Oxford handbook of public management* (pp. 182–208). Oxford University Press.

Breslin, R. A., Pandey, S., & Riccucci, N. M. (2017). Intersectionality in public leadership research: A review and future research agenda. *Review of Public Personnel Administration, 37*(2), 160–182. https://doi.org/10.1177/0734371X17697118

Bullock, J., Young, M., & Wang, Y. (2020). Artificial intelligence, bureaucratic form, and discretion in public service. *Information Polity, 25*(4), 491–507. https://doi.org/10.3233/IP-200223

Burnes, B. (2006). Kurt Lewin and the planned approach to change: A reappraisal. In J. W. Gallos (Ed.), *Organization development* (pp. 133–157). Jossey-Bass.

Center for Public Impact. (2021). *Human learning systems: Public service for the real world* (Multiple authors). Retrieved June 16, 2021, from www.centreforpublicimpact.org/assets/documents/hls-real-world.pdf

Cheung, A. (2005). Service charters and customer empowerment in public services. *Public Management Review*, 7(3), 313–319. https://doi.org/10.1080/14719030500180765

Clark, D. (2000). Citizens, charters and public service reform in France and Britain. *Government and* Opposition, *35*(2), 152–169. https://doi.org/10.1111/1477-7053.00021

Criado, J. I., & Gil-Garcia, J. R. (2019). Creating public value through smart technologies and strategies from digital services to artificial intelligence and beyond. *International Journal of Public Sector Management, 32*(5), 438–450. https://doi.org/10.1108/IJPSM-07-2019-0178

Cummings, S., Bridgman, T., & Brown, K. G. (2016). Unfreezing change as three steps: Rethinking Kurt Lewin's legacy for change management. *Human Relations, 69*(1), 33–60. https://doi.org/10.1177/0018726715577707

Denhardt, J. V., & Denhardt, R. B. (2015a). The new public service revisited. *Public Administration Review, 75*(5), 664–672. https://doi.org/10.1111/puar.12347

Denhardt, J. V., & Denhardt, R. B. (2015b) *The new public service: Serving, not steering*. Routledge.

Denis, J. L., Langley, A., & Rouleau, L. (2005). Rethinking leadership in public organisations. In E. Ferlie, L. Lynn, & C. Pollitt (Eds.), *The Oxford handbook of public management* (pp. 446–467). Oxford University Press.

De Sousa, W. G., De Melo, E. R. P., De Sousa Bermejo, P. H., Sousa Farias, R. A., & Gomes, A. O. (2019). How and where is artificial intelligence in the public sector going? A literature review and research agenda. *Government Information Quarterly, 36*, 101392. https://doi.org/10.1016/j.giq.2019.07.004

De Vries, M. S. (2016). *Understanding public administration*. Palgrave Macmillan.

Dierendonck, D., & Patterson, K. (Eds.). (2018). *Practicing servant leadership: Developments in implementation*. Palgrave Macmillan.

Dzhurova, A. (2020). Symbolic politics and government response to a national emergency: Narrating the COVID-19 crisis. *Administrative Theory & Praxis, 42*(4), 571–587. https://doi.org/10.1080/10841806.2020.1816787

Eurofound. (2020a). *Living, working and COVID-19*. COVID-19 Series. Publications Office of the European Union. Available at: www.eurofound.europa.eu/sites/default/files/ef_publication/field_ef_document/ef20059en.pdf

Eurofound. (2020b). *Telework and ICT-based mobile work: Flexible working in the digital age*. New forms of employment series. Publications Office of the European Union. www.eurofound.europa.eu/sites/default/files/ef_publication/field_ef_document/ef19032en.pdf

Felstead, A., & Henseke, G. (2017). Assessing the growth of remote working and its consequences for effort, well-being, and work-life balance. *New Technology, Work, and Employment, 32*(3), 195–212. https://doi.org/10.1111/ntwe.12097

Fountaine, T., McCarthy, B., & Saleh, T. (2021, Summer). Building the AI-powered organization. *Harvard Business Review*, Special Issue, 10–19.

Fung, A. (2015). Putting the public back into governance: The challenges of citizen participation and its future. *Public Administration Review, 75*(4), 513–522. https://doi.org/10.1111/puar.12361

Galanti, T., Guidetti, G., Mazzei, E., Zappalà, S., & Toscano, F. (2021). Work from home during the COVID-19 outbreak: The impact on employees' remote work productivity, engagement and stress. *Journal of Occupational and Environmental Medicine, 63*(7), E426–E432. https://doi.org/10.1097/JOM.0000000000002236

Gjaltema, J., Biesbroek, R., & Termeer, K. (2019). From government to governance . . . to metagovernance: A systemic literature review. *Public Management Review*. https://doi.org/10.1080/14719037.2019.1648697

Guy, M. E., & Rubin, M. M. (Eds.). (2015*). Public administration evolving*. Routledge.

Hamel, G., & Zanini, M. (2020). *Humanocracy: Creating organizations as amazing as the people inside them*. Harvard Business Review Press.

Hood, C. (1991). A public management for all seasons. *Public Administration, 69*(1), 3–19.

Hood, C. (1995). The "new public management" in the 1980s: Variations on a theme. *Accounting, Organizations and Society, 20*(2–3), 93. https://doi.org/10.1016/0361-3682(93)E0001-W

Hood, C. (2004). The middle aging of new public management: Into the age of paradox? *Journal of Public Administration Research and Theory, 14*(3), 267–282. https://doi.org/10.1093/jopart/muh019

Hood, C., & Dixon, R. (2016). Not what it said on the tin? Reflections on three decades of UK public management reform. *Financial Accountability & Management, 32*(4), 409–428. https://doi.org/10.1111/faam.12095

Irving, J. A. (2018). Leader purposefulness and servant leadership. In D. van Dierendonck & K. Patterson (Eds.), *Practising servant leadership: Developments in implementation* (pp. 25–42). Palgrave Macmillan.

Jalonen, H., Kokkola, J., Laihonen, H., Kirjavainen, H., Kaartemo, V., & Vähämaa, M. (2021). Reaching hard-to-reach people through digital means—citizens as initiators of co-creation in public services. *International Journal of Public Sector Management, 34*(7), 799–816. https://doi.org/10.1108/IJPSM-01-2021-0008

Jensen, P. H. (2020). Experiments and evaluation of public policies: Methods, implementation and challenges. *Australian Journal of Public Administration, 79*(2), 259–268. https://doi.org/10.1111/1467-8500.12406

Junginger, S. (2017). *Transforming public service by design: Re-orienting policies, organisations and services around people*. Routledge.

Kinder, T., Stenvall, J., Six, F., & Memon, A. (2021). Relational leadership in collaborative governance ecosystems. *Public Management Review*. https://doi.org/10.1080/14719037.2021.1879913

Kleiner, A. (2008). *The age of the heretics: A history of the radical thinkers who reinvented corporate management*. Jossey-Bass.

Klijn, E. H., & Koppenjan, J. (2016). *Governance networks in the public sector*. Routledge.

Lapsley, I. (2009). New public management: The cruellest invention of the human spirit? *A Journal of Accounting, Finance and Business Studies*, *45*(1), 1–21. https://doi.org/10.1111/j.1467-6281.2009.00275.x

Lember, V., Brandsen, T., & Tõnurist, P. (2019). The potential impacts of digital technologies on co-production and co-creation. *Public Management Review*. https://doi.org/10.1080/14719037.2019.1619807

Lewin, K. (1935). *A dynamic theory of personality*. McGraw-Hill.

Lewin, K. (1936). *Principles of topological psychology*. McGraw-Hill.

Lilienthal, D. E. (1967). *Management: A humanist art*. Carnegie Institute of Technology.

López, D. J., Vergara, P., & Roa, M. S. (2018). Attributes of the humanist director: The exercise of virtues as a possible scenario for the constitution of humanist enterprise. *The Journal of Social Sciences Research*, *4*(10), 146–152. https://ideas.repec.org/a/arp/tjssrr/2018p146-152.html

López-De-Ipiña, D., Emaldi, M., Aguilera, U., & Pérez-Velasco, J. (2016). Towards citizen co-created public service apps. *Lecture Notes in Computer Science (Including Subseries Lecture Notes in Artificial Intelligence and Lecture Notes in Bioinformatics)*, *10070*, 469–481. https://doi.org/10.1007/978-3-319-48799-1_51

Lowe, T., French, M., Hawkins, M., Hesselgreaves, H., & Wilson, R. (2020). New development: Responding to complexity in public services—the human learning systems approach. *Public Money & Management*. https://doi.org/10.1080/09540962.2020.1832738

Luciano, F. (2020). Artificial intelligence as a public service: Learning from Amsterdam and Helsinki. *Philosophy & Technology*, *33*(4), 541–546. https://doi.org/10.1007/s13347-020-00434-3

Luna-Reyes, L. (2017). Opportunities and challenges for digital governance in a world of digital participation. *Information Polity*, *22*(2–3), 197–205. https://doi.org/10.3233/IP-170408

Lynn, L. E. (2005). Public management: A concise history of the field. In E. Ferlie, L. Lynn, & C. Pollitt (Eds.), *The Oxford handbook of public management* (pp. 27–50). Oxford University Press.

March, J. G. (1978). Bounded rationality, ambiguity and the engineering of choice. *Bell Journal of Economics*, *9*(2), 587–608. www.jstor.org/stable/3003600

Mazzucato, M. (2021). *Mission economy: A moonshot guide to changing capitalism*. Allen Lane.

Meier, K. J., & Hill, G. C. (2005). Bureaucracy in the twenty-first century. In E. Ferlie, L. Lynn, & C. Pollitt (Eds.), *The Oxford handbook of public management* (pp. 51–71). Oxford University Press.

Melé, D. (2003). The challenge of humanistic management. *Journal of Business Ethics*, *44*(44), 77–88. https://doi.org/10.1023/A:1023298710412

Melé, D. (2016). Understanding humanistic management. *Humanistic Management Journal*, *1*(1), 33–55. https://doi.org/10.1007/s41463-016-0011-5

Mintzberg, H. (1973). *The nature of managerial work*. Harper & Row.

Mintzberg, H. (1990, March–April). The manager's job: Folklore and fact. *Harvard Business Review*. Retrieved June 27, 2021, from https://hbr.org/archive-toc/3902

Mintzberg, H. (2009). *Managing*. Berrett-Koehler Publishers, Inc.

Morgan, D. F., Ingle, M. D., & Shinn, G. W. (2019). *New public leadership: Making a difference where we sit*. Routledge.

Morse, R. (2010). Integrative public leadership: Catalyzing collaboration to create public value. *Leadership Quarterly, 21*(2), 231–245. https://doi.org/10.1016/j.leaqua.2010.01.004

Moynihan, D. P., & Landuyt, N. (2009). How do public organizations learn? Bridging cultural and structural perspectives. *Public Administration Review, 69*(6), 1097–1105. https://doi.org/10.1111/j.1540-6210.2009.02067.x

Orazi, D. C., Turrini, A., & Valotti, G. (2013). Public sector leadership: New perspectives for research and practice. *International Review of Administrative Sciences, 79*(3), 486–504. https://doi.org/10.1177/0020852313489945

Osborne, D., & Gaebler, T. (1992). *Reinventing government.* Penguin Press.

Osborne, S. P. (2006). The new public governance? *Public Management Review, 8*(3), 377–387. https://doi.org/10.1080/14719030600853022

Osborne, S. P. (2018). From public service-dominant logic to public service logic: Are public service organizations capable of co-production and value co-creation? *Public Management Review, 20*(2), 225–231. https://doi.org/10.1080/14719037.2017.135046

Pollitt, C. (2003). *The essential public manager.* Open University Press.

Power, M. (1997). *The audit society: Rituals and verifications.* Oxford University Press.

Reuschke, D., & Felstead, A. (2020). Changing workplace geographies in the COVID-19 crisis. *Dialogues in Human Geography, 10*(2), 208–212. https://doi.org/10.1177/2043820620934249

Savory, C. (2010). Patient and public involvement in translative healthcare research. *Clinical Governance: An International Journal, 15*(3), 191–199. https://doi.org/10.1108/14777271011063823

Schillemans, T. (2011). Does horizontal accountability work? Evaluating potential remedies for the accountability deficit of agencies. *Administration & Society, 43*(3), 387–416. https://doi.org/10.1177/0095399711412931

Searle, J. R. (2010). *Making the social world: The structure of human civilization.* Oxford University Press.

Senge, P. (1990). The leader's new work: Building learning organizations. *Sloan Management Review, 32*(1), 7–23. https://sloanreview.mit.edu/article/the-leaders-new-work-building-learning-organizations/

Senge, P. (2020). Commentary: Why practicing a system's perspective is easier said than done. *Applied Developmental Science, 24*(1), 57–61. https://doi.org/10.1080/10888691.2017.1421429

Sennett, R. (2013). *Together: The rituals, pleasures and politics of cooperation.* Penguin Books.

Shearer, E., Stirling, R., & Pasquarelli, W. (2020). *Government AI readiness index 2020.* Canada's International Research Centre. Retrieved July 2, 2021, from https://static1.squarespace.com/static/58b2e92c1e5b6c828058484e/t/5f7747f29ca3c20ecb598f7c/1601653137399/AI+Readiness+Report.pdf

Sorrentino, M., Sicilia, M., & Howlett, M. (2018). Understanding co-production as a new public governance tool. *Policy & Society, 37*(3), 277–293. https://doi.org/10.1080/14494035.2018.1521676

Stanley, J. (2010). Philosophy of language. In D. Moran (Ed.), *The Routledge companion to twentieth century philosophy* (pp. 382–437). Routledge.

Tett, G. (2015). *Silo effect: The peril of expertise and the promise of breaking down barriers.* Simon & Schuster.

Thomassen, J., Ahaus, K., van de Walle, S., & Nabitz, U. (2012). An implementation framework for public service charters: Results of a concept mapping study. *Public Management Review, 16*(4), 570–589. https://doi.org/10.1080/14719037.2012.726062

Torfing, J., & Triantafillou, P. (2013). What's in a name? Grasping new public governance as a political-administrative system. *International Review of Public Administration, 18*(2), 9–25. https://doi.org/10.1080/12294659.2013.10805250

Van Der Wal, Z. (2017). *The 21st century public manager*. Palgrave Macmillan.

Van Der Wal, Z. (2020). Being a public manager in times of crisis: The art of managing stakeholders, political masters, and collaborative networks. *Public Administration Review, 80*(5), 759–764. https://doi.org/10.1111/puar.13245

Van Der Wal, Z., Nabatchi, T., & de Graaf, G. (2015). From galaxies to universe: A cross-disciplinary review and analysis of public values publications from 1969 to 2012. *American Review of Public Administration, 45*(1), 13. https://doi.org/10.1177/0275074013488822

Van Noordt, C., & Misuraca, G. (2020). Exploratory insights on artificial intelligence for government in Europe. *Social Science Computer Review*, 1–9. https://doi.org/10.1177/0894439320980449.

Van Wart, M. (2003). Public-sector leadership theory: An assessment. *Public Administration Review, 63*(2), 214–228. https://doi.org/10.1111/1540-6210.00281

Van Wart, M. (2013a). Administrative leadership theory: A reassessment after 10 years. *Public Administration, 91*(3), 521. https://doi.org/10.1111/padm.12017

Van Wart, M. (2013b). Lessons from leadership theory and the contemporary challenges of leaders. *Public Administration Review, 73*(4), 553–565. https://doi.org/10.1111/puar.12069

Van Wart, M. (2017). *Leadership in public organizations: An introduction*. Routledge.

Van Woerkom, M., Bakker, A. B., & Leiter, M. P. (2021). Editorial: Positive psychology in organisations. *Journal of Occupational and Organizational Psychology, 94*(2), 221–229. https://doi.org/10.1111/joop.12350

Virtanen, P., Stenvall, J., Kinder, T., & Hatem, O. (2018). Do accountabilities change when public organisations transform to service systems: A new conceptual approach. *Financial Accountability & Management, 34*(2), 166–180. https://doi.org/10.1111/faam.12149

Virtanen, P., & Tammeaid, M. (2020). *Developing public sector leadership: New rationale, best practices and tools*. Springer. https://doi.org/10.1007/978-3-030-42311-7

Virtanen, P., & Yli-Viikari, T. (2021). Exogeneous shocks, resilience and the evolution of public governance, the case of Finland. In A. Farazmand (Ed.), *Global encyclopedia of public administration, public policy, and governance*. Springer. https://doi.org/10.1007/978-3-319-31816-5_4180-1

Vogl, T. L., Seidelin, C., Ghanesh, B., & Bright, J. (2020). Smart technology and the emergence of algorithmic bureaucracy: Artificial intelligence in UK local authorities. *Public Administration Review, 80*(6), 946–961. https://doi.org/10.1111/puar.13286

Waldman, M. H. (2006). Evidence-based medicine: How to translate research into patient care. *Journal of the American Podiatric Medical Association, 96*(4), 374–377. https://doi.org/10.7547/0960374

Weber, E. P. (1999). The question of accountability in historical perspective: From Jackson to contemporary grassroots ecosystem management. *Administration and Society, 31*(4), 451–494. https://doi.org/10.1177/00953999922019201

Wheeler, L. (2008). Kurt Lewin. *Social and Personality Psychology Compass, 2*(4), 1638–1650. https://doi.org/10.1111/j.1751-9004.2008.00131.x

Zuboff, S. (2019). *The age of surveillance capitalism: The fight for a human at the new frontier of power*. Profile Books.

# 4 The systemic nature of society as the context for human-centred public leadership

## 4.1 Systemic nature of change

In December 2010, Mohammed Bouazizi, a Tunisian fruit dealer, was totally fed up with rampant corruption and growing inequality in his home country. The dissatisfaction the young man had long felt turned into a desperate act in Sidi Bouzid when Bouazizi, publicly humiliated by the local police, committed suicide. Bouazizi's act has been widely considered as the starting point of what was later termed 'the Arab Spring' uprising. Although there was a long period of dissatisfaction behind the uprising, the suicide became something of a watershed and was followed by the escalation of dissatisfaction into a social movement that overthrew those in power. Just two weeks after the suicide, Tunisia's long-time president, Zine el-Abidine Ben Ali, was driven into exile. The protest movement was not confined to Tunisia but spread rapidly across the Middle East and North Africa. One of the main drivers of its proliferation was social media, which allowed citizens to communicate with each other instead of following the government-controlled media (Papacharissi, 2015).

Bouazizi's suicide served as a leverage point with surprising effects. By the end of February 2010, the Arab Spring had spread to more than ten countries across the region. The pressure on the government was fierce, but so were the measures taken by those in power. In Syria, for example, the protest did not lead to the resignation of President Bashar al-Assad but to one of the greatest humanitarian crises of the 21st century. From this chapter's perspective, the Arab Spring provides an example of a development that has an identifiable starting point and whose consequences can be characterised as systemic. At the same time, it is a question of the expectations and demands of individuals, the collective faith of the community in the possibility of change and the cracks in the power structures of society. The Arab Spring was not just an uprising, it also clearly displayed features of systemic change.

Systemic change inevitably renders more complex the contextual settings of public leadership. It does so by increasing the likelihood that small events induce large and unexpected consequences. For example, many public leaders have faced situations where a single ill-judged tweet or private remark

DOI: 10.4324/9781003205791-4

has sparked a surge of negative publicity. This is at least partly due to the new hybrid media environment, where meanings are made through circulating content from one arena to another (Chadwick, 2013). Mass media absorbs content generated and disseminated in social media platforms, and social media discussions reflect what has been said on TV news and in newspaper editorials. While every sensation takes on a logic of its own, they are often based on utterances taken out of context and shaped to fit the narrative of those who want to create discord. Reported speech is typically exaggerated and deliberately misconstrued to delegitimise the speaker's arguments and ideas. It is also worth noting here that negative publicity is not necessarily limited to the behaviours of public leaders but may also create a need to scrutinise public organisations. Due to this nonlinearity, it is possible that the management systems and decision-making processes will be questioned because of actions taken by individual leaders. This is because nonlinearity implies that the behaviour of the system does not necessarily depend on the values of the initial conditions.

Systemic change refers to the simultaneous changes in operational models, structures, and their interactions (Stroh, 2015). It implies a need to change all levels of a system—from the social to the political and further to the environmental. Systemic change cannot be delegated to individual actors, as it is a matter of development in the interactions between actors, both good and bad. Systemic change is not always triggered by discrete or identifiable events. Extreme acts such as suicides will be remembered, but at the same time they also direct our gaze too easily to the visible side of change, ignoring the hidden underlying drivers. The tension between the visible and the hidden can be addressed using an iceberg metaphor. As we all learn at school, only a fraction of the iceberg is visible to our eyes, with most of its mass below the surface. It is possible that in systemic change too, only a portion of the problem manifests itself as clearly distinguishable events. Perhaps the mechanisms that produce visible events and prevent them are anchored in both social structures and the mental models of individuals. If so, the understanding of systemic change will inevitably remain partial unless we also pay attention to the properties of the factors beneath the surface and, above all, to their interdependencies. Following Meadows (2008), a distinguished environmental scientist and systems thinker, it is important to carefully observe the system, perceive its interaction dynamics, and recognise its pulse.

Kania et al. (2018) provide a systemic perspective on systemic change focusing on factors and circumstances that enable change. According to them, several factors contributing to systemic change can be identified which in turn can be structured into three levels of change. The structural level of systemic change consists of policies, practices, and resources. The structural level materialises as societal institutions, management practices, and regulatory solutions that enable and limit the interaction of actors. It also specifies the distribution and allocation of tangible and intangible resources. At the level of relational change, two key factors here are the connections between actors and the dynamics of power. The number of relationships and the quality of connections determine the influence we are exposed to, while the dynamics of power determine whose voice is heard. At the level of transformative change, it is a question of the mental models of individuals, those deep-rooted ways that make us take things for granted and that guide our thinking, what we do and what we say.

The systemic nature of change challenges conventional ways of sense-making and cuts through many levels of human activity. For example, public administration cannot be structured through a system lens as a machine built vertically (national, regional, local) and horizontally (branches, sectors, industries). Instead, it is a network of interdependencies, based not only on formal competences but also on the actors' abilities to deal with phenomena arising in the political, economic, technological, and cultural arenas and at their interfaces. This leads us to ask, does systemic change also tell us a story of increasing complexity?

## 4.2 Has societal complexity really increased?

The dominant narrative draws a picture of ever-increasing complexity. There are nuanced differences in the descriptions, but what most of them have in common is that the increase in the number and diversity of ideas, events, and actors generates developments that are difficult to predict. Rapidly moving climate change, the unforeseen consequences of ubiquitous digitalisation, changing geopolitical landscapes, and surprising political and social movements are widely used examples of the increasingly complex nature of modern societies. Unsurprisingly, there is no shortage of research that attempts to capture the 'nature' of complexity. Often it has explicitly or implicitly been taken for granted that the contemporary present represents a kind of complexity that has not been seen previously. Mintzberg (1993, p. 34), for example, has described the present moment bias sarcastically as follows:

> in the 1960s, organizations were implored to plan because the stable 1950s were gone; in the 1970s they were told how comparatively stable were the 1960s, in the 1980s there were writers who claimed that techniques such as the Boston Consulting Group's growth share matrix worked in the 1970s because, unlike the 1980s, these were stable years.

In a similar vein Grint (2022, p. 5) questions the idea of the certainty of the good old days by juxtaposing the many uncertainties of our time (e.g., the COVID-19 and the Global Financial Crisis of 2008) with the uncertainties in the past (e.g., the rise of the Nazis to power in 1933 and the Russian Revolution in 1917). He concludes that there has never been a kind of predictability of events which justifies calling a certain period of history the Age of Certainty.

If we put sarcasm aside, can we really say that societal complexity has increased? To elaborate the question further, it is useful to separate ontology from epistemology. In the philosophy of science, ontology refers to understanding the properties of the reality, whereas epistemology refers to knowing the reality. While the ontology asks 'what that is', the epistemology asks, 'how do we know what that is?' Approaching the tendency towards complexity through ontology and epistemology, it can be argued that complexity arises, on the one hand, from our conflicting conceptions of the nature of the reality and, on the other, from the different requirements concerning the evidence that verifies to us the nature of that reality. The dual challenge of complexity manifests itself in the form of wicked problems—i.e., problems have no definitive formulation; solutions are not true or false; there is no test for a solution; every solution has a consequence; they do not have simple causes; and they have numerous possible explanations, which in turn frame different policy responses (Rittel & Webber, 1973). In a nutshell, wicked problems increase uncertainty, complexity, and divergence (Head, 2022, p. 21). Recent decades have seen rapid growth in the use of the wicked problem approach in research. A Google Scholar search shows that in the 1990s the approach attracted some 516 studies, in the 2000s, around 3,500 studies, but by the 2010s we were already at over 16,000 such studies.

The wicked problems approach has been popular across a wide variety of research questions. It has been used, for example, for understanding organisational strategies (e.g., Camillus, 2008), housing planning (Adams, 2011), ethics (e.g., Heimer, 2013), climate change (e.g., Perry, 2015), public governance (e.g., Daviter, 2017), health and social care (e.g., Will et al., 2019), and policy evaluation (Termeer & Dewulf, 2019). Some have even identified 'super' wicked problems characterising them as problems which have the following features: "time is running out; those who cause the problem also seek to provide a solution; the central authority needed to address it is weak or non-existent; and, partly as a result, policy responses discount the future irrationally" (Levin et al., 2012, p. 123). While the research designs varied, the common denominator within them is that wicked problems are understood as subjective, in the sense that everyone involved had an equally 'valid' opinion about it. This growth in the number and diversity of perspectives however implies that complexity *has* increased. This, in turn, begs the question of how to deal with this complexity.

## 4.3 Dealing with complexity

Long before Mintzberg, Appleby (1954) forwarded the idea that the advance of civilisation is a progression in complexity. According to him, the division of labour and specialisation increasingly differentiated persons in terms of experience, functions, and learnings. Consequently, while many things became possible, it also became obvious that the realisation of potentials cannot be based on fragmented expertise but rather on interdependencies between experiences, functions, and learnings. For Appleby, it is these dependencies which produce increased societal complexity. Appleby was one of the first scholars who analysed societal complexity through the lens of dependencies. Moreover, he was not the last scholar to emphasise the role of dependencies as a root cause of complexity. In fact, since about 1990, there has been a veritable flood of research on complexity: Paul Cilliers, David Byrne, Ralph Stacey, and Eve Mitleton-Kelly, to name but a few, have spoken about emergent structures and the processes and outcomes that arise from the interaction of two or more entities. While they all have slightly different perspectives on complexity, they do however share the core idea that the emergent whole cannot be understood based on what is known about its constituent parts. In other words, the emergent whole is more or less than the sum of its parts. The mainstream complexity-informed literature claims that it is not the size of the whole that matters. More important than the number of parts—individuals and organisations—is the intensity of interaction between them. Complexity arises from relations, not from attributes. The everyday life of a long-married couple, to put it bluntly, can be as complex as a strategy process in a large public organisation. In addition to agency, several artefacts such as norms and institutions also play an important role. This is because no action takes place in a social vacuum but is in many ways made possible and limited by the structures that frame it.

Complexity thinking has evolved as a multidisciplinary approach in which comprehensive, holistic thinking replaces a worldview, an approach that emphasises simplifying causal relations and reductionism alongside linear reasoning, control over issues, and predictability (e.g., Cilliers, 1998; Geyer & Rihani, 2010; Byrne & Callaghan, 2014). In spoken language, complexity infers a situation or a problem that is difficult to understand or complicated to handle. It is comparable to something that should be fixed. In complexity thinking, complexity refers to a basic property of a system. In other words, it is neither good nor bad.

Contrary to the ideal of certainty and predictability, complexity thinking implies that change and uncertainty are basic properties of a complex world and therefore all simplifications must fail. One of the key promises of complexity thinking is that it may explain why the whole is more (or less) than the sum of the parts and how all its components come together to produce overarching patterns as the system evolves and adapts (Mitleton-Kelly, 2003; Stacey, 2010). For Byrne (1999), complexity thinking represents a type of progress, by which more phenomena can be understood enabling individuals and communities to influence, if not control, their lives and societies.

Complexity thinking has also contributed to management and leadership studies in many ways. Richardson (2008), for example, emphasises the importance of 'managerial attitude' by which he refers to the shift from a linear, simplistic, attitude to a nonlinear complex one. The shift is not easy as it challenges many strongly held assumptions of, and expectations for, management. As such, complexity thinking encourages managers to study the philosophical underpinnings of their choices. Richardson (2008, p. 22) characterises managers' work as constituting decisions concerning

> which information is required to make a particular decision; how to interpret that information for the purposes at hand, and even choose what the actual purpose might be, as well as what the issue is that needs to be decided upon.

Complexity thinking offers him a scientific way to affect how the common sense of managerial work evolves over time in general and in the context of individual managers' mindsets in particular. While stressing the scientific roots of complexity thinking, he eventually ends up joining those who have propagated the idea that management is as much an art as it is a science.

The artistic side of management is visible, for example, in the work of Uhl-Bien and Arena (2017, 2018), who also propose a complexity-based leadership approach. They envision enabling leadership combining two opposite logics of action. Operational leadership focuses on generating efficiency through the organisation's formal functions, whereas entrepreneurial leadership pursues innovation by the linking up of diverse agents. Enabling leadership operates in the nexus between operational and entrepreneurial leadership. Uhl-Bien and Arena point out that while many managers practice enabling leadership, what is lacking is a leadership language to describe it. This, in turn, has led to misunderstandings of those who have engaged in enabling leadership. Uhl-Bien and Arena conclude that enabling leadership allows for the emergence of organisational adaptability, i.e., the ability to find a balance between exploitation (using existing knowledge, skills, and processes to produce results) and exploration (creating new knowledge, skills, and processes to innovate) (see March, 1991 for more on exploration and exploitation). A search for adaptability can be seen as one of the common denominators of complexity-informed management and leadership. Joosse and Teisman (2021), for example, propose the concept of 'complexification management'. Their main argument is that instead of avoiding complexity, managers should embrace it. Complexification management is a strategy that can be used to revitalise locked processes generated by simplification. Complexification management may increase organisational adaptability as it helps to unlock ineffective path-dependency. Success cannot however be guaranteed, but perhaps the odds can be improved.

Unsurprisingly, the use of complexity thinking in the context of leadership has also been criticised. Rosenhead et al. (2019, p. 35), for example, point out that complexity thinking has inspired 'motherhood' statements which are "for the most part general and non-specific, and offered with a sense of being unchallengeable within the offered framework of (complexity) ideas". They conclude that while complexity researchers claim the legitimacy of science, they also tend to reject certain key denominators of science. In so doing, they "want to have [their] scientific cake and eat it" (Rosenhead et al., 2019, p. 16).

Without belittling the critique, it is assumed here that complexity-informed studies provide potentially useful approach to public leadership. While the 'complexity lens' should not be understood as a panacea that will solve all the challenges thrown up by the complexification of society (as is the case also with many other approaches), it nevertheless has significant leverage power to guide thinking holistically. Instead of 'either/or' thinking, it favours a 'both/and' attitude. In complexity thinking, ideas and things are seen as *phenomena*, rather than as sliced pieces.

One of the most important lessons of complexity thinking is that it enlarges the sphere of public leadership from the organisation to the service ecosystem. In addition to enacting good governance practices within the organisation, public leaders are expected to manage 'upwards, outwards, and downwards' (Moore, 1995). According to Osborne et al. (2021, p. 669), public leaders need to consider institutional level factors such as norms and values on public service delivery, the service level factors including the role of service processes, organisational actors, and the local community on value creation, as well as individual-level factors, specifically, the relationship between the individual and public service delivery. Increasingly, the value of public services is co-created in complex interactions within the ecosystem instead of the dyad interactions between individual public service organisations and service users.

## 4.4 From pieces to phenomena

New phenomena constantly emerge in the political, economic, and cultural arenas and their interfaces. In addition, existing phenomena take on new shapes. Social phenomena emerge from the interconnectedness of things and events, which makes it difficult to find easy solutions. Climate warming, demographic change, the marginalisation of youth, immobility and obesity, and pandemics are examples of complex and interconnected phenomena which have also challenged many conventional and functional-based approaches to management and leadership in public organisations. It is common for these phenomena that, while they challenge existing knowledge, they also produce conflicting interpretations. In the debate around the marginalisation of youth, for example, two extremes can be identified: on the one side are those who see marginalisation as a logical consequence of individuals (bad) choices, while on the other are those who think that it is always a question of discriminatory social structures. Unsurprisingly, the marginalisation of youth is therefore an example of a phenomenon whose administrative compartmentalisation and lack of holistic understanding are likely to produce more problems than solutions. No one can say with certainty what event, occurrence, or situation will, ultimately, lead to marginalisation. A marginalised young person has his or her own will, which influences what actions he or she takes, or fails to take. There is no natural law which dictates the development of social phenomena. Instead, dealing with the phenomena requires the recognition and understanding of the patterns of systemic dynamics. Otherwise, there is a danger that we might unwittingly be contributing to the very problems we want to solve (Stroh, 2015).

Poorly understood societal phenomena can become costly at the societal level causing a loss of well-being, perceived happiness, and prosperity measured at the individual level. Let us look at immobility as a phenomenon. It cannot be explained by individual factors. Instead, immobility is affected by several different things whose cause-and-effect relationships are difficult to discern. The causes and consequences of immobility can be identified in different parts of society. Fragmented decisions made in housing, transportation, and education constitute unintended and detrimental consequences in employment and social and health care. In Finland, for example, it has been estimated that low levels of physical activity, excessive sitting at work and at home, and overall poor physical fitness cost society at least € 3 billion a year, when considering health and social care costs, productivity costs, the loss of income tax revenues, unemployment benefits, and the costs of social exclusion (Vasankari et al., 2018). The problem here is that there is no comprehensive 'sports policy' which could effectively bring together different aspects of immobility nor a competent agency whose responsibility covers the various potential policies relevant to the phenomenon. Instead of developing a set of individual services to tackle immobility, the phenomena-based view favours focusing on societal structures and practices as well as the norms and beliefs that contribute to immobility, at both the individual and community levels. This necessitates cross-border and cross-administrative collaboration within the service ecosystem, calling also for new leadership meta-skills, such as the art of guiding the interaction.

It is also worth noting here that accepting a planning and delivery mechanism based on societal phenomena necessitates accepting increased complexity and reduced generalisability (Von Krogh et al., 2012). Hambrick (2007, p. 1346), for example, has stated that exclusively relying on the concepts and explanatory mechanisms provided by a particular theory may become an obstacle to understanding the multidimensionality of real-life phenomena. If not careful, there is a danger that "our field's theory fetish prevents the reporting of rich detail about interesting phenomena for which no theory yet exists", he warns. It is possible that the phenomena also challenge the idea of social psychologist Kurt Lewin that "nothing is as practical as a good theory" (Lewin, 1945, p. 129). This is not to say that theories of social phenomena have become obsolete. Rather, the question is that the conceptualisation of cross-border phenomena requires the crossing of disciplinary boundaries, or at least a close interdisciplinary dialogue. Previously non-existent or poorly understood phenomena cannot be captured by information that is reducible from previous knowledge (Nissani, 1995).

The limitations of our understanding are largely due to the mental models we apply which, in turn, are rooted in a time when things and phenomena were—at least seemingly—clearly delineated and settled. Senge (2006) suggests that our mental models are an invisible cognitive and cultural condition for systemic change. In other words, the way we perceive, interpret, and frame phenomena is dependent on our mental models. Systemic change is about shifting the conditions that are holding the problem in place (Kania et al., 2018). Hardly ever is our ability to apply phenomenon-based thinking and challenge our mental models more crucial than in times of crisis and unexpected events, in other words, in situations where resilience is critical.

## 4.5 The many faces of resilience

Resilience has been studied extensively as an individual-level phenomenon, often by the methods used in psychological research. The concept has been used in these studies to refer to the adaptability of the human mind. In organisational and leadership research, resilience has been specifically linked to coping with both man-made and natural disasters (e.g., Weick, 1993; Pearson & Clair, 1998). More recently, resilience has been linked to the continuity of organisations' operations in an uncertain, complex, and rapidly changing operating environment (e.g., Bennett & Lemoine, 2014; Välikangas, 2010). Although resilience always implies that something adverse has happened, a perturbative situation can also be seen as an opportunity. As British wartime prime minister Winston Churchill once said, "never let a good crisis go to waste". Churchill, with the help of economists such as John Maynard Keynes and William Beveridge, pushed the visionary work during the war that "defined the peace and shaped the fortunes of generations to come" (Goldin, 2021, p. 5). More generally, the crisis can be seen as a mirror that reveals problems in procedures and/or in structures whose fixing is also beneficial in normal conditions. While not every crisis is a turning point, they may, however, act as a catalyst that accelerates the change already happening (Haas, 2020).

Duchek (2020) has identified three approaches in organisation-driven resilience research. First, in the recovery-focused approach, resilience is portrayed as an organisation's ability to return to pre-crisis normalcy. This kind of 'bouncing back' way of thinking assumes that resilience is "a fundamental quality to respond productively to significant change that disrupts the expected pattern of event" (Horne & Orr, 1988, p. 31). To bounce back, organisations are expected to be able to absorb the impact of the unexpected event(s) and accommodate disturbances without failure (Linnenluecke & Griffiths, 2012). Second, the adaptation-oriented approach rejects the idea of normality, thus resilience is seen as organisational learning which is activated by crisis. Instead of 'bouncing back' the approach stresses 'bouncing forward'. Lengnick-Hall et al. (2011, p. 244) described the resilience organisation's ability to "engage in transformative activities to capitalize on disruptive surprises that potentially threaten organizational survival". Third, from the foresight perspective, resilience manifests itself as proactive preparedness for various crisis situations. The resilient organisation has the capacity to anticipate and adjust to the operational environment (Ortiz-de-Mandojana & Bansal, 2016). Precursor resilience, as Boin and van Eeten (2013, p. 431) term it, "prevents budding problems from escalating into a full-blown crisis or breakdown".

It can be assumed then that the resilience of public organisations consists of proactive preparedness, recovery from crisis, and adaptation to the 'new normal'. However, resilience in public organisations may have additional special features. According to Duit (2016), for example, the challenge here is the need for a continuous balance between resilience and good governance principles, such as transparency, legitimacy, and accountability. In a similar vein, Stark (2014) emphasises the tension between rules and improvisation. In addition, Zhang et al. (2018) and Plimmer et al. (2021), among others, have pointed out that there is a certain degree of rigidity in public sector organisations in relation to transforming the threats and opportunities identified in the operating environment into adaptive actions. This rigidity also hampers public these organisation's ability to make use of solutions developed elsewhere. For example, during the corona pandemic, public organisations in many countries have often been accused of being incapable of identifying, accepting, and disseminating solutions created by citizens and local communities. Contrary to the general trend towards the co-creation of public services (e.g., Brandsen et al., 2018), the tendency during the crisis has been to rely on centralised, top-down steering. Adapting Latour's (1987, p. 10) idea of legitimacy, it seems that the solution has been seen to work when all the relevant people were convinced, not when ordinary people witnessed the workable solutions. Campbell (2021) provides an interesting approach to the legitimacy of public organisations in need of resilience. In contrast to efficiency-enhancing resilience (i.e., public managers seek efficiency or effectiveness gains through improving internal processes or exploiting opportunities in the organisation's environment), Campbell (2021, p. 220) stresses the need for legitimacy-enhancing resilience, in which new processes are "adopted and partnerships formed based on their potential to change the legitimacy of the organization". In line with the idea of this book, Campbell links legitimacy-oriented resilience to the human side of enterprise (see McGregor, 1960). Instead of external incentives and sanctions, Campbell suggests that resilience can be strengthened when leaders persuade, inspire, and empower their subordinates. Campbell's argument appears though somewhat too straightforward. At the start of the COVID-19 crisis, there was an information deficit and the task governments faced was to build a test-and-trace structure to combat spread before the vaccine was created. This was the same problem faced in the 19th century when public health systems (to combat infectious diseases) were first created.

Seen through Lewin's (1947) classical change management model, resilience parallels the development in which social equilibrium drifts into chaos, which in turn allows the emergence of a new social equilibrium. Lewin's idea of the process of unfreeze-change-refreeze is however rather problematic in the context of systemic change for three reasons. First, it assumes change as a process has a starting point and a point of termination. Second, it implies the idea that actors are responsible for propagating the awareness of change and of transforming it into action. Third, depicting change as a periodic process is flawed because it suggests that resilience can be decomposed into components which can be activated when needed. In contrast to periodic phases, individual change agents, and reductionism, systemic change manifests itself as an ongoing, never-ending, and circular process. This comes with consequences. Instead of searching for one optimal equilibrium state, resilience will be proven as one's ability to navigate through several simultaneous equilibrium states. How can this be done? How should resilience be addressed in terms of a societal-level phenomenon?

## 4.6 Complexity-informed interpretation of societal resilience and public leadership

The more complex the world becomes, the more need there is for societal resilience. Leaning on Haavik (2020) and Redding (2020), societal resilience can be defined as society's capacity to cope with unexpected events and to shape social institutions in a way that improves their preparedness. Societal resilience materialises as a *multisystemic* phenomenon (Ungar, 2021) involving people, organisations, processes, institutions, relations, values, and norms in the various subsystems, including politico-administrative, socio-cultural, economic and technological, and regulatory systems. A resilient society can recover after a disturbance and develop new capabilities to adapt to a changing environment. Societal resilience also implies that what is needed is something more fundamental than just 'bouncing back' or 'bouncing forward'. Goldin (2021), for example, points out that 'bouncing back' suggests that we would be heading in the same direction that brought the adversities we are facing, while 'bouncing forward' assumes that we are leaping ahead along in the same direction. Instead of 'rebooting' the system, societal resilience calls for systemic change.

The benefits of societal resilience are unquestionable, but how can societal resilience be achieved in the first place? Can resilience never be solved because we do not have access in advance to the list of all of the problems society could potentially face? These are not easy questions because of the multisystemic nature of this issue. Unsurprisingly, complexity-informed approaches have recently spread into resilience research. Normandin and Therrien (2016) deployed the principles of complexity thinking in introducing a framework for capturing the interdependent dynamics of stability and adaptability inherent to resilience. According to them, resilience can be strengthened by promoting favourable order (e.g., to develop regulation) and favourable disorder (e.g., to improve adaptation) while opposing unfavourable order (e.g., to avert rigidity) and unfavourable disorder (e.g., to avoid chaos). Leaning on the extensive research literature, Normandin and Therrien contribute by providing several favourable order factors and favourable disorder factors. Meek and Marshall (2018) used complexity thinking to study the resilience of the metropolitan area's water management system. They identified several attributes of so-called spatial complexity when they referred to the domain of interacting agents, networks, and systems influencing outcomes of water management governance. They conclude (Meek & Marshall, 2018, p. 1102) that "rather than understand or approach spatial scarcity from a reductionist perspective of control through simplification . . . a complexity-informed approach requires more administrative reliance and trust on the emergent and adaptive outcomes of spatial complexity". Bristow and Healy (2015), in turn, approached economic crisis and the adaptive capacities of regional actors through complexity thinking. They suggest that complexity thinking helps to understand who has agency within regional economies, how agency functions, and specifically what shapes how agents adapt, respond, and react to crises. They argue in favour of the co-evolutionary behaviour of agents within their regional contexts (See also, Exhibit 1).

The aforementioned studies suggest that complexity thinking does show some potential in the search for the building blocks of societal resilience. Instead of an exhaustive analysis, we focus later on some key aspects of complexity, which we think have explanatory power in the context of societal resilience and public leadership.

First, societal resilience should be conceptualised as an emergent whole that arises from the interaction between actors. Societal resilience cannot be reduced to its parts. The whole is considered a new entity. While resilience cannot be designed "it can [nonetheless] be exercised and cultivated" (Dahlberg, 2015, p. 547). Different levels of social resilience are interconnected and have an impact on each other's actions. In other words, what happens at the micro level influences the macro level and *vice versa*. Meso-level structures also play a crucial role as they act as mediators between the micro and macro levels. For example, changes in individual (micro level) behaviour are reflected in changes in the activities of organisations (meso level) and, when a certain threshold is exceeded, changes are transmitted out into society (macro level). Second, self-organisation enables constant adaptation to the changes in environment. Self-organisation occurs when systems exchange information, act, and continuously adapt to others' actions, rather than following the imposition of an overall plan by a central authority. According to Berkes (2007), self-organisation can be supported by focusing on strengthening community-based management, building cross-scale management capabilities, strengthening institutional memory, and nurturing learning organisations and adaptive co-management. Third, diversity

**EXHIBIT 1 Managing the COVID-19 pandemic as an example of societal resilience.**

When the COVID-19 pandemic hit the world, people's daily lives changed dramatically. It soon became very evident that all around the globe, public management and service production were in trouble in this new health crisis due to the complex social transformations caused by the pandemic. The pandemic pointed out governments' inability to engage in pre-disaster learning that would prepare them for situations like this. While some sort of pandemic was forecast (e.g., Henig, 2020; Daszak, 2020), governments and administrations were not prepared for the transboundary consequences of COVID-19 (Bryce et al., 2020). Adapting Haas (2020), the pandemic can be seen as a catalyst that has the power to accelerate the systemic change already ongoing. Some have suggested that COVID-19 is not just a pandemic but a syndemic (Horton, 2020). This means that the escalating health threat, the impacts of control measures, and their interactions with all other health problems and social determinants (e.g., employment, education, income) are treated as one whole.

According to international assessments, Finland succeeded in handling the first three waves of the pandemic quite well (Milne, 2020; Der Spiegel, 2021). After the initial fumbling, the public authorities developed a reasonably effective corona strategy. At the heart of the hybrid strategy, as it was called, were targeted measures and the effective implementation of The Emergency Powers Act and Communicable Diseases Act. To support the lifting of restrictive measures, the hybrid strategy applied the test, trace, isolate, and manage principle. This helped to prevent the uncontrolled spread of the epidemic.

The strategy also had its flip side. The restrictive measures had different consequences on different industries. Various segments of the population were treated differently, for example, at the beginning of the pandemic the older adults were strongly encouraged to stay sheltered. Many experts were also concerned about children and young people's mental health. In addition, many communication problems between the various branches of the public authorities as well as between the authorities and the citizenry were identified. Lähteenmäki-Smith et al. (2021) speak of a paradox whereby they refer to the indications of the governance practices becoming *both* less and more systems driven. In addition to ensuring the Rule of Law, the pandemic sparked in Finland a lively debate about the government's ability to be proactive and one step ahead of real-time processes.

Nonetheless, Finland's approach—shutting down rapidly but not totally to get the pandemic under control—has been one of the most successful in Europe and Finland's infection rates have been one of the lowest on the continent (as of November 2021). There is no single reason for the success. Probably though, one of the key things here has been the systemic approach to pandemic governance. The emergence of the societal resilience displayed by Finnish society was based on three factors: general trust, accountable institutions, and common values. According to the OECD's 2021 survey, Finns' general level of trust in fellow citizens and in social institutions has not been shaken at any stage during the pandemic. Although the restrictions caused many problems in people's everyday lives, acceptance of government action was high. Instead of unanimity, citizens understood the seriousness of the situation and were willing to compromise on their own well-being and the vested interests for the security of society and the continuity of its activities. Moreover, the Government's popularity remained strong during the pandemic.

The success in fighting the pandemic can be assessed through various perspectives. In contrast to many countries, in Finland the pandemic has not caused strong dividing lines between different groups. Lähteenmäki-Smith et al. (2021) assess that while there were many uncertainties related to the spread of the virus, the operational capacity of health system, and the social and economic costs of restrictive measures, the open communication strategy adopted by the Government and health authorities was largely accepted and appreciated by both citizens and societal stakeholders alike. In addition to the establishment of a COVID-19 epidemic situation modelling group by the Ministry of Social Affairs and Health, there were positive signs of cross-sectoral coordination, for example, in the form of human resources mobilisation. Overall, it can be concluded that Finland succeeded relatively well in *enabling* the emergence of societal resilience.

can be seen as a prerequisite source for unpredictable self-organising and the emergence of novelty. On the one hand, without diversity there is no difference that makes a difference. With diversity comes more opportunities for self-organisation. On the other hand, diversity also enables redundancy which, in turn, helps systems to cope with adversity. A diverse system with redundant resources can compensate for processes that have failed.

Fourth, feedback affects the system's behaviour. The feedback loops between different levels either accelerate or balance the change (Coleman, 1990). A circular dependency relationship is typical in feedback processes, meaning that the result of the previous situation is the stake in the following one. In other words, what has happened before is included and continues to impact what happens later. Fifth, trust is needed to connect diverse actors and to underscore the legitimacy of actions. Through trust, the system can reduce the level of complexity emerging from the self-organising interaction processes. It has been claimed that trust is tested first—only after that is the system able to process meanings (Luhmann, 1995). It is a question of both the trust between individuals and individuals' trust in social institutions (Cairney & Wellstead, 2021). Sixth, although change develops through a series of different phases, behaviour is constrained by its reigning attractor(s). An attractor is a complex system's organising principle which limits a system to a pattern of behaviour (Mitleton-Kelly, 2003). In practice, an attractor can be a shared system of meanings or rules, an organisational culture, or even a set of values that determine the future of humanity, such as ecological thinking and human rights. Due to the existence of attractors, each systemic change process has its own characteristic set of behaviours and development paths.

While complexity thinking points to the necessary conditions for societal resilience, this approach alone may not be sufficient. It is possible that societal resilience is an elusive concept, whose meaning is difficult to define exhaustively. Ungar (2021) uses the metaphor of tangram (a Chinese dissection puzzle) in describing the equifinality and multi-finality of the composition of resilience. Equifinality refers to multiple means to attain a single outcome, whereas multi-finality manifests as multiple means to attain many different outcomes. Like a dissection puzzle, where a set of pieces can be assembled in different ways to produce two or more distinct geometric shapes, also societal resilience can be manifest in many shapes. What is beneficial in one context however can be detrimental in another. This kind of contingency speaks in favour of a complexity-informed approach to societal resilience. Building upon Dahlberg (2015), Ungar (2021), and many others, we suggest that while societal resilience cannot be predicted or designed, it can be exercised and cultivated. Accepting emergence, promoting self-organisation, ensuring diversity, understanding feedback loops, strengthening trust, and utilising attractors may not guarantee societal resilience, but neglecting them probably inhibits its development (e.g., Uhl-Bien & Arena, 2018).

## 4.7 Synthesis—the nature of current complexity in public policies and leadership

It has been argued that the qualitative shift in environmental challenges has delivered us into the age of the 'new normal' (Mithani, 2020). While the issue of resilience has already been exhaustively addressed in the study of organisations, what is missing is a system-level approach to resilience (Ungar, 2021). In this chapter, we have deployed complexity thinking in order to illustrate the context—i.e., complexity by nature—of societal resilience and the elements that produce societal resilience—i.e., complexity by design. Context complexity arises in the interdependencies of things, ideas, people, and organisations within and between the macro, meso, and micro levels and between and within multiple and incompatible institutional arrangements. Phenomena are considered complex when they are tightly intertwined and affect each other's functioning. Design complexity, in turn, manifests itself as organisational structures and processes that help to deal with this complexity. According to the law of requisite complexity (Boisot & McKelvey, 2011), organisational complexity must match the external complexity it confronts. In other words, the more complex nature becomes, the more complex a design is required. What seems simple in principle is not necessarily so in practice. This is because the operating environment is "not some objective variable that determines a response but rather an 'issue' to be constituted into a whole variety of 'problems'" (Grint, 2005, p. 1470). The failure in interpretation comes in the form of the simplification of complexity or the complexification of simplicity.

Societal resilience includes the tasks of preserving what exists and of enabling the emergence of novelty. In the context of systemic change, the litmus test for societal resilience is, on the one hand, how the change is interpreted at different levels of society and, on the other, what kind of action can be achieved based on the interpretation. We have challenged a view of resilience based on preparedness, anticipation, and adaptation, emphasising that in complex systems (as most societies can now be considered to be) resilience arises from the interaction structures of system components and the emergence that arises from them. Systemic change does not take place in a social vacuum but is a consequence of evolving change in the landscape through path dependencies and attractors. However, a system that appears to be both complex and chaotic may have repetitive formulas and patterns that can be made visible through system understanding and analysis. As such, we suggest that the elements of societal resilience can be understood through emergence, self-organisation, diversity, feedback, trust, and attractors.

While complexity thinking should not be taken as a silver bullet, it provides a useful approach to finding the balance between different organisational tensions (e.g., between efficiency and innovation). It guides us to think of organisational adaptability both as a structure that emerges from interaction and as a process that is affected by that structure. However, each organisation must find its own recipe for adaptive capability, not least because each organisation has its own historical development path that ultimately determines what is possible and what is not. Adapting Weick (1993), we tend to think that both *déjà vu* and *vu jádè* are always present in leadership and organisational life. Organisations and their leaders are required not only to deal effectively with things that are already familiar but also to throw themselves into situations in which they have no previous experience. The operational environment is not only a context that frames what an organisation is able or unable to do but also at the same time, an interpretation produced in various organisational acts. The interpretation of the operating environment both consciously and unconsciously guides organisational activities. What is crucial, therefore, is that the understanding created in the interpretation is congruent with the opportunities and threats that genuinely affect the operating environment. Perhaps the ultimate value of complexity thinking is that it guides us to ask essential questions and helps us imagine the desired future.

Although the desired future can take several forms, there is a maxim that increasing complexity cannot be addressed effectively through the command-and-control approach. The command-and-control style works in contexts where there are objectively defined good solutions to problems. When the goal is shared, situational awareness agreed and information available, there is no need for the complexification of management practices (cf. Joosse & Teisman, 2021). In cases of systemic change however things get wicked. Contradictory goals, conflicting interests, and complicated interactions speak in favour of coping with complexity instead of taming it (cf. Daviter, 2017). They also stress the need for developing public leaders' meta-skills (see Chapter 5).

Human-centred leadership provides a useful approach to dealing with and perhaps even embracing this complexity. It does so by emphasising the responsive interaction processes existing between leaders and their followers. Human-centred leadership builds on trust, which is critical for self-organisation and the utilisation of the diversity of ideas and actors. Instead of focusing on actions taken by leaders, the human-centred approach assumes that leadership is enacted within the service ecosystem.

## References

Adams, D. (2011). The "wicked problem" of planning for housing development. *Housing Studies*, *26*(6), 951–960. https://doi.org/10.1080/02673037.2011.593128

Appleby, P. H (1954). Managing complexity. *Ethics*, *64*(2), 79–99. https://doi.org/10.1086/290927

Bennett, N., & Lemoine, J. G. (2014). What a difference a word makes: Understanding threats to performance in a VUCA world. *Business Horizons*, *57*(3), 311–317. https://doi.org/10.1016/j.bushor.2014.01.001

Berkes, F. (2007). Understanding uncertainty and reducing vulnerability: Lessons from resilience thinking. *Natural Hazards*, *41*, 283–295. https://doi.org/10.1007/s11069-006-9036-7

Boin, A., & van Eeten, M. J. G. (2013). The resilient organization. *Public Management Review*, *15*(3), 429–445. https://doi.org/10.1080/14719037.2013.769856

Boisot, M., & McKelvey, B. (2011). Complexity and organization-environment relations: Revisiting Ashby's law of requisite variety. In P. Allen, S. Maguire, & B. McKelvey (Eds.), *The Sage handbook of complexity and management* (pp. 279–298). Sage. https://dx.doi.org/10.4135/9781446201084

Brandsen, T., Steen, T., & Verschuere, B. (Eds.). (2018). *Co-production and co-creation. engaging citizens in public services*. Routledge. https://doi.org/ 10.4324/9781315204956

Bristow, G., & Healy, A. (2015). Crisis response, choice and resilience: Insights from complexity thinking. *Cambridge Journal of Regions, Economy and Society*, *8*(2), 241–256. https://doi.org/10.1093/cjres/rsv002

Bryce, C., Ring, P., Ashby, S., & Wardman, J. K. (2020). Resilience in the face of uncertainty: Early lessons from the COVID-19 pandemic. *Journal of Risk Research, 23*(7–8), 880–887. https://doi.org/10.1080/13669877.2020.1756379

Byrne, D. (1999). *Complexity theory and the social sciences: An Introduction.* Routledge. https://doi.org/10.4324/9780203003916

Byrne, D., & Callaghan, G. (2014). *Complexity theory and the social sciences.* Routledge. https://doi.org/10.4324/9780203519585

Cairney, P., & Wellstead, A. (2021). COVID-19: Effective policymaking depends on trust in experts, politicians, and the public. *Policy Design and Practice, 4*(1), 1–14. https://doi.org/10.1080/25741292.2020.1837466

Camillus, J. S. (2008). Strategy as a wicked problem. *Harvard Business Review, 86*(5), 98–101.

Campbell, J. W. (2021). Evolution and change in public organizations: Efficiency, legitimacy and the resilience of core organizational elements. In T. A. Bryer (Eds.), *Handbook of theories of public administration and management* (pp. 220–233). Edward Elgar Publishing. https://doi.org/10.4337/9781789908251.00030

Chadwick, A. (2013). *The hybrid media system: Politics and power.* Oxford University Press. https://doi.org/10.1093/acprof:oso/9780199759477.001.0001

Cilliers, P. (1998). *Complexity and postmodernism.* Routledge. https://doi.org/10.4324/9780203012253

Coleman, J. S. (1990). *Foundations in social theory.* Harvard University Press.

Dahlberg, R. (2015). Resilience and complexity conjoining the discourses of two contested concepts. *Culture Unbound,* 7, 541–557. https://doi.org/10.3384/cu.2000.1525.1572541

Daszak, P. (2020, February 27). We knew disease X was coming: It's here now. *New York Times.*

Daviter, F. (2017). Coping, taming or solving: Alternative approaches to the governance of wicked problems. *Policy Studies, 38*(6), 571–588. https://doi.org/10.1080/01442872.2017.1384543

Der Spiegel. (2021, July 7). Finland best at handling pandemic. *Der Spiegel.* https://yle.fi/uutiset/osasto/news/der_spiegel_finland_best_at_handling_pandemic/12017084

Duchek, S. (2020). Organizational resilience: A capability-based conceptualization. *Business Research, 13*, 215–246. https://doi.org/10.1007/s40685-019-0085-7

Duit, A. (2016). Resilience thinking: Lessons for public administration. *Public Administration, 94*(2), 364–380. https://doi.org/10.1111/padm.12182

Geyer, R., & Rihani, S. (2010). *Complexity and public policy: A new approach to 21st century politics, policy and society.* Routledge. https://doi.org/10.4324/9780203856925

Goldin, I. (2021). *From global crisis to a better world.* Sceptre.

Grint, K. (2005). Problems, problems, problems: The social construction of "leadership". *Human Relations, 58*(11), 1467–1494. https://doi.org/10.1177/0018726705061314

Grint, K. (2022). Critical essay: Wicked problems in the age of uncertainty. *Human Relations.* https://doi.org/10.1177/00187267211070770

Haas, R. N. (2020, April 7). The pandemic will accelerate history rather than reshape it: Not every crisis is a turning point. *Foreign Affairs.*

Haavik, T. (2020). Societal resilience—clarifying the concept and upscaling the scope. *Safety Science, 132.* https://doi.org/10.1016/j.ssci.2020.104964

Hambrick, D. C. (2007). The field of management's devoting to theory: Too much of a good thing? *Academy of Management Journal, 50*(6), 1346–1352. https://doi.org/10.5465/amj.2007.28166119

Head, B. W. (2022). *Wicked problems in public policy: Understanding and responding to complex challenges.* Palgrave Macmillan.

Heimer, C. A. (2013). "Wicked" ethics: Compliance work and the practice of ethics in HIV research. *Social Science & Medicine, 98*, 371–378. https//doi.org/10.1016/j.socscimed.2012.10.030

Henig, R. M. (2020, April 4). Experts warned of a pandemic decades ago: Why weren't we ready? *National Geographic.*

Horne, J. F. & Orr, J. E. (1988). Assessing behaviors that create resilient organizations. *Employment Relations Today, 24*(4), 29–39. https://doi.org/10.1002/ert.3910240405

Horton, R. (2020). Offline: COVID-19 is not a pandemic. *The Lancet, 396*(10255), 874. https://doi.org/10.1016/S0140-6736(20)32000-6

Joosse, H., & Teisman, G. (2021). Employing complexity: Complexification management for locked issues. *Public Management Review, 23*(6), 843–864. https://doi.org/10.1080/14719037.2019.1708435

Kania, J., Kramer, M., & Senge, P. (2018). *The water of systems change.* www.fsg.org/publications/water_of_systems_change

Lähteenmäki-Smith, K., Manu, S., Vartiainen, P., Uusikylä, P., Jalonen, H., Kotiranta, S., Lintinen, U., Annala, M., Gronchi, I., Leppänen, J., & Mertsola, S. (2021). *Government steering beyond 2020: From regulatory and resource management to systems navigation.* Publications of the Government's Analysis, Assessment and Research Activities.

Latour, B. (1987). *Science in action: How to follow scientists and engineers through society.* Harvard University Press.

Lengnick-Hall, C., Beck, T., & Lengnick-Hall, M. (2011). Developing a capacity for organizational resilience through strategic human resource management. *Human Resource Management Review, 21*(3), 243–255. https://doi.org/10.1016/j.hrmr.2010.07.001

Levin, K., Cashore, B., Bernstein, S., & Auld, G. (2012). Overcoming the tragedy of super wicked problems: Constraining our future selves to ameliorate global climate change. *Policy Sciences, 45*, 123–152. https://doi.org/10.1007/s11077-012-9151-0

Lewin, K. (1945). The research center for group dynamics at Massachusetts institute of technology. *Sociometrics, 8*, 128–135. https://doi.org/10.2307/2785233

Lewin, K. (1947). Frontiers in group dynamics: Concept, method and reality in social science; social equilibria and social change. *Human Relations, 1*(1), 5–41. https://doi.org/10.1177/001872674700100103

Linnenluecke, M. K., & Griffiths, A. (2012). Assessing organizational resilience to climate and weather extremes: Complexities and methodological pathways. *Climate Change, 113*, 933–947. https://doi.org/10.1007/s10584-011-0380-6

Luhmann, N. (1995). *Social systems.* Stanford University Press.

March, J. G. (1991). Exploration and exploitation in organizational learning. *Organization Science, 2*(1), 71–87. www.jstor.org/stable/2634940

McGregor, D. (1960). *The human side of enterprise.* McGraw-Hill.

Meadows, D. H. (2008). *Thinking in systems: A primer.* Chelsea Green Publishing.

Meek, J. W., & Marshall, K. S. (2018). Cultivating resiliency through system shock: The Southern California metropolitan water management system as a complex adaptive system. *Public Management Review, 20*(7), 1088–1104. https://doi.org/10.1080/14719037.2017.1364408

Milne, R. (2020, September 24). How Finland kept COVID in check. *Financial Times.*

Mintzberg, H. (1993). The pitfalls of strategic planning. *California Management Review, 36*(1), 32–47. http://dx.doi.org/10.2307/41165733

Mithani, M. A. (2020). Adaptation in the face of the new normal. *Academy of Management Perspectives, 34*(4), 508–530. https://doi.org/10.5465/amp.2019.0054

Mitleton-Kelly, E. (2003). *Complex systems and evolutionary perspectives on organizations: The application of complexity theory to organizations*. Pergamon.

Moore, M. (1995). *Creating public value*. Harvard University Press.

Nissani, M. (1995). Fruits, salads, and smoothies: A working definition of interdisciplinarity. *Journal of Educational Thought, 29*, 119–126. www.jstor.org/stable/23767672

Normandin, J. M., & Therrien, M.-C. (2016). Resilience factors reconciled with complexity: The dynamics of order and disorder. *Journal of Contingencies and Crisis Management, 24*(2), 107–118. https://doi.org/10.1111/1468-5973.12107

OECD. (2021). *Drivers of trust in public institutions in Finland*. OECD Publishing.

Ortiz-de-Mandojana, N., & Bansal, P. (2016). The long-term benefits of organizational resilience through sustainable business practices. *Strategic Management Journal, 37*, 1615–1631. https://doi.org/10.1002/smj.2410

Osborne, S. P., Powell, M., Cui, T., & Strokosch, K. (2021). New development: "Appreciate-engage-facilitate"—the role of public managers in value creation in public services ecosystems. *Public Money & Management, 41*(8), 668–671. https://doi.org/10.1080/09540962.2021.1916189

Papacharissi, Z. (2015). *Affective publics: Sentiment, technology, and politics*. Oxford University Press. https://doi.org/10.1093/acprof:oso/9780199999736.001.0001

Pearson, C. M., & Clair, J. A. (1998). Reframing crisis management. *Academy of Management Review, 23*(1), 59–76. https://doi.org/10.2307/259099

Perry, J. (2015). Climate change adaptation in the world's best places: A wicked problem in need of immediate attention. *Landscape and Urban Planning, 133*, 1–11. https://doi.org/10.1016/j.landurbplan.2014.08.013

Plimmer, G., Berman, E. M., Malinen, S., Franken, E., Naswall, K., Kuntz, J., & Lofgren, K. (2021). Resilience in public sector managers. *Review of Public Personnel Administration*. https://doi.org/10.1177/0734371X20985105

Redding, G. (2020). Societal resilience: China and Japan. *Management and Organization Review, 16*(3), 485–493. https://doi.org/10.1017/mor.2020.33

Richardson, K. E. (2008). Managing complex organizations: Complexity thinking and the science and art of management. *Emergence: Complexity & Organization, 10*(2), 13–26. www.researchgate.net/publication/267683222_Managing_Complex_Organizations_Complexity_Thinking_and_the_Science_and_Art_of_Management

Rittel, H., & Webber, M. (1973). Dilemmas in a general theory of planning. *Policy Sciences, 4*(2), 155–169. https://doi.org/10.1007/BF01405730

Rosenhead, J., Franco, L. A., Grint, K., & Friedland, B. (2019). Complexity theory and leadership practice: A review, a critique, and some recommendations. *The Leadership Quarterly, 30*(5), 101304. https://doi.org/10.1016/j.leaqua.2019.07.002

Senge, P. (2006). *The fifth discipline: The art & practice of the learning organization*. Random House.

Stacey, R. (2010). *Complexity and organizational realities: Uncertainty and the need to rethink management after the collapse of investment capitalism*. Routledge.

Stark, A. (2014). Bureaucratic values and resilience: An exploration of crisis management adaptation. *Public Administration, 92*(3), 692–706. https://doi.org/10.1111/PADM.12085

Stroh, D. P. (2015). *Systems thinking for social change: A practical guide to solving complex problems, avoiding unintended consequences, and achieving lasting results*. Chelsea Green Publishing.

Termeer, C. J. A. M., & Dewulf, A. (2019). A small wins framework to overcome the evaluation paradox of governing wicked problems. *Policy and Society, 38*(2), 298–314. https://doi.org/10.1080/14494035.2018.1497933

Uhl-Bien, M., & Arena, M. (2017). Complexity leadership: Enabling people and organizations for adaptability. *Organizational Dynamics, 46*(1), 9–20. https://doi.org/10.1016/j.orgdyn.2016.12.001

Uhl-Bien, M., & Arena, M. (2018). Leadership for organizational adaptability: A theoretical synthesis and integrative framework. *The Leadership Quarterly, 29*(1), 89–104. https://doi.org/10.1016/j.leaqua.2017.12.009

Ungar, M. (2021). Modelling multisystemic resilience: Connecting biological, psychological, social, and ecological adaptation in contexts of adversity. In M. Ungar (Ed.), *Multisystemic resilience: Adaptation and transformation in contexts of change* (pp. 6–34). Oxford University Press. https://doi.org/ 10.1093/oso/9780190095888.001.0001

Välikangas, L. (2010). *The resilient organization: How adaptive cultures thrive even when strategy fails*. McGraw-Hill.

Vasankari, T., Kolu, P., Kari, J., Pehkonen, J., Havas, E., Tammelin, T., Jalava, J., Koski, H., Pihlainen, K., Kyröläinen, H., Santtila, M., Sievänen, H., Raitanen, J., & Tokola, K. (2018). *Costs of physical activity are increasing—the societal costs of physical inactivity and poor physical fitness*. Publications of the Government's analysis, assessment and research activities 31/2018. Prime Minister's Office.

Von Krogh, G., Rossi-Lamastra, C., & Haefliger, S. (2012). Phenomenon-based research in management and organization science: When is it rigorous and does it matter? *Long Range Planning, 45*(4), 277–298. https://doi.org/10.1016/j.lrp.2012.05.001

Weick, K. E. (1993). The collapse of sensemaking in organizations: The Mann Gulch disaster. *Administrative Science Quarterly, 38*(4), 628–652. https://doi.org/10.2307/2393339

Will, T., Hujala, A., Laulainen, S., & McMurray, R. (2019). *The management of wicked problems in health and social care*. Routledge. https://doi.org/10.4324/9781315102597

Zhang, F., Welch, E. W., & Miao, Q. (2018). Public organization adaptation to extreme events: Mediating role of risk perception. *Journal of Public Administration Research and Theory, 28*(3), 371–387. https://doi.org/10.1093/jopart/muy004

# 5 Nurturing human-centredness through public leadership meta-skills

## 5.1 Increasing importance of meta-skills

Previous chapters have outlined the ongoing transformation of the working environment of public administrations and public organisations more generally, as well as their response to these developments. Previous chapters have also looked at how the theoretical and practical understanding of public leadership has evolved. Consequently, public leadership and public sector institutions of the 2020s are working in a world where connections between actors and the dynamics of power matter more than ever and where holistic thinking works better than reductionism or linear reasoning. As such, a poor understanding of overarching societal phenomena can both become costly and cause a significant loss of well-being, fundamentally inhibiting the capability to tackle unexpected future developments.

Achieving a better level of social impact for public policy and public services in a complex world calls for a leadership approach that allows for and favours organisational adaptability. This does not necessarily apply only to public organisations but calls for the creation of the capacity for co-leadership and co-creation between public organisations in cross-cutting societal issues while also taking along other sectors of society, including private businesses and non-governmental organisations and citizens. The task is not however easily accomplished, given that public organisations are often substance-bound and silo-based in terms of their division of labour, legal codes, regulations, and the traditionally conservative way in which they are usually applied. A new vocabulary and working practices are therefore required to elevate horizontal accountability and human-centeredness as the core rationale of the public leadership.

Several important questions follow on from these observations. How are these new capabilities and attitudes built among civil service leaders and managers? And to what extent is this readiness already prevalent among top-level public service leaders? Although public servants and leaders tend to be well-educated people, we cannot assume that this kind of profound shift towards enabling and bridgebuilding for co-created change happens by itself and without consciously cultivating and appreciating the skills and structures accelerating the change.

DOI: 10.4324/9781003205791-5

Public organisations at different levels of governance around the globe are known to be cradles of the committee and bureaucratic culture. Deliberation is often institutionalised in public committees where civil servants, interest group representatives, and experts participate. However, anyone with any experience of the way in which the public sector works in practice knows that far too often these committees and networks do not work as platforms of mutual learning or as the generators of new solutions to interagency issues (e.g., Feiock, 2013; Krick & Holst, 2018; Arganoff, 2006).

Committees often operate as negotiation platforms, safeguarding the organisational status quo, rather than exploring new insights for wicked problems in a spirit of creating new solutions (Annala et al., 2020). Committees are generally constituted by established parties or opinion groups, where the members are merely representatives of their background organisations, rather than co-creators of common goals and solutions. The same spirit of 'zero-sum game' can be found in forums between different branches of government. So, collaborative leadership, joint learning, and solution-building do not happen by themselves just because there is a broad range of representation around the table. To succeed in co-operating beyond the sectoral and substantial boundaries in tackling the complex societal phenomena in an impactful way, the development and adoption of leadership meta-skills are essential. Leadership meta-skills are needed to facilitate cross-sectoral collaboration as an incubator of systems change. Adopting and developing meta-skills is also important from the human-centred point of view and in terms of increasing the public sector's ability to generate services based on the actual needs of service users. In general, this requires using existing structures and resources in a new way and gathering different parties for co-creating non-compartmentalised services. This boundary-spanning and cross-cutting co-creation does not happen without deployment of the meta-skills that ease cross-contextual co-operation and renewal.

## 5.2 Origins and the evolution of leadership meta-skills

Meta-skills refer to generic and transferrable leadership competencies and skills, which reveal themselves in the interactional choices of those who steer cooperation or participate in it (Virtanen & Tammeaid, 2020). Meta-skills are present in both the skills and attitudes that guide interaction. Meta-skills enhance reciprocal and dynamic connections between actors. Leadership meta-skills are particularly important since leaders generally set the pace in terms of organisational procedures and culture. Leaders actively support and enable public organisations in their drive for transformation towards human-centeredness, which itself nourishes public organisations to renew themselves. The capability to build and steer the fruitful cross-sectoral co-creation of new solutions to cross-cutting societal issues manifests itself in meta-skills in everyday working life.

Meta-skills are characterised as that level of leadership skills lying above the traditional way to approach the contents of leadership via strategic leadership, process management, planning procedures etc. Meta-skills draw attention to the fact that in addition to making choices on what is done, how that is done also makes a difference—both to the people involved and in terms of the societal results. Meta-skills refer to capabilities that are overarching and transferable from one operating environment (government silo) to another. As leadership skills, they can be characterised as taking agency and responsibility in building future-driven reciprocal cooperation. Meta-skilfulness is required in undertaking systems change and enabling organisational or network learning and should therefore be in the interests of successful public sector leadership (Virtanen & Tammeaid, 2020, 2021).

Until recently, leadership research has not paid much attention to meta-skills though leadership meta-skills do share similarities with theories of shared leadership (Bolden, 2011) which reminds us that leadership is a social process and with distributed leadership (Fitzgerald et al., 2013) which underlines the notion that leadership is not the monopoly or responsibility of just one person or authority. The concept of metacognition (Metcalfe & Shimamura, 1994) approaches leadership through collective consciousness and the personal or collective assumptions that guide our thinking. Meta-governance (Gjaltema et al., 2019) in its turn notes that for enhanced accountability, transparency, and the trustworthiness of governance, there is a clear need for coordination and leading together across the sectors and different levels of governance (Virtanen & Tammeaid, 2021). Van Wart's typology of public meta-skills approach (discussed in Chapter 3) resembles collaborative leadership, transformative leadership, self-organising, and networked leadership. The tradition of authentic leadership has also raised some of the same perspectives. Building upon van Wart, meta-skills thinking appears to have common features grounded in community change management and organisational learning (Van Wart, 2017, p. 177). These approaches are interested in how to enable organisations, practitioners, and service users to work together in a more cooperative and trust-based manner.

Putting things together, then, the public leadership meta-skills approach rests upon four substantial roots: socio-constructive theories of knowledge creation and renewal, the co-creation view of systems change, the philosophy and practice of reframing taken from the Solution-Focused approach, and the virtue ethics and strengths approach stemming from positive psychology.

The socio-constructive approach to organisational learning emphasises that knowledge creation is a holistic process, where interaction, emotions, perceptions, bodily experiences, and thinking merge. In this view, leadership always represents itself as relational between human beings, and the role of our assumptions is highlighted, since they largely create the world which we are able later to discover (Cooperrider, 2017; Hersted & Gergen, 2013). Nonaka and Takeuchi have presented similar ideas in their SECI-process of organisational knowledge creation consisting of socialisation, externalisation, combination, and internalisation (Nonaka & Takeuchi, 1995) highlighting the importance of creating *ba*, a shared space and time conducive to the development of new understanding. Murtonen and Lehtinen for their part highlight the role of social support as the key mechanism of adult learning and development (Murtonen & Lehtinen, 2020).

The co-creation view of systems change emphasises the role of co-discovery and common learning journeys involving not only the service users but also other stakeholders (Akhilesh, 2017; Ind & Coates, 2013) as well as the role of interactive leadership i.e., the "dynamic that produces adaptive outcomes in a social system" (Uhl-Bien et al., 2007, p. 306).

As an approach to change, this highlights the reality that legitimacy is built socially and that many small streams flowing in the same direction make for powerful systems change (Virtanen & Tammeaid, 2020). According to Papi-Thornton and Cubista (2019), inducing systemic change requires the development of self-awareness as well as social/emotional intelligence, empathy, and a desire to promote systems-level impacts, shifting the orientation from mainstream, short-term, individualistic success. It also benefits from working with diverse worldviews and committing to and prioritising the health and vitality of human systems, learning systems tools, frameworks and participatory methods, and from focusing on applied practice, rather than theoretical understanding alone. This could mean, for example, developing skills through field-based learning and flexibility to adapt to the emergent factors of ever-shifting systems instead of relying on long-term planning or forecasting. Within the field of policy design, this calls for relying on co-creation and experimental learning as policy design quality criteria (de Smedt & Borch, 2021). It is easy to agree with Ind and Coates (2013), who hold the view that co-creation practice about change brings together psychotherapy, management science, innovation and open innovation, design, intent, and emergence, as well as creativity practice.

Solution-Focused philosophy and the practice of reframing lay the foundation for meta-skills in several ways. It draws attention to the potential of human interaction to create a desired future and to utilise the skills often associated with one area of life in other situations (Kim Berg & Szabó, 2005). The roots of the Solution-Focused approach in human psychology highlight the importance of dispelling limiting beliefs of what is possible, obligatory, or true in any given situation. The same applies to common and shared beliefs, convictions, and opinions. This kind of reframing can happen via fruitful interaction and the Solution-Focused manner of doing it by simultaneously strengthening interactional relationships, and building trust is a key factor in co-creating change and promoting holistic thinking, rather than reductionism and linear reasoning.

The Solution-Focused approach differs from many other approaches to change-making by taking a future-driven (i.e., teleological) stand instead of a causal one, trusting in emergence rather than pre-planning and utilising variety instead of looking for rigorous consensus (Virtanen & Tammeaid,

2020). All of these are key features in the promotion of change, making human-centred rather than decision-maker-centred choices. Solution-Focused practice offers various ways to combine individual, organisational, and societal aspirations (e.g., Dierolf, 2014; Tammeaid, 2020). In the context of systems change, the Solutions-Focused approach understands that a sustainable change cannot be forced or ordered and that we cannot change other people either. What we can do is promote high-quality interaction and change the circumstances towards a more favourable direction such that they become a space of mutual learning and purposeful cooperation (Bateson, 2015; McKergow, 2021).

An essential part of the change-making power of meta-skills stems from virtue ethics, something which positive psychology has in recent decades introduced in a new form that can be easily utilised in organisations and leadership. Positive psychology looks at human activity through the medium of strengths and hidden strengths to be developed. In this view, good and wise deeds result from judgement that takes both emotions and factual reasoning into account. Nor is thought alone enough to be a virtue but turning good intentions into activities generates good results. From a meta-skills viewpoint, leadership is manifested more in deeds than as personal qualities.

This element introduces a new feature to the long tradition of leadership theories by challenging the search for a person with a certain type of leadership qualities, instead focusing on what leaders do and what kinds of interactions they provoke in their surroundings. People's diversity is genuinely a useful reality both in the Solution-Focused and positive psychology views. This implies that different individuals can succeed in a leadership role. Leadership meta-skills argue that the desire to create fruitful interactions between various people and groupings, to explore things from different perspectives, and to build solutions that open new thinking and new ways of acting are essential.

In Chapter 2, we discussed morality and the human ability to carry out both good and bad deeds. Both positive psychology and the Solution-Focused approach make the deliberate choice to build circumstances where peoples' best qualities come to the forefront. "The art of being wise is the art of knowing what to overlook," says American psychologist William James (James, 1890, p. 865) in his famous quote. Not everything deserves to be covered, looked at, or explored when we involve ourselves in the task of systems change-making. Focusing on virtues and good deeds primarily feeds better impulses to the connections between actors and the dynamics of power. The deliberate choice of building trust makes for a more resilient society and better accountability. There is a distinctive relationship between ethics and societal resilience (Varona, 2021), and at this point also lies the catalytic power of leadership meta-skills.

According to Dutton et al. (2010), a more virtuous work-related identity can alter individuals' preferences in terms of building connections to others and facilitating the cultivation of social resources. This represents an important move to increase trust and appreciation. Echoing Dutton et al. (2010), the focus on building virtuous qualities also strengthens social resources on the evaluative, developmental, and structural levels by generating increased understanding of others—including outgroups—encouraging the formation of new relationships, disclosing more information, discovering shared perspectives, and acting in a more authentic manner. Moreover, as Fredrickson (2013) has shown in her seminal research of positive emotions, such emotions strengthen actors' mental, physical, and social resources. Flexibility in operational terms increases and the opportunities to learn and create something new, even in challenging and fragmented situations, improves. Highlighting strengths, signs of progress, and positive deviations reinforces the inherent ability of human communities to work together to address the issues ahead and create something new. Shifting the spotlight to strengths and opportunities breaks the traditional setup, where change is seen as a difficult, often externally generated, compulsion to change.

Developing meta-skills offers a promising opportunity for governments and public organisations more generally to improve their policy design by moving away from seeking a prescribed procedure, a lean consensus, or a predictable single future towards the possibility of multiple transition pathways. It also provides a platform for developing an enabling and human-centred leadership style both inside public organisations and in relation to other organisations and society. Contextual integrative thinking and joining resources for human-centred change are necessary for government to meet the challenges of the 2020s. Highlighting the importance of meta-skilling makes explicit the notion that success in systems change does not occur in a vacuum. Meta-skills and the interactional design they bring to public sector leadership are essential for successful change-making.

## 5.3 Public leadership meta-skills typology

Meta-skills manifest themselves in relation to the environments in which people use them. Instead of producing attribute lists of general meta-skills, the more appropriate approach is to focus on which meta-skills in different operating environments promote cross-contextual interaction and renewal. Based on earlier research related to leadership meta-skills (Virtanen & Tammeaid, 2020, 2021), this section discusses six public leadership meta-skills—their contents, meaning, and value while also testing them empirically.

The idea of public leadership meta-skills was born and developed during six long-term "Renewing Public Sector—Enabling Leadership" leadership training courses operated by the Finnish Innovation Fund Sitra and conducted in Finland for 140 senior government officials during the period 2017–2018. The focus here was to strengthen enabling and cross-sectoral leadership among top civil service leaders (Permanent State Secretaries, Under-Secretaries of State, Director Generals, and other senior-level members of ministry staff) supporting leadership capabilities to take an active role in the transformations needed within the context of government work in the 2020s. When designing the courses, it was important to identify the primary characteristics and transformational challenges of public administration in the 2020s as well as the leadership competencies required for successful governance. During the six separate leadership courses (each consisting of around 22–25 participants), leadership meta-skills emerged as a useful conceptual tool with which to capture cross-governmental cooperation and human-centred leadership. The public leadership philosophy and practice embedded in the leadership training curricula as well as the leadership training methodology is more thoroughly described in Virtanen and Tammeaid (2020). Based on the long-term leadership courses that incubated the idea of public leadership meta-skills, six leadership meta-skills were subsequently identified. They are, learning to learn, the systems approach, dialogical positioning, harnessing thinking skills, reaching out to practice, and upholding an enabling mindset (see Fig. 5.2).

According to the tacit knowledge provided by the training courses as well as decades of experience as a leader, civil servant, coach, and consultant within the government working environment, these six meta-skills build capacity to facilitate good trans-contextual interaction and promote integrative change and renewal which are a prerequisite for tackling a variety of cross-cutting societal issues regardless of public sector branch.

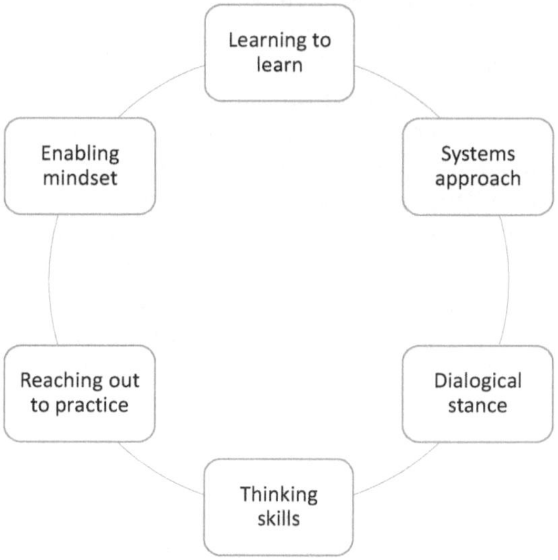


*Figure 5.1* Public leadership meta-skills.

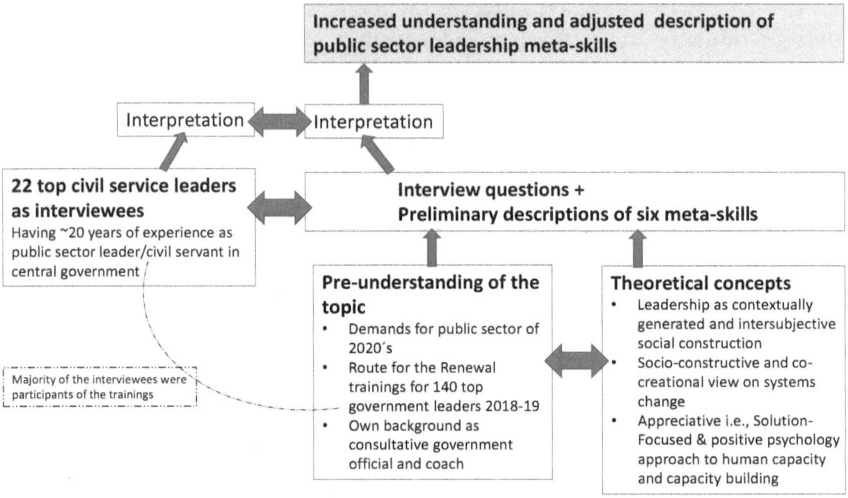


*Figure 5.2* Empirical research logic.

Additionally, these identified meta-skills enable public sector renewal and a broadening of the scope of government interventions and policy implementation while lacking them can easily undercut any existing aspirations for renewal.

*Learning to learn* encompasses public leaders' engagement and interaction with the changing world. It also conveys the idea of a learning attitude that relates both to everyday tasks and comprehensive policy implementation processes. Leadership is a process of constant learning as well as of showing an example and fostering learning in others. An important component of learning to learn is the ability to view one's own activities as part of a larger context and finding new and constructive ways to be and act as part of the emerging entity. Kallio (2020) points out that development in adulthood can include both progress and regression and that these processes often take place retrospectively. Furthermore, basic cognitive mechanisms, motivational factors, concepts, beliefs of learning, teaching, and the nature of knowledge affect development and learning abilities during adulthood. The role of collaborative knowledge building in learning processes as well as the metacognitive understanding of one's own learning, motivation, and beliefs supporting the learning process are all integral parts of learning to learn (Murtonen & Lehtinen, 2020).

*The systems approach* brings together public leaders and public organisations in a web of interaction with various other societal actors. Achieving change constitutes a process and requires new kinds of joint sensemaking, interaction, and feedback loops. In the systems approach, the illusion of controlling human systems—and public organisations—to carry out tasks much as a piece of machinery does with expected performance outcomes is replaced by an extensive understanding that every part of a system affects and operates as part of the whole. Actions made as part of the system can be enabling or opportunity-reducing. Instead of describing and mapping the properties of the system, it is more important to see each other as part of the system and ask what we want to create together. This meta-skill is based on the same argument as this whole book: public sector, society, and leadership can best be understood and improved by looking at how the different parts interact with each other and how they are integrated. Systems thinking is not a uniform field of study and in the context of meta-skills systems thinking refers first and foremost to the dynamics of open systems and people acting in networks of responsive feedback structures (Stacey, 2010). This insight lays the groundwork for our exploration of societal phenomena from a multidisciplinary and multi-player point of view (Ståhle et al., 2020).

*The dialogical stance* incorporates reciprocal human-to-human relationship with all people despite status or role but also as a practical skill to build dialogical interaction. Good leadership is not apart from, or above, the organisation but fulfils its overarching role in relationships. Dialogue as an actionable skill conveys the idea of building adaptive spaces for comprehensive and enlarged understanding and cognition of different experiences and contexts to arise. Facilitating joint sensemaking and bridgebuilding improves the conditions for change. The dialogical stance describes the change of leadership from an authoritarian and status-based culture to a more informal human-to-human relationship approach despite the different roles people continue to inhabit in an organisation or around a common task. This same shift has been the primary focus of the Human Relations movement on leadership outlined in Chapter 2. Furthermore, the thorough and favourable impact of the dialogical stance in communication between human beings has been described in detail, for example, in Buber's (1937) classic distinction between the I-Thou relationship and the I—It relationship and in Isaacs' (2007) seminal work about dialogue and the art of thinking together.

*Thinking skills* refer to the ability to detach oneself from familiar thought patterns and consider things from diverse, new, and even surprising perspectives. Harnessing thinking skills increases the ability to critically examine one's own as well as other generally shared beliefs and established ways of perception and building solutions. To identify what is essential and meaningful in different circumstances helps us to make choices in real situations. This however requires mental flexibility in its broadest sense, i.e., perception, knowledge building, creativity, and positive emotions. Geoffrey Vickers has described the human mind as an act of artistry, where intuition and rationality are always involved. Steve de Shazer, the central figure in the development of the Solution-Focused approach, refers to Vickers' definition noting that the "human mind has available to it at least two different modes of knowing and it uses both in appropriate and inappropriate combinations in its endless efforts to understand" (de Shazer, 2016, p. 55).

Kallio (2020) points out that attaining the ability to engage in contextual integrative thinking is the target of cognitive development and learning in adulthood. It requires an understanding of the multiplicity and plurality of viewpoints, opinions, explanations, and domains and acts as a prerequisite for the making of wise decisions and conclusions. An important Solution-Focused adjunct to thinking skills is the development of an ability also to choose a 'not-knowing-position' or 'beginners mind' even in a familiar situation and, by that means, to generate new understanding or to lead thinking back to the fundamentals (Malinen, 2004).

*Reaching out to practice* makes explicit attempts to find new ways of working quickly, open-mindedly, constantly learning, and thereby shaping the future through active involvement. Consequently, it brings with it the idea of acting as a partner in networks and ecosystems, building partnerships and providing good conditions for the implementation of decisions. Too often, there is a gap between strategic decision-making and the operational level activity in public organisations. This gap needs to be overcome and one possible way to accomplish this is to adopt the novel and collaborative ways of the human-centred approach—to place yourself in a dialogue with staff and service users. Reaching out to practice brings about experiential learning, which is also an effective means of change in public organisations. Conditions, connections, and directions can also be changed by simply changing the tone and space for interaction and in that way, creating new kinds of dynamics (Bateson, 2015; Stacey, 2010). It is a surprisingly counterintuitive way of inducing change due to beliefs like 'the plan has to come before action', 'theory is more valuable practice', and 'learning is a cognitive process (only)'. Both the long tradition of experiential learning (Kolb & Fry, 1975) and the enactive approach to learning portrayed in the Solution-Focused approach remind us that interacting with the world is an embodied and holistic endeavour enabling change (McKergow, 2021). Within the field of leadership, the recent development of social learning labs has reinforced this view of putting things into practice. Wenger-Trayners (2021) describes 'systems convening' as a crucial form of leadership in the 21st century, making explicit the idea of leadership as convening, involving narrative work, legitimacy work, boundary stretching, identity work supporting personal transformation, agency and power works, as well as articulating value. Indeed, the Design Council in the UK has recently revised its systems design framework by adding the supporting role of leadership to established design processes like the double diamond. They also highlight the skills and abilities of narration and connection in their model (Drew, 2021)

*The enabling mindset* is the breeding ground for seeing, taking, and pinpointing new opportunities; creating new ways of working and interaction; and, even more importantly, appreciating the natural transformative capacity that human beings and communities possess. Change begins with the assumptions people bring with them. Paying attention to opportunities even in a gloomy situation, as well as to the strengths and capabilities of the people involved, increases the functionality and developmental capacity in any change. The enabling mindset creates space for success and for proceeding towards the common goal in various ways instead of striving for one uniform solution or deciding on behalf of others. As a leadership stance, it means making room for others to flourish. The enabling mindset forms the core of Solution-Focused thinking. Gearing the mindset towards possibilities and enabling rather than problems and constraints is fundamental in breaking from mechanistic and narrow reason-effect thinking approaches (Grant et al., 2012). It opens the gates to everyday creativity and the non-linear space of opportunity. In order not to end up just fixing the failures in respect of current 'solutions,' we must look to what we want to create in terms of the direction of the mission, the purpose of our actions, and the desired future, rather than simply looking at the problems. When approaching issues with an enabling mindset, there are usually more resources than expected, fewer hindrances than expected, and more room for actions (Virtanen & Tammeaid, 2020). Moreover, as Vickers notes, the importance of values through which we see others is clear (see Ison, 2005; Williams, 2005): our humanity hinges on our capacity to respond and to do so aptly, by creating appreciative systems for human society. In the context of public policy issues, the enabling mindset can be recognised by changing problem-focused definitions (describing poor development and its serious ramifications) into workable future targets (what we want to see happening and what the enablers of that development) are, while, at the same time, changing our passive view of the world into one of active action. It is important then not just to look at public policies as ways to repair a problem but rather as ways to co-create new and relevant solutions.

The aforementioned meta-skills were subjected to empirical testing in 2021 when 22 high-ranking Finnish civil servants were interviewed (see, Exhibit 2).

## 5.4 Public leaders' narratives about leadership meta-skills

### *5.4.1 Research logic*

The semi-structured theme interviews of top civil service leaders were conducted as virtual, recorded interviews lasting from 45 to 60 minutes between December 2020 and June 2021. The interviews were a phenomenological

**EXHIBIT 2 Empirical research about public leadership meta-skills in Finland.**

To understand how public leadership meta-skills fit into the ways in which public sector leaders themselves make sense of their work, role, and everyday endeavours, a series of interviews were conducted in Spring 2021. We interviewed 22 high-ranking civil service leaders working in the central government in Finland.

All of the interviewees had held civil service careers spanning several decades, mainly in leadership positions and all had held positions in different branches of government. At the time of the interviews—Winter 2020 and Spring 2021—they all had ministerial leadership positions or were leading central government agencies. Twelve of the interviewees were men, twelve women. Seven of them were, or had during their recent career, held the position of Secretary of State or Under-Secretaryof State. In general, most of the interviewees were Director Generals representing all 12 government ministries[1] of Finland. Three interviewees were Director Generals of central government agencies, and one represented another central government institution. To contextualise the Finnish case, we should note that, on the one hand, the Finnish Government refers to the body which convenes for the general governing of the country, consisting of the Prime Minister and other ministers, while on the other, it is also the decision-making body for governmental and administrative matters consisting of the Government plenary session and twelve ministries. For Finland it is typical to have a multi-party government for a maximum of four years at a time. Each ministry is responsible for the preparation of matters within its mandate and for the proper functioning of administration. They also guide the performance of around 40 specialised government agencies. Altogether, the Finnish central government has around 74,000 employees, of whom roughly 6,000 work in the twelve ministries. The number of top civil service leaders is around 150–160 in total.

Public administration leadership culture and public administration structures in Finland have traditionally been based on Neo-Weberian State-type arrangements in which authority is exercised through a disciplined hierarchy of impartial officials although traces of New Public Management with an emphasis on market-type mechanisms, performance targets, and outsourcing and New Public Governance with an emphasis on the government's ability and willingness to work and govern across agencies are also visible in the Finnish Governmental tradition. From the perspective of public sector leadership development, the Finnish model can be labelled as a combination of egalitarian management model and an elitist one. Over the years, Finland has been among the 'best in class' in terms of the other Nordic countries in the OECD and EU comparisons in terms of the efficiency and effectiveness of public administration and its functions (Virtanen & Tammeaid, 2020).

and hermeneutical effort to understand public sector leadership and the enablers of success in public sector functions as well as an attempt to bring some new understanding to the multidisciplinary nature of public sector leadership. The main aim of the interviews was to put to the test the hypothetic concept of public sector leadership meta-skills as exercised by highly experienced public sector leaders who, due to the nature of their work duties, have a good vantage point across the whole gamut of the government's functions. Thematic clustering of the material gathered from the informants led to a content analysis (Puusa, 2020; Braun & Clarke, 2006), bringing up first how the informants interpret the concept and practice of public sector leadership meta-skills (Pessoa et al., 2019) and, second, the resemblances and regularities in the whole sample of interviews of these experienced Finnish public sector leaders.

A standard interview structure was sent to every interviewee beforehand to enable them to familiarise themselves with the theme in advance. The interview structure included a general definition of meta-skills, a hypothetic assumption of the impact of meta-skills on public leadership, i.e., improving the capacity for renewal of the public sector and broadening the scope of policy choices, descriptions of the six meta-skills assumed important based on our pre-understanding of the issue, and the following questions:

1. *What do you think of these six meta-skills? How important do they seem to you in your own work? Does possessing them help or does lacking them complicate your work?*
2. *How do these meta-skills apply to you as a leader: How and where have they developed, or have you consciously developed them?*
3. *Do you consider it important that these meta-skills be developed more widely across government/public administration? If so, by what kind of measures?*
4. *What else do you wish to say?*

The interviews were conducted on a confidentiality basis to support the authenticity of the interview material. The confidentiality issue was important, given the high rank of the interviewees and the obvious fact that a limited number of people hold such high-ranking positions within the Finnish government structure, thus making it rather easy to identify the people concerned potentially impacting their proclivity to speak freely etc. To undertake a thematic clustering of the interview material, all the interviews were transcribed. The material gathered was used to identify answers to the following questions: do these experienced public sector leaders find the concept of meta-skills relevant and understandable; how do they react to the list of six meta-skills; would they group, define, or verbalise them in another way or do they see some meta-skills as being more relevant to them than others; how do they see the relationships between different meta-skills; what kinds of definitions and/or examples do they associate with each of the six meta-skills; what has the use of (assuming they were identified) these meta-skills brought to their everyday leadership and central government work; can, in their experience, meta-skills help the public sector to undergo renewal and broaden of scope of policy choices; how do they see the development of meta-skills in their own career and how do they rate the level of the six meta-skills in the public sector in general; do they consider developing meta-skills to be important in public administration and if so, through what kinds of measures; and, finally, what else do they want to say about the issue?

The interviews were conducted during a particularly difficult period, given the ongoing global COVID-19 crisis and an extensive period of remote work in government functions. These special circumstances were however reflected in the interviews to only a small extent since the interviewees were all long-term civil service leaders with experience from different government/cabinet periods. Moreover, the shift to remote work had, due to the country's state of technical readiness, been relatively smooth, compared to that of many other countries. The interviews coincided with the mid-term period of the cabinet's existence, which enabled the task of gathering the latest insights of the government-level leadership quite fruitful.

### *5.4.2 The value of putting emphasis on leadership meta-skills*

The first surprise emerging from the interviews was how unanimously the interviewed leaders agreed with the idea of the existence and importance of leadership meta-skills. Some of the interviewees critically questioned whether all six meta-skills were on the same level or whether some are more personal or are even meta-skills of meta-meta-skills. Others noted that these are not the definitions they themselves would have given, but despite that these six meta-skills did make sense to them. A solid majority of the interviewees agreed with the idea and list of six public leadership meta-skills, and several described them as reflecting extremely well the important features of successful public sector leadership.

Some interviewees echoed traces of personality and feature theories behind their perception on leadership, but most detected by themselves that leadership meta-skills refer to dynamic and processual leadership capabilities that appear in interaction. All the interviewees agreed that unlike in most private sector companies, public sector leadership is about succeeding together over organisational and institutional fences. There was a unanimous understanding of the importance of cross-sectoral cooperation over organisational and thematic borders, both to make better use of the capacity of the civil service *cadre* and to achieve policy formations and decisions more in line with citizen and societal needs. Dialogical stance was the most familiar of the six meta-skills to these Finnish leaders. It was understood merely as conducting discussions with different stakeholders. Dialogue in a deeper sense—as deep listening and co-creation—appeared less in the interviewees' answers but was however recognised by a few of them. "This is something machines can't do and will therefore be the most essential leadership skill in the future", noted a Director General with around 40 years of experience in both ministerial and government agency leadership. "Leadership that is not based on dialogue is just a hippo—highly paid people's opinion", continued a Secretary of State with a working-life-spanning ministerial leadership career.

The importance of learning to learn both in leadership positions and in public sector organisations more generally was also widely recognised by the interviewees as was the role of the leader to show the way forward in terms of that development. A Secretary of State put the importance of the learning attitude in a nutshell by saying that

> *without learning to learn not a single organisation can respond to the issues it should be dealing with. It is hard to see how an organisation not constantly learning could be more than mediocre. Leaders' meta-skills are at the same time meta-skills of the whole organisation. We should put much more weight on them in selection.*

An enabling mindset was the most difficult meta-skill to grasp for the interviewees. Deep understanding of this meta-skill was portrayed in the answers of those few who had received formal training in terms of coaching or Solution-Focused practice. Some leaders however portrayed an intuitive understanding of the enabling stance. Most associated the enabling mindset with strengths-based leadership that had been part of the 'Renewing Public Sector—Enabling Leadership' training programmes and told us that the paradigm shift to spotting and using strengths had permanently changed their approach to leadership. The enabling mindset notion had also brought with it remarkable effects in organisational culture, as described by a Director General with ministerial affiliation and around 15 years of experience from both government agency and ministerial organisations:

> *The internal culture of our ministry starts with people's strengths. And they are recognised and encouraged. This is reflected in work motivation, flexibility and group dynamics. Colleagues appreciate other people's strengths and build on them. It is impactful and we have it as a culture. We do not talk much about it, but it is part of our organisation. It enables us to create new things and frees up action. Work engagement and energy comes from it. Sometimes there are huge and sometimes smaller issues to deal with, but ownership is created for both. It also comes up in networks, at the national level or in networks of like-minded countries.*

Some of the interviewees had undertaken profound changes in their organisations based on the idea of enabling. For example, the change of the former internal administrative services to enabling services. Thinking skills was the meta-skill that divided the interviewees most. It was either named 'the best', 'the most important', or the most unfamiliar of all meta-skills.

> *Without intellectual curiosity nothing is achieved except leading the old in an outdated way,*

summarised one Secretary of State with over 30 years of leadership experience from several government branches. An Under-Secretary of State with over 30 years of leadership experience from different government branches emphasised that the

> *Societal relevance of organisations that can't think and co-create together disappears.*

Reaching out to practice provoked a somewhat more scattered response, although all the interviewees recognised the problem between strategy and practice and the difficulty of maintaining a dynamic relationship between them. One Director General with ministerial affiliation and over 20 years of leadership experience described the process of reaching out to practice in the following way:

> *Public administration leaders need to make at least three levels of reflection on how to put a policy into practice and how to communicate it. First is the political framework, the opportunities, the constraints, the institutions, how to get it accepted there. For many things there is also some kind of procedure in legislation, but when we talk about an experiment or any other new model of*

*policymaking or cooperation, we must think how to adapt it to that political reality. And secondly. you must think about how it will be understood in there in your own civil servant silo and thirdly how it will be co-created with other branches of government and society. All these pieces should still fit together so that they do not lead in different directions. This all comes back to systems thinking and to the fact that, if you don't get politicians to see or believe or take an interest to it, it just doesn't happen. But this is how ecosystems are built.*

A Secretary of State with over 30 years of leadership experience from several government branches reminded us of the long timespan of change-making:

*Many are looking for profound and visible changes without understanding that a sustainable change is achieved by small steps and in a systemic manner. Structural changes can of course be implemented overnight, but the behavioural change of actors which in private companies take months, takes years in the public sector. And then cultural change that is said to take 3–5 years, even 7, in the private sector, takes much more time again in the public sector. You must understand that if you make a structural change in order to be quick, it leads to conscious efforts of leading the behavioural change for months and the cultural change for the coming years. And you must be constant in doing it, otherwise the organisation pulls back into the old ways.*

Table 5.1 summarises how the interviewees saw the various enablers and hindrances in respect of nurturing and developing meta-skills in government leadership and what kinds of amendments they made to the model. One of the motivations for carrying out the interviews was to find out how much public sector leaders use meta-skills and in what kinds of circumstances. According to the interviews conducted, almost all interviewed leaders used meta-skills both in internal leadership (own organisation) and in leading their government branches (performance management of governance sectors), as well as in cross-sectoral co-operation between public sector branches, other sectors, and society more generally. Only three of the 22 interviewees made use of meta-skills mainly internally and within their own branch of government, while one interviewee was only using meta-skills internally. Broad use of leadership meta-skills is portrayed as taking a role as an enabling co-ordinator or initiator and the one who actively brings different stakeholders together. Good experiences of broad cross-sectoral policy preparation had been gathered for example in preparing nation-wide strategies for digitalisation, comprehensive security, health security, and informal ecosystem forums and municipal dialogues.

The motivations behind restricting the use of meta-skills to one's own department or organisation were expressed in terms of perceptual experiences of discouragement within the organisation to cross-sectoral working, looking at official duties from a broader perspective, and investing time and effort into renewing the organisation's ways of working. Those who reported strong notions of this kind in terms of a discouraging organisational culture had, interestingly, developed different responses to it. One reported simply accepting the situation and silently envying colleagues working for other government organisations where the socio-cultural possibilities for systems thinking and action were better. Another had adopted a strategy of outspokenness, publicly raising questioning of the choices made and other possibilities available, despite lame response from the surrounding organisation. The third's strategy had been to actively seek inspiration and support from peers from other organisations to 'get themselves going' and change the culture of their own organisation, too. All three raised the importance of joint structures such as training, co-creation labs, and the increased use of cross-sectoral policy planning to encourage all government organisations to adopt ways of working that better respond to the needs of the 2020s and 2030s.

Considering the hierarchical composition of government organisations, it was no surprise that the interviewees who held positions at the Secretary of State or Under-Secretary of State levels had the best opportunities to set the pace for the renewal of working methods and open-minded organisational culture even though they were also facing most pressure from the political leadership.

It is also noteworthy that citizen or service users were not really mentioned during the interviews focusing on leadership meta-skills with top-level civil servant leaders, whose role is to concentrate on strategic policy issues at the state level, i.e., quite far from the experiential world of a single citizen or public service user. Clearly, in terms of timespan, policy planning reaches out far into the future from the perspective of immediate government service experiences. Nevertheless, all public policies have a direct effect on individual citizens and different groups in society as well as on the operating conditions of private companies. As such, it is crucial to keep the ordinary citizen, the multiplicity of life situations, and the various players in mind when sketching policy guidelines and contents. Harnessing meta-skills serves as a vehicle to place oneself in someone else's position while keeping at least an imaginary citizen and a variety of viewpoints in mind while engaging in the ongoing task of strategic policy work. In addition, it is also important to poke holes in decision-makers bubbles by consciously arranging occasional opportunities for direct dialogue with other sectors of society, the citizen, and possible service users. Direct encountering at its best widens all the participants' views of the world and of its possible futures, as well as illuminating the actual issues others have to deal with. This kind of cross-border encounter rarely succeeds without good meta-skills. Since 'citizens' or 'service users' are generally unwieldy and often amorphous groups to approach from the policy planning side, the best examples provided by the interviewees talked about the thorough segmentation of affected parties in relation to the policy issues at hand and of keeping regular contact with actors in both the third and private sectors within the respective policy fields.

### *5.4.3 Bureaucratic culture and rigid organisational structures*

This sample of top-level civil servant interviews suggested that the leadership conditions restricting even the top leader's opportunities for human-centred leadership and elevating horizontal accountability reside, on the one hand, in statutory blindness residing in public sector organisational cultures and on the other in the tense relationship between the political level and civil service leaders. Dealing successfully with both pressures seems to be the key to public sector leadership's ability to generate renewal and broaden the scope of human-centred policy choices.

The interviewees talked about many incidents where boundary stretching and finding a way through to the established interpretations of the legal framework had looked like an impossible journey, but persistence in asking for the backgrounds to legal conclusions had paid off. Experienced leaders ensured that future-oriented far-sightedness is required in order to engage in constructive questioning of the prevailing legalism across the sector and in holding the societal target in mind at the crossroads of decision-making. It is important to note here that asking, for example, two regional authorities to pool their expertise in order to work together in a complex permit granting process (outside their usual functional area) does not require breaking laws but merely understanding that the functions of an authority are meant to ease, not inhibit, the functioning of society. Far too often, the authorities are beholden to their own administrative strictures or to/for other authorities and the main target of the work imperceptibly shifts, for example, to avoiding complaints from the administrative court rather than fulfilling a constructive role in society. Moreover, the most enlightened representatives of the courts now note that the role of the civil servant has changed. A good civil servant and civil service leader is proactive, flexible, and takes the initiative within the framework of current laws and regulations.

According to the interviews, this shift is ongoing but needs upholding and consistency of application across public sector organisations. Some interviewees noted that proceeding with opportunities for purpose-oriented work within the public sector is crucial for the public sector's ability to attract skilful leaders and a skilled workforce. There was also a common notion that the legalistic framework surrounding public sector organisations is sometimes used as an excuse for not acting or to justify short-term political wins or other benefits. When describing the relationship between political level and civil service leadership, which in practice co-lead central government ministries, the findings of the interviewees were divided into two minor narratives and one dominant one. The first minor narrative highlighted the civil service leaders' role in serving the changing political leadership to the best of its abilities. That was reflected, for example, in statements like the following by an interviewed Director General with ministerial affiliation and over 20 years of leadership experience

> *sometimes our role is to help the minister to make really stupid decisions—in cases where they insist.*

In contrast, the second minor narrative highlighted the balancing role played by civil servants. Historically, before Finland gained its independence, the civil servant's opportunity to prolong decisions and hinder processes served the country well while it has also been observed that there may be a need for them to play this role again were authoritarian and populistic political tendencies to gain a foothold on the political scene. The dominant narrative, however, settled on a point somewhere in between these views. All interviewees nevertheless agreed that relationships at the political level are often tense and confusing.

In principle, the two-pronged leadership of the government is an asset. It unites the long experience and means of societal change-making of the civil servants with the political goals of the electorate chosen in the normal democratic manner. For this combination to be successful, 'appreciation of the other' is required from both sides. Problems habitually emerge around the lack of recognition of the importance of this leadership alliance and the concomitant lack of appreciation and dialogue this carries. Public policy planning and implementation need careful elaboration and where preparations are made only in political or in civil services siloes, this often results in problems and misunderstandings. Haste, a lack of dialogue, proceeding only on ideological bases without a reality check and pre-set tight commitments were widely identified as characteristic of many of the present-day policy processes initiated by political leaders. On the other hand, the interviewees admitted that the ability to provide opportunities to open up alternative ways forward had not always been characteristic of the civil service side either.

Dysfunctional relationships between political and civil service leaders are also reflected in the uneven organisational cultures of the various ministries. According to the interviewees, some of the ministries are very reluctant to draw up even long-term strategic guidelines without political involvement.

Since political power is often more interested in short (cabinet time) than long-term objectives, while most of the issues ministries take care of never appear on political agendas, some ministries can be said to function as partly directionless in terms of their long view. The decision-making opportunity in different issues is distributed to single civil servants, often lacking a view and/or experience of anything other than a narrow, specialised field. That severely undermines opportunities for human-centred and holistic policy and decision-making and the ability to address societal issues in general. In other ministries, the preparation of public policies and policy implementation are however led more in the spirit of consciously involving all the relevant stakeholders in cooperation. The interviewees highlighted here the relevance and impact-driven approach to forming meaningful preparatory processes, instead of narrow expert thinking and/or representative committees easily freezing thinking and action with a vested interest to preserve the status quo.

The relationship between political and civil service leadership is a characteristic feature of government ministries but traditionally much less so of government agencies. Instead, in recent decades, the role of government agencies in Finland has been to act as independent authorities providing expert knowledge within specialised fields while serving people and businesses in licencing, registration, or approval matters. The interviews show however that there have been attempts to impose a more politicised approach to those matters dealt with by government agencies, thus 'nudging' decision-making in a more politicised direction The coming years will show whether these developments were intensified because of the unusual circumstances of the Covid-19 pandemic, because of tendencies within certain political parties or whether this simply reflects a more general trend in terms of a politicising culture.

### *5.4.4 Jumping over restrictive organisational 'hurdles'*

Maintaining a focus on 'the big picture' was mentioned by the interviewees as the primary success strategy in terms of serving society and societal development from a human-centred perspective. It is however important to note that 'the big picture' is not something a successful leader only internalises but rather they communicate it regularly within their own organisation and with outsiders and are eager to discuss it in a dialogical manner with various people. These everyday leadership actions both increase the quality of leadership and decision-making and serve also as fertile ground for cultural change in terms of pondering issues, decisions, and guidelines from multiple perspectives. One part of this 'big picture' is a leader's ability to swap 'hats' between the strategic and operational levels. Losing sight of the operational reality easily leads to decisions stemming from different realities from those who are affected most by the decisions or those in roles who must implement them. According to the interviewees, it takes a conscious effort to maintain this link to the operational side of things, but it always pays to do so, since without an appreciation of the reality 'on the ground' dialogue easily dies. Four of the interviewees pointed out that the big picture should also include, far more so than it currently does, an appreciation of the international and global scenery. According to their findings, both internal and cross-sectoral discussions and situational pictures tend to focus on domestic affairs, often forgetting the broader international circumstances affecting Finland as with any other country.

Another emergent success factor mentioned by several interviewees was the need to better understand the role of civil society. Civil society refers both to the organised third sector and to self-organising free citizen activism utilising the Internet, social media, and information openness, primarily seeking concrete collaboration for self-directed immediate goals (Mäenpää & Faehnle, 2018). Working together with civil society creates a new kind of challenge and opportunity for the government. For public sector leadership, it means increased openness and elevated readiness to open the background to decision-making. Although it is hard, at the ministerial level, to regularly hold discussions directly with the citizenry, maintaining an enabling mindset in terms of their indirect interventions with the citizenry is an important part of succeeding in these challenging tasks. This can mean, for example, encouraging test beds, sandboxes, and voluntary codes, i.e., self-regulation, without legislation, allowing for greater flexibility in different geographical areas and, in general, establishing legitimacy for the creation of more human-centred services while harnessing the political will for change. At the city and/or municipal level, the opportunities to create space for local bottom-up initiatives and decision-making may be even wider.

A third success factor broadly emerging from the interviews was the importance of forging a good working relationship with the mainstream and social media. To keep the big picture in focus while supporting transparency, any public sector leader in the 2020s has to be active, or at least reachable, by media and in general also on social media. Those interviewees with long experience in government leadership positions however had serious doubts about whether it was possible to uphold fruitful relationships with either. Both media spheres have gradually begun to resemble each other and are increasingly stamped by hyperbole and polarisation. On occasion, this leads to the demonising of individuals and organised campaigns of attack stemming from various motivations, from personal and political motives to intentional attempts to cause instability in society. So, one of the success factors in terms of human-centred leadership is—counterintuitively—keeping media and social media in particular in their place and not letting them distort the views and trust of the citizenry, or society more generally.

In critical situations, leaders should then ask for professional help with communications.

Since the Solution-Focused approach provides an important cornerstone for the concept of leadership meta-skills it was interesting to track Solution-Focused signs of thinking and behaviour in the descriptions the interviewees provided of their everyday work as public sector leaders. A remarkable finding here was that more than half of the interviewees featured Solution-Focused thinking and behaviour in their answers, although only 1–2 have received any formal training in the Solution-Focus approach. This finding implies that decades of experience in demanding leadership positions in public sector working environments, characterised by multi-stakeholder involvement, gradually guides successful leadership practice towards Solution-Focused thinking and behaviour. 'Solution-Focused' is a wording sometimes appearing in the vocabulary of the Finnish central government. It is often however used erroneously to mean equal to provide a ready-made solution to someone else's (i.e., externalised) problem. The interviewees did not necessarily use the word but rather expressed descriptions of Solution-Focused co-created solution formation, in their daily work as public sector organisation leaders. In so doing, they demonstrated the power one leader can have in stretching the boundaries of tradition and in finding new ways forward. In complex situations, any leader can assume that agency and use it to tackle the co-creation challenge with the resources they have and with the meta-skills they already possess.

As a general observation, the interviews conducted reinforced the notion that the six meta-skills examined form a whole, where one meta-skill is difficult to detach or elevate above the others. It is, for example, essential that policy implementation is practised in such a way that the interaction between strategic decision-making and operational activities remains open and two-way, i.e., dialogical and that the promotion of learning and thinking skills in the day-to-day running of an organisation takes place in an enabling rather than in criticising or discouraging spirit. Faithfully to their Solutions-Focused roots, the six meta-skills discussed in this chapter help build the human-centred change that activates both the known and previously unrevealed knowledge and capabilities already residing in people, builds rapport and motivation in relation to the target before bringing in research or other external knowledge or boundary conditions created by legislation, including financial resources or anything else. In so doing, it facilitates the human capacity and collective intention vital for the making of good decisions (Searle, 2010). The six meta-skills together create a platform to transform the hard codes of organisational culture and ways of working, i.e., social norms, budgeting, and type and extent of the data and information used in sensemaking and decision-making. Meta-skills shift the focus of the common tasks to the future and what is wanted instead of focusing on how have things have been done thus far. Legitimacy is built socially, and change happens by changing the interaction process. Practising meta-skills then helps public sector leaders to ask better questions.

### *5.4.5 Opportunities for public management development*

The up-to-date empirical research on the role of meta-skills in the work of Finnish high-ranking public sector leaders presented in the previous section provides a promising result in terms of the importance of possessing and harnessing meta-skills in public sector leadership to achieve more holistic and human-centred governance.

The interviews conducted gave a government-wide picture of meta-skills as part of the self-understanding and agency of those civil service leaders responsible for the betterment of society at the ministerial and partly also at other central government levels. More empirical research is, however, needed to grasp the role of meta-skills in the leadership of other public sector spheres i.e., other kinds of leadership positions and within central government and the public sector more generally, especially at the regional and municipal administration levels. Staff and citizen views of the meta-skilfulness of the leadership would also be interesting to gauge more fully. The extension of the interview pool to include the administrations of other countries would provide the necessary clarification in terms of our understanding of the role of leadership meta-skills in other societies and cultures.

One finding that does however require further research according to the Finnish answers is the question of whether the government ministries, which together form the government in an administrative sense, can be successfully understood within a conceptual framework and with the theoretical tools of organisational research. The interviewees confirmed the perception that despite their similar status and role in government composition, the ministries that form the central government of Finland are a collection of very different organisations with utterly different organisational cultures and ways of working. There are remarkable differences between the ministries in terms of their organisational and operational cultures, as well as in their ways of working with politicians, administration, citizen, and their own field of substance. The construction of the government's central bodies differs to some extent from country to country—even when considering only those countries ruled in a democratic manner—as noted in Chapter 2. The Government of Finland represents a government body consisting of independent ministries. So, despite being a decision-making entity and despite knowing how important cross-sectoral governance is, can the government in the broad sense be called an organisation and does it function as such?

Looking at the most recent organisational scholarly research, the government entity comprising of ministries taking care of their sectoral fields and government central agencies working within those fields could be defined as a 'nine-headed' *hybrid organisation* as in the ancient legend of the Hydra (Johansson & Vakkuri, 2017). It could also be termed a *bi-modal organisation*, which successfully balances a certain amount of organisation with short-term actions of *autopoesis* and fluid social networks (Smith & Sharicz, 2013). It is also possible to look at it as ubiquitous in contemporary governance arrangements provoking Institutional Collective Action dilemmas crossing jurisdictions and institutional contexts (Feiock, 2013).

One possibility is to call it a *nested organisation* reminding us of a Russian doll (Blavoukos & Bourantonis, 2017). From the systems change perspective, Colding and Barthel (2019) bring up the importance of looking at the actual practices to achieve good results in a nested organisation and understanding the critical link between complex and dynamic ecosystems, adaptive management practices, and institutions. The concept of dynamic fractal organisations also provides one possible way to look at the government entity. But taking the ability to integrate and synthesise tacit and explicit knowledge and create *phronesis* along the way as the signifiers of a fractal organisation (Nonaka et al., 2014), it would be an exaggeration to say that governments are fractal organisations. From the point of view of human-centred leadership that would however make for a lucrative goal. When the need for horizontal accountability and better capacities to look at policy issues from the perspective of the citizen or end user are widely recognised—as is the case in Finland—there have been some attempts in recent years to create co-ordinating horizontal structures between ministries. Most of the interviewees however acknowledged that this process of harmonisation has begun at the wrong end, i.e., through attempts to unify procedures in financial, personnel, and technical matters. Choosing that route has created increased frustration when the actual shortcoming is in the fuzzy and uncoordinated leadership model with unclear relationships between political level and civil service leaders and low incentives for cross-sectoral cooperation. In multi-party government, the political leaders tend to experience low incentives for cooperation since there is a tendency for ministers to rival each other in terms of political visibility or quick social media wins in matters that would demand the coordinated cooperation of several ministries to find new solutions to complex problems. In some cases, the difficulties relating to horizontal accountability can be exacerbated by civil service leader's ingrained sectoral views, so human-centred horizontal policy making does not happen without investing in the new mindset recognising the need for co-creation both within the political and civil service leaderships. Succeeding in precipitating a paradigm shift from the traditional subdivided ways of thinking and functioning towards human-centredness is not a technical endeavour but something that needs leadership.

An interesting question emerges here in relation to how much the need to renew the administration and public leadership appears on political agendas, although government ministers are, in principle, also leading the ministries as organisations during their periods in the cabinet. In practice, Secretaries of State usually fulfil that role, while the development of administration and governance practices seldom finds its way onto the party-political agenda. This seems to be one reason for the persistence of the status quo in terms of the way in which the government administration is organised. Interviewees from a few ministries report on several remarkable developments, including the restructuring of ways of working and investing in leadership development after acquiring ministerial permission to elevate those issues onto the work agenda.

In summary, there is a clear need for the civil service and political leaderships to keep each other in a close embrace. This generates better quality administration and policy preparation for the political leaders and enables civil service leaders to lead their organisations and networks to be more in line with the demands of the 2020s. Extended efforts to promote good quality dialogue and mutual appreciation in the spirit of co-creation are however required to succeed in this goal.

## 5.5 Support structures for cross-sectoral leadership

Achieving better public policy outcomes and producing better services in a complex world is not an easy task to fulfil. As discussed earlier, it is not only the societies that are complex but also the governments, while their resilience emerges from the interaction between actors (Ungar, 2021). This interaction cannot be planned, but it can be exercised and cultivated (Lowe & Plimmer, 2019; Stacey, 2010). Leadership is about purposeful action and making room for personal and organisational renewal.

According to the interviews, interaction between the different parts of the system has increased, and it is not generally understood that working in silos does not lead to a result where the different parties are satisfied. Judging from this, we can take it that governance is moving in a positive direction and that understanding of the 'big picture' has significantly increased. Using the classification of Searle (Searle, 2010; see also Chapter 2) we can say that there is a wide *collective recognition* of the need to work together towards common goals. The Finnish civil services leaders interviewed here highlighted various examples where they have been engaged in patching the dysfunctionalities of siloed and formal procedures by initiating new kinds of discussion forums, preliminary preparation, and ecosystem building across the boundaries between government and other sectors of society.

For this development to be strengthened, public leaders need at least two things: encouragement, incentives, and supporting structures for cross-sectoral co-operation and the evolution of meta-skills to ensure that the inevitably colliding viewpoints and complex decisions are made in circumstances that enable fruitful interaction and increase the opportunities to find new solutions.

Asking for the creation of structures to support the cross-sectoral work promoting human-centredness is not an easy task within the public sector, where good intentions can be derailed through over-regulation or imposition. A situation where either the administrative structure or legislation does not encourage cross-sectoral policy preparation is therefore now unviable. According to the interviews, coordinated and co-created policy-formation in Finnish central government has occasionally been better during some governmental periods due to the existence of particularly skilful Secretaries of State at the Prime Minister's office interested in promoting solutions supporting co-leadership. The government capacity for leadership and co-ordination should not, though, rely on the skills, capabilities, and interests of one person. Political positions do not necessarily attract people with leadership and working life experience. According to the interviewees, strengthening the dialogue and real co-ordination first on the highest strategic level between the ministries with the lead of Prime Minister's office would be an important step to further support this process. Also highlighting the principle of broad-based policy preparation and favouring it in practice (not only on paper) would give the required signal for cultural change.

Without any supporting structures, it happens easily that the so-called secondary gains (van Edmond, 2003) run over understanding and intentions to use the possibility one has for changing the traditional script and choosing a more novel way of action. Secondary gains here refer to psychological phenomena in terms of pondering the pros and cons of different means of action and not making decisions with the end user in mind but deciding in favour of traditional part-optimising ways of working because it is easier, more familiar, less time-consuming, and socially simpler, thus delivering short-term gains to the decision-maker. Hämäläinen et al. refer to the same kinds of challenges in their work on systems intelligence (Hämäläinen et al., 2014).

From the viewpoint of socio-cultural learning, the least effective way of inducing change is demanding or ordering somebody to do something. Setting new socio-cultural norms by means of inclusive, engaging working methods which allow for variety and adaption and trusting people's abilities are far more effective in changing working practices (Murtonen & Lehtinen, 2020).

The work of central government is far from characteristic of uniform or production type of work (Johansson & Vakkuri, 2017). Rather, governance is more like craft work, which takes place in often quite discrete environments built around various complicated and complex societal issues. As such, it is hard to govern by means of strictly uniform structures. This observation was again confirmed by the interviewees. Investing in leadership meta-skills provides a platform for the promotion of cross-sectoral human-centred leadership within government bodies. It is an investment in shifting the policy planning of complex and intertwined issues from a top-down and performance-based focus to a co-creation and context-based one.

Leadership meta-skills are human support structures that take organisations and networks into dynamic new spaces, upholding pockets of creativity and renewal, often called *adaptive spaces* (Uhl-Bien & Arena, 2018; Uhl-Bien et al., 2007) or *ba*, where context-based mutual learning happens (Nonaka et al., 2016). The quality of human action is decisive in people's willingness to engage in communities and their willingness to provide their best knowledge and abilities for common use—also in challenging situations of boundary crossing—both in terms of government work and in any other professional surroundings (Murtonen & Lehtinen, 2020; Scalzo & Fariñas, 2019; Törmänen et al., 2021). This type of co-creation increases opportunities to achieve *phronesis*, the classical Aristotelian notion of mature knowledge creation and decision-making stemming from the aspiration to make human life better (Kristjánsson et al., 2021; Tynjälä, 2020). In terms of cross-sectoral leadership, all agents compose together the circumstances for what is possible and what is not for each other. Therefore, it is important that meta-skills are promoted widely among leadership groups.

## 5.6 Synthesis—public leadership meta-skills provide a passage to navigate complex leadership contexts

Leadership meta-skills are sensemaking and bridgebuilding tools that seek common ground despite the existence of different perspectives. They widen the opportunities for different viewpoints to be understood on a deeper level, promote positive dialogue widening flexible mindsets, breaking down biased attitudes and the space between polarities. Meta-skilled bridgebuilding requires abandoning a monopoly of truth and taking the initiative with an outlook that some researchers refer to as 'intellectual humility', i.e., understanding that one's own beliefs might be wrong or only partially true (e.g., Leary et al., 2017). Meta-skilled bridgebuilding is far from grandiose in terms of leadership moves but merely reflects the idea that it is the small details of communication that make the difference and turn the task into a common endeavour (see Table 5.1 to indicate the detailed analysis about the organisational enablers and hindrances related to the use of leadership meta-skills).

The meta-skills presented, discussed, and empirically analysed in this chapter contribute to the emergence of a future-oriented, dynamic, and opportunity-taking organisational and leadership culture. Achieving real-life change is a challenge for most leaders, whether they are piloting organisational renewal, implementing public policy, or tackling any other major challenge. In all cases, co-creation, harnessing the potential of the different parts of the system towards a common goal smooths the way. It is not created by seeking uniformity but by creating the conditions for success for different people and different stakeholders.

It is important to note that human-centeredness involves both internal and external leadership, the first focusing on fostering and nurturing a human-centred leadership style within one's own organisation as well as the network of organisations forming the public sector while the second leads human-centred public policy work involving the end-user and citizen perspective. Both leadership tasks are hard to succeed in without good meta-skills promoting productive co-creation in the twists and turns of our complex world.

The empirical case from Finland presented in this chapter sheds light on how experienced senior public sector leaders themselves interpret these meta-skills, how they define the importance of meta-skills in building human-centred, strengths-based, and flourishing organisations, constituting joint sensemaking and collaboration cutting across organisational boundaries and compartmentalised sectors within the public administration. The support structures for and hindrances to the harnessing of meta-skills were also addressed in the context of cross-sectoral public organising and leadership.

The process of working together with many stakeholders and different people cannot be planned, but leadership meta-skills help to guide progress agilely in the midst of action. This way of managing renders organisations and networks much more resilient during both sudden and predictable changes in their operating environments. It places everyone in the role of a responsible actor in relation to future goal attainment.

After getting acquainted with case studies on public service co-creation, it is easy to become lulled into the belief that co-creation is easy and happens on its own, when the right mix of stakeholders is put in a room together and provided with marker pens and a flipchart. Bridgebuilding does not however come without skills, nor without risk, the possibility for disappointment or, ultimately, of failure. The prospect of success is increased by developing both leadership meta-skills and practical coaching, co-creation, and facilitation skills. More important than methods, however, is the mindset displayed in the context of leadership meta-skills, which consists of an appreciative perception of human capabilities and mutual trust-building. As described earlier, meta-skilfulness does not guarantee success in all situations, but it does gather the available resources to use and increase the likelihood of success. Succeeding with the promotion of co-creation also involves an understanding that change is always a process, not a one-time event. Harnessing leadership meta-skills builds success in fulfilling the ultimate task of the public sector: making life better. What the concept of meta-skills brings to leadership development will be discussed later, in Chapter 7 (Reforming public leadership through learning).

*Table 5.1* Public leadership meta-skills definitions by the Finnish top civil service leaders.

| *Enablers for nurturing and developing in government/public leadership* | *Hindrances for nurturing and developing in government leadership* | *Ideas and amendments* |
|---|---|---|
| **1. Learning to learn**<br>• **Working in different organisations (organised and unorganised rotation)**<br>• **Out-of-the-box experiences, using all events at work as opportunities for learning**<br>• **Positive curiosity and deep listening**<br>• **Recruiting development potential to organisations, not experts of narrow fields**<br>• **General interest in social issues nationally and globally (and not only in own field)**<br>• **Involving oneself in international co-operation**<br>• **Understanding that wisdom does not reside in one's own head, own office, or in the board**<br>• **Interest in people and human behaviour**<br>• **Arranging and guarding opportunities to concentrate on and delve deeper into issues**<br>• **Bringing the learning component to all processes**<br>• **Peer-support and learning from others (training and informal)**<br>• **Own ability to deepen into new issue quickly**<br>• **Ability to scrutinise one's own emotions and perceptions**<br>• **Courage to break the social pattern of hastiness**<br>• **Lifting up what we have learned already, where proceeded**<br>• **Creating connections and networks for mutual learning also with institutions outside one's own field** | Time, place, and energy for learning in pressured work<br>Lack of understanding of the importance of learning<br>Training organised in classroom based and teacher-focused manner<br>Attitudes and discouragement by colleagues and employees, who have not renewed their competences for years<br>Rigid structures and hierarchy of the government bodies restricting learning and thinking<br>Ossified perceptions of human development possibilities | Highlighting the importance of learning as every civil servant's duty<br>Arranging brown bag lunches around different issues<br>Using collaborative ICT-platforms for processing information together<br>Regular 'lessons learned' moments in the working community<br>Providing opportunities for the personnel to expand into previously unknown field |

| | | |
|---|---|---|
| **2. Systems approach**<br>• **Seeing oneself and the actions of one's own organisation as part of the bigger scenery, taking the helicopter perspective**<br>• **Requirements of the demanding policy formation work with strong contextual elements and many stakeholders**<br>• **Good experiences of broad-based policy preparation**<br>• **Increased understanding of phenomena-based approach within government**<br>• **Defining 'leadership of the whole' as the primary duty of all director generals**<br>• **Understanding that citizen's needs continually develop over time not working only here and now, but towards the future**<br>• **Not 'performing expertise' but helping the government to achieve its societal goals**<br>• **Understanding that everything new is born on interfaces between different fields**<br>• **Examples of strong interdependencies (good and bad)**<br>• **Understanding that horizontal impacts are as important as vertical ones.**<br>• **Developing organisational ability for agile and flexible way of working proactively**<br>• **Acting as the initiator in bringing different stakeholders together**<br>• **Opening channels of communication and discussion with civil society and the private sector**<br>• **Understanding that the essence of leadership is not portrayed in management systems and calculations, but in attuning it to developments in the world**<br>• **Interdisciplinarity, also within the academic world**<br>• **Investing time and energy in visioning and foresight**<br>• **Turning attention to how I can personally increase trust, openness, and appreciation to different viewpoints**<br>• **Investing in opening up the reasons behind decisions, also in issues that are approached more emotionally than with factual reasoning in society** | Rigid and subdivided administrative structures<br>Fragmented structure of the central government, lack of joint goal setting and ability to form long-term joint goals<br>The multiple functions of the public sector (from legislative to market-based service provision)<br>Academic fields and education keeping up siloed thinking and knowledge development<br>Fear of making mistakes<br>Tradition of performance-based management and trust in waterfall model of implementation<br>Organisational defences based on emotional grounds<br>Lack of genuine co-operative mindset between different government organisations<br>Lack of supporting structures and incentives<br>Tradition of narrowing leadership down to management processes<br>Raising leadership and decision-making above the organisation or the society<br>Exaggerated administrative burden (e.g., documentation requirements) directing the leadership time and effort to irrelevant details<br>Increased politicisation of decision-making | Systems understanding is most powerfully learned through experience, harder to learn as a theoretical concept |

(*Continued*)

*Table 5.1* (Continued)

| *Enablers for nurturing and developing in government/public leadership* | *Hindrances for nurturing and developing in government leadership* | *Ideas and amendments* |
|---|---|---|
| **3. Dialogical stance**<br>• **Patience to listen and desire to understand**<br>• **Discussing from the same level with everybody and meeting different opinions in a positive way**<br>• **Going through the trouble to achieve dialogue with those who do not think alike**<br>• **Giving space to others and not presenting one's own ideas first**<br>• **Informal culture of the Finnish administration**<br>• **Long tradition of involving NGOs and companies in strategy talks**<br>• **Investing time in answering letters from the general public**<br>• **Choosing appreciative leadership style**<br>• **Showing own example is dialogical leadership and in breaking expectations of omniscient boss**<br>• **Highlighting that all employees despite different responsibilities have an important role in common success**<br>• **Understanding that the dialogical way may seem slower, but it is quicker in the end due to better commitment, taking time for it**<br>• **Making sure that all participate and take part in meetings**<br>• **Investing in creating common targets despite differences**<br>• **Highlighting the importance of thorough discussion, not rushing to conclusions**<br>• **Understanding that there is no 'pure knowledge' anywhere, also experts opinions differ according to (and within) the field. Dialogue is a prerequisite for knowledge creation and decision-making** | The non-dialogical government organisational culture only 20 years away<br>Traditions and expectations of hierarchical all-knowing management<br>Tradition of impropriety to discuss matters of another unit/ministry/organisation<br>Lack of actual skills, although understanding of the importance of dialogue is there<br>Old school leaders who take badly opinions differing from their own<br>Misunderstanding that a decision-making process cannot be dialogical<br>Populism and lack of dialogical tradition in the organisational intranet, media, social media and politics<br>Lots of development room to get rid of the deceptive illusion of efficiency of virtual meetings and make virtual meetings more dialogical | Making use of opportunities for coaching, development, and feedback in terms of getting better at involving personnel and other people<br>Using digital platforms for having dialogue with remote units, stakeholders, and the civil society<br>Learning coaching leadership style<br>Learning from the discussive and appreciative culture of international organisations<br>Restoring the opportunities for dialogue after the period of virtual work during Covid-19 pandemic |

| | | |
|---|---|---|
| **• Giving a model of deep listening in meetings and negotiations**<br>**• Developing one's own skills to create ba-spaces**<br>**• Learning to ask better questions and in such a way that provokes curiosity and creativity**<br>**• Learning conflict resolution skills**<br>**• Being explicit in one's own behaviour so that other people feel that they can express, without fear, what they think**<br>**• Understanding that listening and appreciating does not mean agreeing with someone's opinions or interpretations** | | |
| **4. Thinking-skills**<br>**• Understanding that there are several relevant angles of entry to any issue**<br>**• Constructive questioning of the underlying assumptions in meetings etc.**<br>**• Establishing a future exploring team in the organisation**<br>**• Harnessing foresight and future modelling**<br>**• Using participatory and multifaceted working methods in regular meetings**<br>**• Using roleplaying and gamification in order to gain new perspectives in committees**<br>**• Organising workshops alongside and as part of meeting-driven policy preparation processes**<br>**• Banning mobile phones and laptops in some meetings and concentrating on interaction and co-thinking**<br>**• Using opportunities to get involved in policy preparation processes outside a familiar field**<br>**• Harnessing one's own ability to be fully present in various situations and connecting to different realities**<br>**• Allowing time to also think of others** | Plethora of issues that should be thought through thoroughly and time pressure is a problematic combination.<br>Increasingly shortening time spans of policy preparation<br>Political pressure and efforts to fit huge transformative challenges into one cabinet period<br>Plethora of information and too little synthetised information using multiple types of knowledge<br>Days consisting of 'tunnels' of short meetings<br>A cultural belief that advanced preparation of stances and statements is a good thing<br>No actual tradition of joint critical review of common established beliefs | Too much leadership time is spent on routine duties, such as reading statements, signing papers etc. Substantial amount of that work should be replaced by using algorithms which are better suited to those kinds of duties.<br>Gathering together newcomers' bright ideas for challenging the current way of working<br>Deteriorating thinking skills is a sign of a decline in the level of civilisation |

(*Continued*)

*Table 5.1* (Continued)

| *Enablers for nurturing and developing in government/public leadership* | *Hindrances for nurturing and developing in government leadership* | *Ideas and amendments* |
|---|---|---|
| • **Recognising one's own biases, perceptions, and basic assumptions and being ready to treat them critically**<br>• **Understanding that achieving wisdom is a process**<br>• **Highlighting that a good decision is not a partial result achieved via rational reasoning but something that connects to the context and entirety in a purposeful way**<br>• **Bearing the silence after an unexpected thought and seeing the change in what is possible and what is not as a process**<br>• **Bearing in mind that we all live in our own bubbles**<br>• **Being able to change one's own mind and re-think bad decisions, thanking people for bringing in good new arguments**<br>• **Purposeful recruiting of people with different backgrounds, different strengths, and different generations**<br>• **Making board meetings a forum of dialogue**<br>• **Forming outside reference groups of people with various backgrounds to challenge our own thinking and that of the organisation**<br>• **Understanding that focusing only on the issues of one's own sector is not enough** | Government silos have been free to cement their own beliefs for too long, thus affecting leadership thinking and preparedness<br>Timidity to have real discussion, fear of someone feeling offended by open discussion<br>Turning a blind eye to hard unsolved matters and hoping that somebody else takes the agency | |
| 5. Reaching out to practice<br>• **Understanding that it is impossible to lead from a strategic ivory tower**<br>• **Showing the big picture, future vision, and strategic goals and making room for employees/people to find different ways to reach them**<br>• **Be very clear if the aim is just to make a decision or to implement it; unfortunately, decisions without any intention to execute are often made in the public sector**<br>• **Creating different possible ways of implementation and engaging people in the process** | | |

| | | |
|---|---|---|
| • **Spreading ownership of the issue/project broadly enough; asking 'what this has to include to make it acceptable'**<br>• **Constant sorting out of what is essential to get involved in and what is not**<br>• **Standing behind the chosen path and ensuring the conditions exist for its implementation**<br>• **Assuring political and stakeholder support for the issue**<br>• **Understanding what the everyday challenges in the field are**<br>• **Thinking about the operational side already in the preparatory phase**<br>• **Understanding that in the citizen interface different priorities are important to those on the strategic level**<br>• **Remembering that planning can be done, but you have to be ready to change the plans according to the context**<br>• **The change process has to 'breathe' along the way. It involves interjections, interim decisions, redirecting the process, and encouragement. This is called stewardship, i.e., leadership**<br>• **Giving up dreams of perfect solutions and settling with 'good enough'**<br>• **Keeping an eye on both the strategic and the operation sides, but remembering to step out of both regularly**<br>• **Good understanding of internal and external networks as a tool of implementation and knowledge resource along the way**<br>• **Understanding that structural changes are quick to implement, but behavioural and cultural changes require years and the constant upholding of the chosen direction**<br>• **Understanding that the choice of the means and ways of implementation provide a strong message in respect of the actual objectives and form organisational culture**<br>• **Remembering that people act rationally from their own point of view**<br>• **Having the ability to summarise the essential for the end-user perspective** | Thinking that decisions implement themselves and leading strategy execution is not necessary (or part of one's own job description)<br>Taking the means of achieving something as a starting point instead of the target<br>Fragmentation and polarisation of the political climate<br>Shifting responsibility to others/other organisations<br>Producing a list of things that cannot be done or are not allowed to be done (due to the legislative framework)<br>Concentrate on systematic visioning and alienating from everyday life<br>Establishing executive boards without operative responsibilities<br>Producing long, specific documentation without understanding the context of the implementation or the end user's perspective<br>Micromanaging | In open systems even small flaws in putting things into practice can cause huge problems, compared to closed systems. In crises, the ability to put things into practice in the society is a crucial ability<br>Sharpening the tools of project management in the public sector |

(*Continued*)

*Table 5.1* (Continued)

| *Enablers for nurturing and developing in government/public leadership* | *Hindrances for nurturing and developing in government leadership* | *Ideas and amendments* |
|---|---|---|
| **6. Enabling mindset**<br>• **Building faith in the future and signalling hope even in difficult situations**<br>• **Maintaining the ultimate target, a better life for citizens, in mind**<br>• **Shifting the focus from control, order, and prohibition to creating the circumstances for people to make their own choices**<br>• **Keeping in the mind a sense of proportion**<br>• **Not saying that something is not possible, but thinking together about what can be done within certain boundaries**<br>• **Not over-regulating the future based on current prejudices, instead making sure that the public sector enables the development of new technology etc.**<br>• **Accepting that all decisions and solutions are not meant to be permanent, sometimes a good enough solution for a few years is the best choice**<br>• **Bottom-up processes instead of top-down**<br>• **Enabling civil servants to work across the entirety of societal business rather than just a narrow field [generalists v specialists]**<br>• **Involving people based on interest in the issue instead of representation**<br>• **Not trying to be an expert in every field but using the expertise and talent all around you**<br>• **Encouraging the crafting of good ways to work so that they lead to agreed results** | Formal leadership and development agreements that do not lead to any actions<br>Tightly regulated HR limits of the public sector sometimes prohibiting sensible shifts of job description | Remembering that nobody is perfect, even the leader: important to add self-compassion and mercy to the list of meta-skills |

- **Understanding that other people do the actual work, not the leader**
- **Seeing and appreciating different strengths in people, not uniformity**
- **Understanding leadership as a role, making it possible for others to flourish and shine**
- **Focusing on people's strengths and building on them, also in performance and development discussions**
- **Starting potential and talent programmes**
- **Helping people to reach their potential and using their agency in a constructive way**
- **Positive perception of human beings**
- **Seeing the nature of people and organisations as becoming (instead of being)**
- **Focusing on developing ways of working and doing things a bit better. Renewing mindsets rather than computer systems**
- **Learning to ask what is well, what is working, and how do we find paths forward.**

## Note

1. Prime minister's office, Ministry of Finance, Ministry of Justice, Ministry of Foreign Affairs, Ministry of Home Affairs, Ministry of Defence, Ministry of Education and Culture, Ministry of Agriculture and Forestry, Ministry of Transport and Communications, Ministry of Economic Affairs and Employment, Ministry of Social Affairs and Health, Ministry of Environment.

## References

Akhilesh, K. B. (2017). *Co-creation and learning*. Springer Briefs in Business. Springer. https://doi.org/10.1007/978-81-322-3679-5_2

Annala, M., Leppänen, J., Mertsola, S., & Sabel, C. F. (2020). *Humble government: How to realize ambitious reforms prudently*. Government's Analysis, Assessments, and Research Activities. https://tietokayttoon.fi/documents/1927382/2158283/Humble+Government.pdf/

Arganoff, R. (2006). Inside collaborative networks: Ten lessons for public managers. *Public Administration Review, 66*(s1), 56–65. https://doi.org/10.1111/j.1540-6210.2006.00666.x

Bateson, N. (2015). *Symmathesy—a word in progress: Proposing a new word that refers to living systems*. Occasional Paper of the International Bateson Institute. https://internationalbatesoninstitute.wdfiles.com/local-files/pub%3Anbateson-symmathesy2015/BatesonN2015-IBIarchive-Symmathesy.pdf

Blavoukos, S., & Bourantonis, D. (2017). Nested institutions. In J. Koops & R. Biermann (Eds.), *Palgrave handbook of inter-organizational relations in world politics*. Palgrave Macmillan. https://doi.org/10.1057/978-1-137-36039-7_14

Bolden, R. (2011). Distributed leadership in organizations: A review of theory and research. *International Journal of Management Reviews, 13*(3), 251–269. https://doi.org/10.1111/j.1468-2370.2011.00306.x

Buber, M. (1937). *I and thou* (R. G. Smith, Trans.). T & T Clark.

Colding, J., & Barthel, S. (2019). Exploring the social-ecological systems discourse 20 years later. *Ecology and Society, 24*(1). https://www.jstor.org/stable/26796920

Cooperrider, D. (2017). The gift of new eyes: Personal reflections after 30 years of appreciative inquiry in organizational life. *Research in Organizational Change and Development,* 25, 81–142. https://doi.org/10.1108/S0897-301620170000025003

de Shazer, S. (2016). Fit. *Journal of Systemic Therapies, 35*(1), 55–59. Originally published in the *Journal of Strategic and Systemic Therapies, 3*(3), 1984, 34–37.

de Smedt, P., & Borch, K. (2021). Participatory policy design in system innovation, *Policy Design and Practice*. https://doi.org/10.1080/25741292.2021.1887592

Dierolf, K. (2014). *Solution-focused team coaching*. Solutions Academy Verlag.

Drew, C. (2021). *Developing our new systemic design framework*. https://medium.com/design-council/developing-our-new-systemic-design-framework-e0f74fe118f7

Dutton, J., Morgan Roberts, L., & Bednar, J. (2010). Pathways for positive identity construction at work: Four types of positive identity and the building of social resources. *Academy of Management Review, 35*(2), 265–293. https://doi.org/10.5465/AMR.2010.48463334

Feiock, R. C. (2013). The institutional collective action framework. *The Policy Studies Journal, 41*(3), 398–425. https://doi.org/10.1111/psj.12023

Fitzgerald, L., Ferlie, E., McGivern, G., & Buchanan, D. (2013). Distributed leadership patterns and service improvement: Evidence and argument from English healthcare. *The Leadership Quarterly, 24*(1), 227–239. https://doi.org/10.1016/j.leaqua.2012.10.012

Fredrickson, B. L. (2013). Chapter one—positive emotions broaden and build. *Advances in Experimental Social Psychology, 47*, 1–53. https://doi.org/10.1016/B978-0-12-407236-7.00001-2

Gjaltema, J., Biesbroek, R., & Termeer, K. (2019). From government to governance . . . to metagovernance: A systemic literature review. *Public Management Review, 22*(12), 1760–1780. https://doi.org/10.1080/14719037.2019.1648697

Grant, A., Cavanagh, M., Kleitman, S., Spence, G., Lakota, M., & Yu, N. (2012). Development and validation of the solution-focused inventory. *The Journal of Positive Psychology*, 7(4), 334–348. https://doi.org/10.1080/17439760.2012.697184

Hersted, L., & Gergen, K. J. (2013). *Relational leading: Practices for dialogically based collaboration*. Taos Institute Publications.

Hämäläinen, R. P., Jones, R., & Saarinen, E. (2014). *Being better better: Living with systems intelligence*. Aalto University Publications.

Ind, N., & Coates, N. (2013). The meanings of co-creation. *European Business Review, 25*(1). https://doi.org/10.1108/09555341311287754

Isaacs, W. N. (2007). Toward an action theory of dialogue. *International Journal of Public Administration, 24*(7–8), 709–748. https://doi.org/10.1081/PAD-100104771

Ison, R. (2005). Geoffrey Vickers 2004: Contemporary applications and changing appreciative settings. *Systems Research and Behavioral Science, 22*, 277–284. https://doi.org/10.1002/sres.691

James, W. (1890). *The principles of psychology* (Vol. II). Etext Conversion Project—Nalanda Digital Library. http://library.manipaldubai.com/DL/the_principles_of_psychology_vol_II.pdf

Johansson, J. E., & Vakkuri, J. (2017). *Governing hybrid organisations: Exploring diversity of institutional life*. Routledge.

Kallio, E. K. (2020). From multiperspective to contextual integrative thinking in adulthood: Considerations on theorisation of adult thinking and its place as a component of wisdom. In Kallio, E. K. (Ed.), *Development of adult learning: Interdiciplinary perspectives on cognitive development and adult learning* (pp. 9–32). Routledge. https://doi.org/10.4324/9781315187464

Kim Berg, I., & Szabó, P. (2005). *Brief coaching for lasting solutions*. W. W. Norton.

Kolb, D. A., & Fry, R. (1975). Towards an applied theory of experiential learning. In C. Cooper (Ed.), *Theories of group processes*. John Wiley & Sons. www.researchgate.net/profile/David-Kolb-2/publication/238759143_Toward_an_Applied_Theory_of_Experiential_Learning/links/57d2aea608ae5f03b48cbdd0/Toward-an-Applied-Theory-of-Experiential-Learning.pdf

Krick, E., & Holst, C. (2018). Committee governance in consensus cultures: An exploration of best practice cases in Germany and Norway. In F. Fredrik Engelstad, C. Holst, & G. C. Aakvaag (Eds.), *Democratic state and democratic society* (pp. 151–174). De Gruyter Open Poland. https://doi.org/10.1515/9783110634082-008

Kristjánsson, K., Fowers, B., Darnell, C., & Pollard, D. (2021). Phronesis (practical wisdom) as a type of contextual integrative thinking. *Review of General Psychology, 25*(3), 239–257. https://doi.org/10.1177/10892680211023063

Leary, M. R., Diebels, K. J., Davisson, E. K., Jongman-Sereno, K. P., Isherwood, J. C., Raimi, K. T., Deffler, S. A., & Hoyle, R. H. (2017). Cognitive and interpersonal features of intellectual humility. *Personality and Social Psychology Bulletin, 43*(6), 793–813. https://doi.org/10.1177/0146167217697695

Lowe, T., & Plimmer, D. (2019). Exploring the new world: Practical insights for funding, commissioning and managing in complexity. *Collaborate.* www.collaboratecic.com/exploring-the-new-world-practical-insights-for-funding-commissioning-and-managing-in-complexity-20a0c53b89aa

Malinen, T. (2004). Interview: The wisdom of not knowing? A conversation with Harlene Anderson. *Journal of Systemic Therapies, 23*(2), 68–77. https://doi.org/10.1521/jsyt.23.2.68.36646

McKergow, M. (2021). *The next generation of solution focused practice stretching the world for new opportunities and progress.* Routledge. ISBN 9780367428839.

Metcalfe, J., & Shimamura, A. P. (1994). *Metacognition: Knowing about knowing.* MIT Press.

Murtonen, M., & Lehtinen, E. (2020). Adult learners and theories of learning. In E. K. Kallio (Ed.), *Development of adult learning: Interdisciplinary perspectives on cognitive development and adult learning* (pp. 97–122). Routledge. https://doi.org/10.4324/9781315187464-7

Mäenpää, P., & Faehnle, M. (2018). Urban civic activism: Solutions for the governance of a self-organising urban community. *Helsinki Quarterly, 2.* www.kvartti.fi/en/articles/urban-civic-activism-solutions-governance-self-organising-urban-community

Nonaka, I., Hirose, A., & Takeda, Y. (2016). "Meso"-foundations of dynamic capabilities: Team-level synthesis and distributed leadership as the source of dynamic creativity. *Global Strategy Journal, 6*(3), 168–182. https://doi.org/10.1002/gsj.1125

Nonaka, I., Kodama, M., Hirose, A., & Kohlbacher, F. (2014). Dynamic fractal organizations for promoting knowledge-based transformation—a new paradigm for organizational theory. *European Management Journal, 32*(1). https://doi.org/10.1016/j.emj.2013.02.003

Nonaka, I., & Takeuchi, H. (1995). *The knowledge-creating company: How Japanese companies create the dynamics of innovation.* Oxford University Press.

Papi-Thornton, D., & Cubista, J. (2019, May 6). Systems change in social innovation education: Why social entrepreneurship and innovation education needs to incorporate systems change concepts, and where educators and institutions can begin. *Stanford Social Innovation Review.* https://ssir.org/articles/entry/systems_change_in_social_innovation_education#

Pessoa, A. S. G., Harper, E., Samogim Santos, I., & Carvalho da Silva Gracino, M. (2019). Using reflexive interviewing to foster deep understanding of research participants' perspectives. *International Journal of Qualitative Methods, 18,* 1–9. https://doi.org/10.1177/1609406918825026

Puusa, A. (2020). *Haastattelutyypit ja niiden metodiset ominaisuudet: Laadullisen tutkimuksen menetelmät ja näkökulmat [Types of interviews and their methodological features: Methods and perspectives of qualitative research]* (P. Juuti & A. Puusa, Eds.). Gaudeamus. ISBN 978-952-345-616-7

Scalzo, G., & Fariñas, G. (2019). Aristotelian phronesis as a key factor for leadership in the knowledge-creating company according to Ikujiro Nonaka. *Cuadernos de Administración, 31*(57). http://dx.doi.org/10.11144/Javeriana.cao31-57.apkfl

Searle, J. R. (2010). *Making the social world: The structure of human civilization*. Oxford University Press.

Smith, P. A. C., & Sharicz, C. A. (2013). The bi-modal organization balancing autopoiesis and fluid social networks for sustainability. *The Learning Organization: An International Journal, 20*(2), 134–152. https://doi.org/10.1108/09696471311303773

Stacey, R. D. (2010). *Complexity and organizational reality: Uncertainty and the need to rethink management after the collapse of investment capitalism*. Routledge.

Ståhle, P., Mononen, L., Tynjälä, P., & Kallio, E. K. (2020). Systems thinking and adult cognitive development. In E. K. Kallio (Ed.), *Development of adult learning: Interdisciplinary perspectives on cognitive development and adult learning* (pp. 191–207). Routledge. https://doi.org/10.4324/9781315187464-12

Tammeaid, M. (2020). "How to build large scale change": Leading the client to go where they want to go. *The InterAction Collection of Solution Focus Practice in Organisations, 12*. www.sfio.org/interaction/2020-1/how-to-build-large-scale-change/

Tynjälä, P., Kallio, K., & Heikkinen, H. L. T. (2020). Professional expertise, integrative thinking, wisdom, and phronesis. In E. Kallio (Ed.), *Development of adult learning: Interdiciplinary perspectives on cognitive development and adult learning* (pp. 156–174). Routledge.

Törmänen, J., Hämäläinen, R. P., & Saarinen, E. (2021). Perceived systems intelligence and performance in organizations. In *The learning organization*. Emerald Publishing Limited. https://doi.org/10.1108/TLO-04-2021-0045

Uhl-Bien, M., & Arena, M. (2018). Leadership for organizational adaptability: A theoretical synthesis and integrative framework. *The Leadership Quarterly, 29*(1), 89–104. https://doi.org/10.1016/j.leaqua.2017.12.009

Uhl-Bien, M., Russ, M., & McKelvey, B. (2007). Complexity leadership theory: Shifting leadership from the industrial age to the knowledge era. *The Leadership Quarterly, 18*(4), 298–318. https://doi.org/10.1016/j.leaqua.2007.04.002

Ungar, M. (2021). Modelling multisystemic resilience: Connecting biological, psychological, social, and ecological adaptation in contexts of adversity. In M. Ungar (Eds.), *Multisystemic resilience: Adaptation and transformation in contexts of change* (pp. 6–34). Oxford University Press. https://doi.org/ 10.1093/oso/9780190095888.001.0001

van Edmond, J. J. (2003). Multiple meanings of secondary gain. *The American Journal of Psychoanalysis, 63*, 137–147. https://link.springer.com/article/10.1023/A:1024027131335

van Wart, M. (2017). *Leadership in public organizations: An introduction*. Routledge.

Varona, G. (2021). Ethics and the resilient society: Examining the role of ethics in building societal resilience. *Academia Letters*, Article 1785. https://doi.org/10.20935/AL1785

Virtanen, P., & Tammeaid, M. (2020). *Developing public sector leadership: New rationale, best practices and tools*. Springer. https://doi.org/10.1007/978-3-030-42311-7

Virtanen, P., & Tammeaid, M. (2021). Public leadership meta-skills. In A. Farazmand (Ed.), *The Global encyclopedia of public administration, public policy and governance*. Springer Nature. https://doi.org/10.1007/978-3-319-31816-5_4176-1

Wenger-Trayner, E., & Wenger-Trayner, B. (2021). *"Systems convening" as a crucial form of leadership for the 21st century*. Social Learning Lab, Sesimbra. https://wenger-trayner.com/systems-convening/

Williams, G. (2005). Geoffrey Vickers: Philosopher of responsibility. *Systems Research and Behavioral Science, 22*(4), 291–298. https://doi.org/10.1002/sres.693

# 6 Reforming government through human-centredness

## 6.1 Diversity and uncertainty lead to 'muddling through'

Government reform is a positively loaded concept. It promises a better future, implying that something that is wrong, corrupt, or unsatisfactory will be removed, improved, or amended. The scale and scope of government reform vary from context to context. On the one hand, there are 'grand' reforms such as the European Green Deal, which aims to make Europe the first climate-neutral continent in the world. On the other, reform can also be focused on specific policy areas, health, education, environment, labour, police, security, defence, and so on.

Some reforms are initiated and implemented in accordance with coherent theoretical underpinnings. The doctrine of New Public Management (NPM), for example, has underpinned reforms in public administration since the late 1970s. By providing business-like tools and styles, it was expected to improve efficiency and accountability in public management (Hood, 1991; Pollitt & Bouckaert, 2004). Studies on NPM-inspired reforms, however, paint a somewhat blurrier picture. While some scholars have deemed NPM to be a useful lens for transferring 'best practices' from one context to another (e.g., Holmes & Shand, 1995; Manning, 2001), several others have warned that reforms cannot be successfully implemented by following the instructions of the NPM 'playbook' nor simply imitating what has been done in different contexts (e.g., Kaboolian, 1998; Savoie, 2002). Mathiasen (1999), for example, has argued that contexts are always politically and culturally unique in a way that imitation is not plausible.

NPM's critics suggest that in addition to intended and foreseen consequences, every reform has potentially unintended and unforeseen consequences. Vedung (2013), for example, points out that sometimes there are unintended consequences and perverse effects (following literally Vedung's vocabulary) even on the target audiences of a reform. This is at least partly due to the fact that the future is always somewhat uncertain. Uncertainty arises because events in the future do not follow the course of past events while knowledge of the future is always incomplete (e.g., Rowe, 1994). In

DOI: 10.4324/9781003205791-6

the context of governmental reform, uncertainty comes in various forms, including uncertainty related to the opportunities offered by the operating environment, the competing aspirations of diverse actors, and lack of evidence of what kinds of solutions can be deemed legitimate.

Adapting Lindblom (1959), reforming can be paralleled with the process of 'muddling through'. That is to say that reform is not a rational process which is completed step by step until the well-defined goal is achieved but rather an incremental process in which solutions are sought out gradually and where incoherent change in policy and practice is the rule, not the exception. The impetus for Lindblom's seminal article was his observation of the gap between the rational decision-making 'ideal' and reality. The planning and implementation of reforms are complex and therefore incomplete. Reform is not just a question of a rational review of the substantive issues of policy action and an objective assessment of the related value issues but also of the practical experience of those responsible for the reform of how the process should be taken forward. Some things are emphasised more, some less. It is, moreover, worth noting here that muddling through did not mean failure for Lindblom but the ability to push things forward. Muddling through is not doomed to failure. In line with Lindblom's 'optimism', several studies have recently been published focusing on policy successes in complex settings. Compton and 't Hart (2019), for example, have edited a book arguing that democratic governments are not so bad at what they do. Based on the evidence from 15 in-depth case studies, they explain how successful public reforms have been taken up and carried out. Somehow public administrations have managed to struggle through and made decent decisions with limited information about cause-and-effect relationships (Peters, 2021, p. 1626).

While Lindblom published his article in the 1950s, its basic message is still relevant and timely. The planning of reforms has taken new forms (e.g., online citizen involvement, see Section 3.8), but the idea of being able to prepare for future administrative reforms in accordance with a rational decision-making ideal does not correspond to reality. As a matter of fact, the participatory and deliberative turn in policy making, albeit with good intentions, has increased the complexity of reforms. From the perspective of this book, the choice is not to fight but rather to embrace complexity.

## 6.2 Government reform as tackling tame and wicked problems with evidence

Muddling through becomes more meaningful the better we understand the reasons that cause uncertainty. This can be done, for example, by focusing on the *manageability* of the reforms. While all reforms are somewhat risky endeavours, some of them are riskier than others. Adapting the seminal work by Rittel and Webber (1973) it is possible to categorise reforms into two types: tame and wicked reforms. *Tame reforms* are characterised by low levels of uncertainty. Problems that need to be solved are unambiguous as the cognitive challenge associated with them is not focused on the outcome but manifests itself in a lack of factual knowledge (Daft & Lengel, 1986). Managing the tame reform is facilitated by the fact that uncertainties in the process are detached from the people engaging in the process. In addition, there are 'right' solutions to given problems and the goals do not change in the process.

Wicked reforms or 'grand challenges' (Eisenhardt et al., 2016), in turn, are associated with more uncertainty and unpredictability. This is due to the interconnectedness of the underlying phenomena. Wickedness arises from the problem of "being able to link cause and effect with any certainty" (Peters, 2021, p. 1627). Typically, there is a lack of, or too much, knowledge and conflicting interests. This opens political debate, both in terms of means and the hoped-for results. In the context of public reform, 'wickedness' denotes competing values and ambiguity, where there are no solutions which are just true or false, just better or worse (Meynhardt, 2021, p. 1633). As interests tend to change over time, wicked reforms require an ability to navigate the complex information environment. The question is not how to solve something but how to cope with it. Building upon Dery (1984), Daviter (2017) characterises coping as a process of never-ending discourse with reality in a way that enables the discovery of yet more facets, more dimensions of action, and more opportunities for improvement.

Reforms can be supported with evidence. In its purest form, evidence-based means that information is put through a critical review process that guarantees that every decision is justified by reference to the best available evidence. As evidence-based decision-making assumes an objectively measurable outcome, it is considered appropriate in matters that do not involve ideological confrontations. For example, in assessing the efficiency of service production, the evidence-based approach works better than in justifying policy guidelines (Head, 2015). The instrumental use of evidence in solving technical problems is deemed more legitimate than the application of evidence to the advancement of political goals (Newman, 2017).

Evidence-based decision-making is not however a panacea. Indeed, it has been criticised on the basis that it emphasises the rationalisation of decision-making in a way that neglects and underestimates its democratic aspect (Parsons, 2002). Several scholars have argued that the political dynamics related to reforms cannot be neutralised even with the most convincing evidence (e.g., Newman & Head, 2017). Since wickedness arises not from the lack of evidence, but the ambiguity of the evidence, it is natural to think, as Cairney (2019) does, that coping with the wickedness of administrative reform is primarily a matter of policy-based evidence. In other words, evidence is sought to support a policy which has already been decided upon (Strassheim & Kettunen, 2014).

Evidence-based decision-making, while it has its own flaws, does however suggest movement in the right direction as it emphasises the process of knowing in formulating and implementing public reforms. Instead of a simple dichotomy of facts versus values, knowing is a socially constructed phenomenon. Instead of being just a means to answer political questions, knowledge "has become a source of questions that need to be politically answered" (Rubio & Baert, 2012, p. 3). The importance of knowledge guides us to reflect on reform as an epistemic work.

## 6.3 Government reform as an epistemic work

It is important to avoid both a naive interpretation of the role of evidence and a cynical scepticism towards politics in the reform process. Too much focus on evidence produces an oversimplified view of reform, whereas emphasising the political dimension of the reform allows even relevant evidence to be ignored. A tension arises between the 'objective' and 'subjective', for example, in the case of well-being, which has multiple indicators. Slightly simplified well-being can be approached either as a lack of financial resources, poor housing conditions, and health problems or as personal challenges such as a lack of close relationships, sense of meaninglessness, and general dissatisfaction with one's life. Poverty is measurable, while unhappiness remains elusive.

From the human-centred leadership perspective the key question arises, how to balance objective evidence with subjective interpretation? A quick answer is that it depends on the nature of the reform. In the case of tame reform, there is a clear link between problem and solution, which allows the reform process to focus on means rather than ends (Daviter, 2017). What is important is the reliability of the evidence generated. The legitimacy of evidence as an element of 'good' decision-making is not questioned. In cases of wicked reform, in turn, the idea of evidence is more problematic. This is because wickedness cannot be approached by using a simple question-answer logic. One aspect of wickedness is that every attempt to solve questions hides within it the seeds of a new issue. Therefore, it is also likely that wicked reform is immune to the 'ultimate solution'. In the words of Lindblom (1979, p. 519), attempts to use problem-solving techniques almost inevitably fail to deliver encompassing solutions and instead produce "ill-considered, often accidental incompleteness". Instead of searching for the 'ultimate solution', what is crucial is the ability to avoid 'premature closure' (Peters, 2015, p. 133). Daviter (2017, p. 581), referring to Turner (1989), points to the importance of remaining cognisant of the fact that in ill-structured problems, the criteria of 'good' is itself part of the problem. It seems that what is 'wicked' may turn into 'super wicked', in a sense that those who cause the problem are also expected to provide a solution (Levin et al., 2012). What seems necessary is that achieving success entails working at least in two areas: there is a need for both craft work which consists of "devising, adopting and implementing programmes and reforms that have a meaningful impact on the public issues giving rise to their existence", and political work which manifests itself as "forming and maintaining coalitions of stakeholders to persuasively propagate these programmes" (Compton & 't Hart, 2019, p. 2).

Alternatively, working on reforms can be seen as *epistemic* work. One useful approach here is provided by Alasuutari and Qadir (2014), who have proposed an epistemic perspective on governance. Their key argument is that "policy-making is always premised on actors' understanding of the world and the situation at hand" and "actors themselves are, likewise, constituted by such understandings" (Alasuutari & Qadir, 2014, p. 70). Epistemic work operates in two dimensions (paradigmatic and practical) and in three layers, which are the ontology of the environment, actors and identifications, and norms and ideals (Fig. 6.1). Accordingly, epistemic work aims to provide answers to the following questions: what is the environment, who are the actors, and what is virtuous or acceptable? The ontology of the environment describes the perspectives through which a common understanding of the prevailing reality is defined and influenced. It is important to note that reality here does not however mean a true picture of the situation, but each actor's perception of the situation as s/he understands it and how communicating the reality image in the network of actors helps to promote the success of one's own perspective in political work (Alasuutari & Qadir, 2019, pp. 24–26). For example, Grint (2022, p. 3) reminds us that the COVID-pandemic is not an objective fact but a socially constructed interpretation of social reality. Instead of consensus, there are different and conflicting views on the legitimacy of lockdowns, vaccination procedures, furlough schemes, face coverings, and so on. Actors and identifications as a

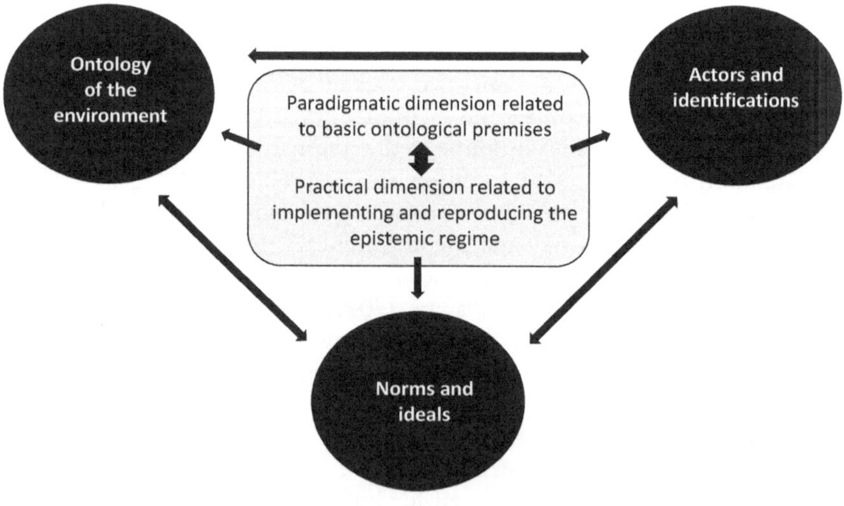


*Figure 6.1* Dimensions and layers of epistemic governance (based on Alasuutari & Qadir, 2014).

concept cover both the actors' own understanding of themselves and their view of themselves and the role of others in relation to the issue at hand. It is a matter of identifying different groups in one's own or another group. The negative hallmark definitions used in politics for other groups, compared to one's own group, are typical examples of identification. On the other hand, the definition of a common agency and group is also widely used in a positive sense to promote identification with goals that are generally considered virtuous and acceptable (Alasuutari & Qadir, 2019, p. 27). Norms and ideals are part of an epistemic work in which an actor seeks to convince others of the legitimacy of his/her views by invoking well-known values, principles, and practices. Norms and ideals emerge and spread effectively when the values can be justified by evidence.

From a governmental reform perspective, epistemic work brings to the fore the need for a human-centred approach. The 'wickedness' of reform results from the actions taken by humans. It is people who initiate reforms, gather information, make decisions, and evaluate outcomes. People debate issues, build coalitions, set agendas, and seek support for their claims for various causes. While they do that to sponsor their agenda and influence their peers, they also become a part of what is in dispute (cf. Turner, 1989). That is to say that the whole and the parts become intertwined. Adapting Haken's (1977) idea of circular causality, Meynhardt (2021, p. 1638) argues that interaction between people leads to the emergence of collective properties, from which individuals cannot simply deny or escape. As discussed previously, the emergent whole is more than the sum of its parts. This means that the emergent whole is not fundamentally an attribute-based but relation-based phenomenon. While the diversity of actors matters, their relations matter more.

## 6.4 Government reform as human-centred sensemaking

Government reforms always encounter and generate a wide range of conflicting interests and tensions. In addition to 'rationally' judged intentions, there are also emotionally inspired hopes and fears. Different views make the management of reform difficult at every phase of the policy cycle (e.g., Jann & Wegrich, 2007), from planning to implementation through to evaluation. What becomes crucial then is how these tensions are framed and how different voices are heard.

Sensemaking refers to the process through which people work to understand issues that are unknown to them. The aim is to frame scattered information pieces and put stimuli into a larger framework of interpretation. This happens through observing, perceiving, and understanding. Karl Weick is widely regarded as a pioneer of sensemaking in organisational research. Weick has addressed sensemaking in several of his works. In his 1995 book, *Sensemaking in Organizations*, he divides sensemaking into seven features which are, identity, retrospective, enactment, social, ongoing, cues, and plausibility.

*Identity* is based on a mechanism of self-referencing, in which the individual and the subjects of the referral are in a recursive relationship with each other. An individual exists in relation to others and his/her environment. What and how they are made sense of depends on the identity of the individual, which in turn modifies the identity of the individual. *Retrospective* means that action is a prerequisite for sensemaking. Meanings can only be given to past events—never to ongoing or future events. It follows from the ambiguity of events and phenomena, in turn, that retrospective sensemaking is always prioritisation based on values and preferences. By the concept of *enactment*, Weick refers to the two sides of sensemaking, namely awareness and action. In addition to perceiving and understanding the existing, sensemaking is at the same time a matter of creating the existing. The environment is not independent of those who interpret it but is always the subject of ongoing sensemaking. Like it or not, our actions depend on what our fellow human beings do and do not do. Therefore, sensemaking is always a *social* process that assumes its form and content in interaction. It is also an *ongoing* process, in the sense that it does not have a start and end point. Significance is implemented during situations and in the flow of events. To choose the essential, in turn, requires the ability to identify *cues*. For Weick, cues are a source of power guiding and limiting the actions of individuals and systems. *Plausibility* is a necessary condition for all activities. The pursuit of punctuality and accuracy often leads to slow movement, which is why it often makes more sense to settle for a sufficiently credible and convincing interpretation. Due to the uncertainty of the information and the ambiguity of the phenomena, sensemaking is always incomplete.

Sensemaking takes place in the way we use language and speak (Weick et al., 2005). Sensemaking is the organisation of phenomena through communication and their shaping to allow for certain kinds of action. It is thus always a matter of choosing one and excluding the other. Particularly in the context of wicked reform, the role of language cannot be exaggerated (cf. Grint, 2022). Instead of 'neutral' naming, events and phenomena are framed as relevant. Lakoff (2006) has defined frames as mental structures of the human mind that are necessary for understanding reality, which are sometimes also exploited in the creation of reality. Frames organise scattered stimuli into whole entities, they shape our thinking and attitudes towards our environment, and they influence the actions we take at any given time. In so doing, frames are social constructs and deep-rooted conventions, which is why we are rarely even aware of their connection to our thinking and action. Lakoff (2006) divides frames into two categories: deep frames shape individuals' worldviews and define what is collectively believed in the community, while issue-defining frames indicate words that are concretely utilised in the framing process. Sensemaking and framing benefit from *diversity*.

## 6.5 Government reform as human-centred diversity

Sensemaking is a process that both produces and depends upon diversity. The combination of the seven features of sensemaking influences what stimuli are perceived in the organisation and what conclusions are drawn from them. Although Weick does not directly discuss the role of diversity in sensemaking, it seems obvious that many of its features are at least indirectly related to diversity. For example, the more diverse the value base used to interpret environment, the more solid the understanding of retrospective events. Similarly, the plausible identification of cues floating in the flow of events depends to a large extent on the diversity of the actors who interpret them and the quality of the interaction. The self-referencing mechanism, in turn, has the effect that the diverse community of actors reflects aspects of its environment that reinforce the diversity of the community. Frames are used to build narratives that can be communicated about phenomena and events and that appeal to recipients. In so doing, they serve as a bridge between interpretation and action and help to separate the acceptable from the unacceptable. The diversity of a community affects the ways and form in which it is framed. The deep frames of a homogeneous community are narrower and more internally cohesive than in heterogeneous communities.

The diversity of actors and relationships can contribute to both sensemaking, which supports interpretation and understanding, and framing, which brings about such action. The value of sensemaking and framing can be concretised as the ability to face the complexity inherent in wicked reforms. The success, however, is not self-evident. It is essential to aim at the creation of shared meanings, as only information that has been identified as meaningful can lead to change (Wheatley, 1999). It is important to point out here that the shared meaning is not imposed by those 'in power'. To be useful, the idea of shared meaning should acknowledge that different people have different world views and, what is more important, is that they have different abilities to see things. This kind of diversity of knowledge and values is crucial for any reform process because it allows for a 'polyphony' of perspectives. Hazen (1993, p. 24), for example, uses polyphony as a metaphor for organisational change. According to him, the metaphor of polyphony "supports inclusive change as it helps us to hear . . . people who speak with another in their own voices".

The idea of polyphony is particularly useful for reform processes for at least two reasons. First, it admits that every actor has their own perspective on the reform at hand. It means that the truth (if any) lies between these multiple perspectives. A wicked-type government reform is subjective in the sense that everyone can have an equally 'correct' opinion about it. By listening to multiple voices, however, it is possible to understand its wickedness and make room for different rationalities (cf. Clegg et al., 2006). Stressing the importance of silent voices, it is possible to avoid the culture that is too monological (Clegg et al., 2006). Second, polyphony not only refers to the fact that everyone has their own point of view but also implies a plurality of values. The process of tackling the wickedness of reform is always political, with people mutually enabling and constraining each other. Instead of seeing different perspectives as static representations that should be receptively noticed, the idea of polyphony emphasises "the creative interaction of contradictory and different voices" (Clegg et al., 2006, p. 14).

With collaborative reflection however comes the question of the tensions involved in the interaction. A plurality of voices does not necessarily contribute to diversity. The combination of tensions inherent in interaction and the interdependence between the actors means that in certain circumstances, even simple things can end up as complex entities. Tackling complexity requires acceptance that no actor alone can control and decide the outcome of *interaction* processes.

## 6.6 Government reform as human-centred responsive interaction

Government reforms do not happen by themselves, they are made by people. One can argue that reform is, basically, managing people-to-people interactions. When it comes to different people, it is obvious that there is also an interaction with different dynamics. While interaction dynamics are different in different situations, what is common is that one actor's actions are both enabled and limited by the other's actions. Luhmann (1995) calls this as a double contingency and emphasises its importance by pointing out that double contingencies are always based on voluntariness. This, in turn, means that there are risks involved in the interaction. The risk of interaction underlines the importance of trust between actors. It is this trust between the actors which ultimately determines how the double contingencies can be harnessed as drivers to overcome the challenges faced by the reformers.

Trust supports knowledge sharing and encourages creativity. Courage is also needed when new ideas are misleading and the direction needs to be revised. This requires that ideas can be questioned and compared and that actors need to be prepared to abandon their own thinking frameworks if necessary (Popper, 1996). For this reason, leaders need to pay attention to the comprehensive and diverse treatment of issues on the agenda. This can be supported by investing in the responsiveness of interaction processes. Underlying the responsive interaction process is the idea of reflexivity, which is based on accepting and understanding that there is not always just one truth and one right solution (Stacey, 2001). For Stacey (2001), complex responsive processes mean the alternation of competition and cooperation in the relationships between different actors. In a similar vein, Giddens (1990) argues that systems renewal requires the reflexive monitoring of knowledge, in which both practices are constantly evaluated in the light of new knowledge and the data itself is subject to re-evaluation. Through reflexivity, actors adapt to their social environment and plan their activities.

Reflexivity is not just about personal, critical evaluation of one's own thinking but also about sharing information and interacting with people (Schön, 1991). It is important to note here that by reflecting alone, one can learn about things concerning one's own work, while by reflecting together, the learning process becomes common (Forester, 1999). The key is not to pay attention to the characteristics of individual actors but to what kind of higher-level behaviour emerges from the interactions between individual actors. Individuals' intentions and choices are important in terms of outcome, but they alone cannot explain what is happening (Stacey, 2009). The intentions and choices of individual actors are the raw material which, when mixed with the intentions and choices of other actors, produces an emergent pattern which is qualitatively more (or less) than the sum of its parts.

The responsive interaction approach brings forward the questions of power and the middle manager's role in the reform process. First, it is critical to acknowledge that power is not based on position but rather is embedded in the dynamics of interaction (cf. Elias, 2001). Power is manifested, for example, in the way in which some actors are involved in knowledge and interaction, while others are excluded. It is ultimately a question of accepting that in complex reforms, rarely does one actor have sufficient power and knowledge to solve wicked problems. Second, it suggests that middle managers can play a key role in creating meanings and content through their own experiences as well as the organisation's various delivery mechanisms (cf. Stacey & Griffin, 2015). Metaphorically speaking, the top management represents the purposive direction for the organisation, while middle managers form its heart. Where the top management is responsible for formulating the strategy, the role of middle managers is to interpret it locally. Through responsive interactions, reformers forge the *value proposition* of the reform.

## 6.7 Government reform as value proposition

One particularly potential line of criticism of New Public Management (NPM) claims that its argumentation is based on linear models of public service delivery and an oversimplified approach to public service management in an increasingly complex and interdependent world (e.g., Osborne, 2018). NPM focused on the effectiveness of public administration and viewed public service outcomes as an element of performance (Yang & Northcott, 2019). Consequently, a concept of 'value' is attached to public service costs, e.g., 'value for money' thinking, specifically associated with how to reduce costs (Kloot & Martin, 2000). In NPM discourse, value is an organisationally driven reason for reforming public services. Congruently, value creation has been a matter of how to arrange operations within public organisations. The more efficiently public services are provided, the more legitimate public organisations are perceived. The contrast is clear when value is approached from the service user's perspective. Inspired by service management and marketing theory (e.g., Vargo & Lusch, 2004), there has been a rapid growth in research focused on citizens' and service users' roles in value creation. Farr (2016), Bryson et al. (2017), Osborne (2018), and Grönroos (2019), to name but a few, approach value creation as an activity where citizens and service users play an active role. They are not just value beneficiaries but value co-creators. Osborne (2018, p. 225), for example, claims that co-creation "assumes an interactive and dynamic relationship where value is created at the nexus of interaction". According to Petrescu (2019) and Strokosch and Osborne (2020), value-creation interactions take place in public service ecosystems consisting of the service specific elements (public service organisations, citizens, and technology) and the broader societal context and the values that underpin it.

Value has become a focal concept in public administration and an eternal question in philosophy. Searching for consensus over the definition of value dates back at least to Aristotle, who addressed the two meanings of value: 'exchange—value' and 'use—value' (Vargo et al., 2008). Aristotle's thinking was influenced by his idea of the differences between objective and physical things and the subjective meanings of the things created in the minds of their users. Adam Smith (2000) elaborated on Aristotle's thinking by bringing the discussion of value creation into the development of economics (Vargo et al., 2008). In his seminal work *The Wealth of Nations* (1776/2000, p. 31), Smith writes that "the word value, it is to be observed has two different meanings, and sometimes expresses the utility of some particular object, and sometimes the power of purchasing other goods which the possession of that object conveys". Congruently with Aristotle, Smith named two forms of value as 'value-in-use' and 'value-in-exchange' (Vargo et al., 2008).

Government reform can be seen as a kind of value proposition, consisting of key promises and advantages for the citizen and other stakeholders. Typically, reforms are launched to change what kinds of services are provided, by whom and to whom. While it is tempting to depict reformers as value creators and citizens as value beneficiaries, the concept of value proposition assumes that value cannot be delivered from creators to beneficiaries. Instead of 'value-in-exchange', Grönroos (2019), Osborne (2018), Eriksson et al. (2020), and many others point out that value is always realised 'in-use', when the user uses the service. This also means that the provider can only offer potential value. Grönroos and Voima (2013) explain the value-creation process by separating three different value spheres, namely, the service provider sphere, the service user sphere, and the joint sphere. According to them, value is created either in the user sphere independently by users or in joint sphere in collaboration between the provider and user. The better the experience fits the needs, expectations, and wishes of the citizen, the more valuable the service is perceived. This kind of subjectivity of value also means that value is never true, it exists only in the eye of the beholder. The ecosystem view also stresses the role of the societal context and the values

## EXHIBIT 3 Value proposition and its complexity in practice—Health and social services reform in Finland

The Finnish health and social services reform will shift the responsibility for organising health and social services and rescue services from the local government level (municipalities) to the regional government level (counties). The reform has been on the political agenda in Finland since almost the beginning of the 2000s. The value proposition of the reform is to ensure that everyone in Finland has equal access to high-quality health and social services. The reform will develop healthcare and social welfare services and reorganise their structure. From a leadership point of view, the reform can be described as a systemic change with a 'complexity twist'. Key challenges include collaboration in service production within the counties, citizen and service user participation, and interaction between the government and counties.

The complexity of the reform emerges from and may take several forms such as conceptual complexity, structural complexity, institutional complexity, ideological complexity, and professional complexity. First, health and social services aim to maintain and improve citizens' well-being. Conceptual complexity results from the multifaceted nature of well-being, and it is influenced by many factors, including physical and mental health, safety and security, relationships, and community (e.g., Halleröd & Seldén, 2013). Second, health and social services are provided by a mix of public-, private-, and third-sector organisations. Structural complexity manifests itself as the anticipated difficulty involved in the design and delivery of services resulting from coordination with multiple government agencies and from the imperative for service integration (e.g., Bode, 2006). Third, public-, private-, and third-sector organisations operate under different institutional arrangements (for-profit, non-profit, or a combination thereof) and partly under different jurisdictions. Institutional complexity arises from different and contrary institutional logics and incoherent pricing and financing policies caused by the decisions made at different government levels (e.g., Saz-Carranza & Longo, 2012). Fourth, health and social services is a politically sensitive issue because it mirrors the core values of the society. Ideological complexity emerges from the value conflicts and tensions resulting from the challenges of balancing 'traditional' governmental values (integrity, neutrality, legality, and impartiality) with 'business-like' values (efficiency, innovation, and effectiveness) (e.g., Jaspers & Steen, 2018). Fifth, the aim is to ensure that services are provided seamlessly to people and that people are given help for their individual needs. This requires service integration, which is easier said than done. Instead of integration, tensions arising between different expertise may lead to professional complexity (e.g., Mennin, 2010).

A brief look at the complexities of the reform qualifies it as "the mother of all domestic reform packages" in Finland (Alter, 2019). Realising the potential of reform requires a new kind of public leadership (Virtanen & Tammeaid, 2020) and an ability to drive through the systemic change that creates the conditions for real-service integration. This requires a shift from sector-specific operations to the facilitation of the phenomenon-based approach. Simultaneously, there is a need to transform service-delivery orientation into value co-creation. The risks of failure are obvious, and they are not limited to the reform as such; it questions the capacity of government to remain an effective actor in complex policy areas (Alter, 2019).

surrounding and legitimising the services. 'Value-in-context' happens when a citizen brings his/her life experiences which are affected by societal values, to a public service encounter (Osborne et al., 2021).

The importance of the experimental dimension of value combined with the assumption that value emerges through interaction begs the question of whether and how value creation can be facilitated through human-centred leadership.

## 6.8 Human-centred leadership as interactive practice

Further to what was said in Chapter 2, it should be noted again that the concept of value is somewhat elusive. It has however proved useful in the context of leadership. There are at least three reasons for this.

First, value helps us to understand human behaviour. People tend to do things they see as valuable. If we understand the rationale that makes things worth pursuing, we are also better able to understand people's motivations to do such things in the first instance. Second, value enables us to understand how people rank things. People tend to value things that give them more utility than others. The better we understand the calculations through which people attach value to things, the better we understand their preferences. Third, through value it is possible to influence peoples' behaviour. As people rank opportunities available to them, it is in the interest of agents to portray their 'choice' as being as worthy as possible. The more valuable something is seen, the more engaged people will be.

Though value can take several forms, its emergence can be supported through leadership, which relies on relationships between leaders and followers, not the characteristics of leaders. Several studies have found that personalised charismatic leaders prefer personal outcomes over presenting a vision for an organisation's future (e.g., House & Howell, 1992; O'Connor et al., 1995). Unsurprisingly, the view that emphasises charismatic leadership has been replaced by approaches that emphasise the shared (e.g., Lambert, 2002) and distributed (e.g., Gronn, 2002) nature of leadership. Despite the small differences in nuances, both leadership approaches share the idea that leadership is enacted through social interaction. In other words, leadership is perceived neither as a characteristic of the individual nor as a characteristic of a relationship between two individuals or between an individual and a group but rather as a social interaction maintained and modified through relations. DeRue and Ashford (2010) suggested that social interactions provide the building blocks for leadership identity construction. They define leadership identity construction as a claiming-granting process. By claiming, DeRue and Ashford (2010, p. 631) refer "to the actions people take to assert their identity as either a leader or follower", whereas granting means "the actions that a person takes to bestow a leader or follower identity onto another person".

Real leadership cannot exist without followers. For Uhl-Bien (2021), this means that leadership is co-creation. Co-creation happens at the nexus of the act of leaders and followers. This means that the dynamics of leadership cannot be understood when the focus is only either on the behaviour of leaders or the on the actions taken by the followers. Co-creative leadership celebrates diversity and promotes an organisation's sensemaking abilities, helping it to adapt to its changing environment. It is, moreover, worth noting here that co-creative leadership is a complex social phenomenon implicitly carrying with it the possibility for both good and bad (Uhl-Bien, 2021, p. 158). Adaption may fail and leadership can occasionally drift towards value co-destruction. In the public service context, value co-destruction typically happens when the interacting parties fail to integrate resources in a mutually beneficial manner (Engen et al., 2021, p. 890). Sometimes this is the result of the conflicting interests between parties (Rossi & Tuurnas, 2021), while on other occasions, co-destruction can be a by-product of good intentions. Leaning on King et al. (2002), Jalonen et al. (2020) suggest that co-destruction may happen even when 'good people' come together in 'good faith' to do 'good things'. In other words, neither leaders nor followers intend to do any harm, but negative outcomes nevertheless emerge from their interactions.

The relationship between leader and followers is a complex one, in the sense that what emerges through interaction cannot be reduced to the characteristics of leaders and followers. Interaction produces leadership which is more or less the sum of its parts. It is obvious that individual acts of leaders and followers have consequences on how leadership is enacted.

## 6.9 Synthesis—the dimensions of human-centredness in reforming government

What value is and how it is created are debatable questions which have inspired academic research across many disciplines. Despite extensive research, consensus over the content of value, its prerequisites, and consequences seemingly, remains out of reach. It seems that the attractiveness of the concept has increased, not decreased, because of its vagueness and ambiguity (Bozeman, 2002). What seems to be clear, however, is that complex government reforms cannot succeed without leadership and followership.

A relational approach to public leadership (shared, distributive, and co-creative leadership) speaks in favour of human-centredness in two ways. First, it assumes that public administration personnel are seen as trusted and as having agency to act upon one another. Agency is understood here as the ability "to create the conditions within which something new can emerge" (Lichtenstein, 2016, p. 4). Second, it emphasises the service user's role as active subjects rather than passive objects. Service users are perceived as value co-creators who have knowledge and experiences to offer. It is in the public administration's interest to hear their voices.

It should also be noted that depicting a reform as complex also involves a potential solution. This is the case because complexity manifests as emergence in which interdependencies between ideas, phenomena, events, and actors allow for the simultaneous development of new and useful approaches that can lead to the fruitful destruction of existing 'good' practices.

It can also be assumed that the more complex the reform, the more values conflict with one another. Thus, from the human-centred leadership approach, one of the key issues in reform processes is to nurture the value pluralism. Incommensurable and incompatible values should not be addressed with the same yardstick. When incommensurability and incompatibility are taken seriously, it means that in addition to objective and measurable evidence reformers are sensitive to different needs, willing to listen to various voices, and capable of making sense of citizens' subjective judgements and lived experiences.

## References

Alasuutari, P., & Qadir, A. (2014). Epistemic governance: An approach to the politics of policymaking. *European Journal of Cultural and Political Sociology, 1*(1), 67–84. https://doi.org/10.1080/23254823.2014.887986

Alasuutari, P., & Qadir, A. (2019). *Epistemic governance: Social change in the modern world.* Palgrave Macmillan. https://dx.doi.org/10.1007/978-3-030-19150-4

Alter, R. (2019). *The center of government in Finland: How to prepare better (for) the future.* Report commissioned by the Finnish Innovation Fund. SITRA.

Bode, I. (2006). Co-governance within networks and the non-profit—for-profit divide: A cross-cultural perspective on the evolution of domiciliary elderly care. *Public Management Review, 26*(4), 551–566. https://doi.org/10.1080/14719030601022932

Bozeman, B. (2002). Public-value failure: When efficient markets may not do. *Public Administration Review, 62*(2), 145–161. www.jstor.org/stable/3109898

Bryson, J., Sancino, A., Benington, J., & Hartley, J. (2017). Towards a multi-actor theory of public value co-creation. *Public Management Review, 19*(5), 640–654. https://doi.org/10.1080/14719037.2016.1192164

Cairney, P. (2019). The UK government's imaginative use of evidence to make policy. *British Politics, 14*, 1–22. https://doi.org/10.1057/s41293-017-0068-2

Clegg, S. R., Kornberger, M., Carter, C., & Rhodes, C. (2006). For management? *Management Learning, 37*(1), 7–27. https://doi.org/10.1177/1350507606060975

Compton, M., & 't Hart, P. (2019). *Great policy success*. Oxford University Press. https://doi.org/10.1093/oso/9780198843719.001.0001

Daft, R. L., & Lengel, R. H. (1986). Organizational information requirements, media richness and structural design. *Management Science, 32*(5), 554–571. www.jstor.org/stable/2631846

Daviter, F. (2017). Coping, taming or solving: Alternative approaches to the governance of wicked problems. *Policy Studies, 38*(6), 571–588. https://doi.org/10.1080/01442872.2017.1384543

DeRue, D. S., & Ashford, S. J. (2010). Who will lead and who will follow? A social process of leadership identity construction in organizations. *Academy of Management Review, 35*(4), 627–647. www.jstor.org/stable/29765008

Dery, D. (1984). *Problem definition in policy analysis*. University Press of Kansas.

Eisenhardt, K. M., Gracbner, M. E., & Sonenshein, S. (2016). Grand challenges and inductive methods: Rigor without rigors mortis. *Academy of Management Journal, 59*(4), 1113–1123. https://doi.org/10.5465/amj.2016.4004

Elias, N. (2001). *The society of individuals*. Continuum.

Engen, M., Fransson, M., Quist, J., & Skålén, P (2021). Continuing the development of the public service logic: A study of value co-destruction in public services. *Public Management Review, 23*(6), 886–905.

Eriksson, E., Andersson, T., Hellström, A., Gadolin, C., & Lifvergren, S. (2020). Collaborative public management: Coordinated value propositions among public service organizations. *Public Management Review, 22*(6), 791–812. https://doi.org/10.1080/14719037.2019.1604793

Farr, M. (2016). Co-production and value co-creation in outcome-based contracting in public services. *Public Management Review, 18*(5), 654–672. https://doi.org/10.1080/14719037.2015.1111661

Forester, J. (1999). *The deliberative practitioner. Encouraging participatory planning processes*. MIT Press.

Giddens, A. (1990). *The consequences of modernity*. Stanford University Press.

Grint, K. (2022). Critical essay: Wicked problems in the age of uncertainty. *Human Relations*. https://doi.org/10.1177/00187267211070770

Gronn, P. (2002). Distributed leadership as a unit of analysis. *The Leadership Quarterly, 13*(4), 423–451. https://doi.org/10.1016/S1048-9843(02)00120-0

Grönroos, C. (2019). Reforming public services: Does service logic have anything to offer? *Public Management Review, 21*(5), 775–788. https://doi.org/10.1080/14719037.2018.1529879

Grönroos, C., & Voima, P. (2013). Critical service logic: Making sense of value creation and co-creation. *Journal of the Academy of Marketing Science, 14*(2), 133–150. https://doi.org/10.1007/s11747-012-0308-3

Haken, H. (1977). *Synergetics: Nonequilibrium phase transition and self-organizations in physics, chemistry and biology*. Springer. https://doi.org/10.1007/978-3-642-96469-5

Halleröd, B., & Seldén, D. (2013). The multi-dimensional characteristics of wellbeing: How different aspects of wellbeing interact and do not interact with each other. *Social Indicator Research, 113*, 807–825. https://doi.org/10.1007/s11205-012-0115-8

Hazen, M. A. (1993). Towards polyphonic organization. *Journal of Organizational Change, 6*(5), 15–26. https://doi.org/10.1108/09534819310072747

Head, B. W. (2015). Toward more "evidence-informed" policy making? *Public Administration Review, 76*(3), 472–484. https://doi.org/10.1111/puar.12475

Holmes, M., & Shand, D. (1995). Management reform: Some practitioner perspectives on the past ten years. *Governance, 8*(4), 551–578. https://doi.org/10.1111/j.1468-0491.1995.tb00227.x

Hood, C. (1991). A public management for all seasons? *Public Administration, 69*(1), 3–19. https://doi.org/10.1111/j.1467-9299.1991.tb00779.x

House, R. J., & Howell, M. (1992). Personality and charismatic leadership. *The Leadership Quarterly, 3*(2), 81–108. https://doi.org/10.1016/1048-9843(92)90028-E

Jalonen, H., Puustinen, A., & Raisio, H. (2020). The hidden side of co-creation in complex multi-stakeholder environment: When self-organization fails and emergence overtakes. In H. Lehtimäki, P. Uusikylä, & A. Smedlund (Eds.), *Society as an interaction space: A systemic approach* (pp. 3–22). Springer. https://doi.org/10.1007/978-981-15-0069-5

Jann, W., & Wegrich, K. (2007). Theories of the policy cycle. In F. Fischer, G. J. Miller, & M. S. Sidney (Eds.), *Handbook of policy analysis*. Routledge.

Jaspers, S., & Steen, T. (2018). Realizing public values: Enhancement or obstruction? Exploring value tensions and coping strategies in the co-production of social care. *Public Management Review, 21*(4), 606–627. https://doi.org/10.1080/14719037.2018.1508608

Kaboolian, L. (1998). The new public management: Challenging the boundaries of the management vs. administration debate. *Public Administration Review, 58*(3), 189–193. https://doi.org/10.2307/976558

King, J., Down, J. T., & Bella, D. A. (2002). Learning to think in circles. *Journal of Management Inquiry, 11*(2), 161–170. https://doi.org/10.1177/10592602011002010

Kloot, L., & Martin, J. (2000). Strategic performance management: A balanced approach to performance management issues in local government. *Management Accounting Review, 11*, 231–251. https://doi.org/10.1006/mare.2000.0130

Lakoff, G. (2006). *Thinking points: Communicating our American values and vision*. Farrar, Straus & Giroux.

Lambert, L. (2002). A framework for shared leadership. *Educational Leadership, 59*(8), 37–40.

Levin, K., Cashore, B., Bernstein, S., & Auld, G. (2012). Overcoming the tragedy of super wicked problems: Constraining our future selves to ameliorate global climate change. *Policy Sciences, 45*, 123–152. https://doi.org/10.1007/s11077-012-9151-0

Lichtenstein, B. B. (2016). Complexity science at a crossroads: Exploring a science of emergence. *Academy of Management Proceedings*. https://doi.org/10.5465/ambpp.2016.38

Lindblom, C. E. (1959). The science of "muddling through". *Public Administration Review, 19*(2), 70–88. https://doi.org/10.2307/973677

Lindblom, C. E. (1979). Still muddling, not yet through. *Public Administration Review, 39*(6), 517–526.

Luhmann, N. (1995). *Social systems*. Stanford University Press.

Manning, N. (2001). The legacy of the new public management in developing countries. *International Review of Administrative Sciences*, *67*(2) 297–312. https://doi.org/10.1177/0020852301672009

Mathiasen, D. G. (1999). The new public management and its critics. *International Public Management Journal*, *2*(1), 90–111. https://doi.org/10.1016/S1096-7494(00)87433-4

Mennin, S. (2010). Complexity and health professions education. *Journal of Evaluation in Clinical Practice*, *16*, 835–837. https://doi.org/10.1111/j.1365-2753.2010.01503.x

Meynhardt, T. (2021). Public value is knowable, public value creation is not. *Administration & Society*, *53*(19), 1631–1642. https://doi.org/10.1177/00953997211053500

Newman, J. (2017). Deconstructing the debate over evidence-based policy. *Critical Policy Studies*, *11*(2), 211–226. https://doi.org/10.1080/19460171.2016.1224724

Newman, J., & Head, B. W. (2017). Wicked tendencies in policy problems: Rethinking the distinction between social and technical problems. *Policy and Society*, *36*(3), 414–429. https://doi.org/10.1080/14494035.2017.1361635

O'Connor, J., Mumford, M. D., Clifton, T. C., Gessner, T. L., & Shane Collennly, M. (1995). Charismatic leaders and destructiveness: An historiometric study. *The Leadership Quarterly*, *6*(4), 529–555. https://doi.org/10.1016/1048-9843(95)90026-8

Osborne, S. P. (2018). From public service-dominant logic to public service logic: Are public service organizations capable of co-production and value co-creation? *Public Management Review*, *20*(2), 225–231. https://doi.org/10.1080/14719037.2017.1350461

Osborne, S. P., Nasi, G., & Powell, M. (2021). Beyond co-production: Value creation and public services. *Public Administration*, early view. https://doi.org/10.1111/padm.12718

Parsons, W. (2002). From muddling through to muddling up: Evidence-based policy making and the modernisation of British government. *Public Policy and Administration*, *17*(3), 43–60. https://doi.org/10.1177/095207670201700304

Peters, B. G. (2015). *Advanced introduction to public policy*. Edward Elgar.

Peters, B. G. (2021). Some optimism about public governance. *Administration & Society*, *53*(10), 1624–1630. https://doi.org/10.1177/00953997211053501.

Petrescu, M. (2019). From marketing to public value: Towards a theory of public service ecosystems. *Public Management Review*, *21*(11), 1733–1752. https://doi.org/10.1080/14719037.2019.1619811

Pollitt, C., & Bouckaert, G. (2004). *Public management reform: A comparative analysis*. Oxford University Press.

Popper, K. R. (1996). *The myth of the framework: In defence of science and rationality*. Routledge. https://doi.org/10.4324/9780203535806

Rittel, H. W. J., & Webber, M. M. (1973). Dilemmas in a general theory of planning. *Policy Sciences*, *4*(2), 155–169. https://doi.org/10.1007/BF01405730

Rossi, P., & Tuurnas, S. (2021). Conflicts fostering understanding of value co-creation and service systems transformation in complex public service systems. *Public Management Review*, *23*(2), 254–275. https://doi.org/10.1080/14719037.2019.1679231

Rowe, W. D. (1994). Understanding uncertainty. *Risk Analysis*, *14*(5), 743–750. https://doi.org/10.1111/j.1539-6924.1994.tb00284.x

Rubio, F. D., & Baert, P. (2012). *The politics of knowledge*. Routledge. https://doi.org/10.4324/9780203877746

Savoie, D. J. (2002). What is wrong with the new public management. In S. P. Osborne (Ed.), *Public management: Critical perspectives* (pp. 263–272). Routledge.

Saz-Carranza, A., & Longo, F. (2012). Managing competing institutional logics public–private joint ventures. *Public Management Review, 14*(3), 331–357. https://doi.org/10.1080/14719037.2011.637407

Schön, D. A. (1991). *The reflective practitioner: How professionals think in action?* Basic Books.

Smith, A. (2000). *The wealth of nations* (orig. 1776). Random House.

Stacey, R. (2001). *Complex responsive processes in organizations: Learning and knowledge creation*. Routledge. https://doi.org/10.4324/9780203361481

Stacey, R. (2009). *Complexity and organizational realities: Uncertainty and the need to rethink management after the collapse of investment capitalism*. Routledge.

Stacey, R., & Griffin, D. (2015). *A complexity perspective on researching organizations: Taking experience seriously*. Routledge. https://doi.org/10.4324/9780203696941

Strassheim, H., & Kettunen, P. (2014). When does evidence-based policy turn into policy-based evidence? Configurations, contexts and mechanisms. *Evidence & Policy: A Journal of Research, Debate and Practice, 10*(2), 259–277. https://doi.org/10.1332/174426514X13990433991320

Strokosch, K., & Osborne, S. (2020). Co-experience, co-production and co-governance: An ecosystem approach to the analysis of value creation. *Policy & Politics, 48*(3), 425–442. https://doi.org/10.1332/030557320X15857337955214

Turner, S. (1989). Truth and decision. In D. Chubin & E. W. Chu (Eds.), *Science off the pedestal: Social perspectives on science and technology* (pp. 175–188). Wadsworth.

Uhl-Bien, M. (2021). Complexity leadership and followership: Changed leadership in a changed world. *Journal of Change Management, 21*(2), 144–162. https://doi.org/10.1080/14697017.2021.1917490

Vargo, S. L., & Lusch, R. F. (2004). Evolving to a new dominant logic for marketing. *Journal of Marketing, 68*, 1–17. https://doi.org/10.1509/jmkg.68.1.1.24036

Vargo, S. L., Maglio, P. P., & Akaka, M. A. (2008). On value and value co-creation: A service systems and service logic perspective. *European Management Journal, 26*(3), 149–152. https://doi.org/10.1016/j.emj.2008.04.003

Vedung, E. (2013). Six models of evaluation. In E. Araral, S. Fritzen, M. Howlett, M. Ramesh, & X. Wu (Eds.), *Routledge handbook of public policy* (pp. 387–400). Routledge. https://doi.org/10.4324/9780203097571

Virtanen, P., & Tammeaid, M. (2020). *Developing public sector leadership*. Springer. https://doi.org/10.1007/978-3-030-42311-7

Weick, K. E. (1995). *Sensemaking in organizations*. Sage.

Weick, K. E., Sutcliffe, K. M., & Obstfeld, D. (2005). Organizing and the process of sensemaking. *Organization Science, 16*(4), 409–421. https://doi.org/10.1287/orsc.1050.0133

Wheatley, M. (1999). *Leadership and the new science: Discovering order in a chaotic world*. Berrett-Koehler Publishers Inc.

Yang, C., & Northcott, W. (2019). Together we measure: Improving public service outcomes via the co-production of performance measurement. *Public Money & Management, 39*(4), 253–261. https://doi.org/10.1080/09540962.2019.1592906

# 7 Reforming public leadership through learning

## 7.1 Updating the assumptions around teaching and learning

### *7.1.1 The potential benefits of traditional classroom learning are questionable*

This book has concentrated its discussions on the challenges of human-centeredness that throw a shadow over the conventional rationale of public sector functions and leadership. An ever-diminishing portion of public sector leadership is now conducted in the 'known-world' with settled case-practices and clear goals, while the capability to act in a wise way under conditions of uncertainty is continually increasing. The ability to learn and renew both personal and common ways of working thus comes to the fore when attempting to reform the public sector to meet the challenges of this increasingly intertwined world.

In these circumstances, a good civil servant and/or civil service leader is proactive and flexible and takes future-oriented initiatives within the framework of laws and regulations, recalling the notion that resilience and new solutions emerge from the interaction between actors (Murtonen & Lehtinen, 2020, p. 101; Ungar, 2021). The possible range of relevant actors here extends from different branches of government to other sectors and the end users of public sector decisions and services. Instead of forming 'best solutions', strategic leadership involves openness to complexity, variety, and adaptation, according to the complexity of the environment (Gershenson, 2014) and context-bound negotiations of local and situational meaning (Hersted & Gergen, 2013; Rosso et al., 2010).

As discussed in Chapter 5, leadership meta-skills, such as the dynamic and processual leadership capabilities that appear in interaction, provide an important opportunity to meet all these challenges head on. But what kind of learning and development in general is required to enhance public sector capabilities for renewal and increased meta-skilfulness in its actions? When looking at the training and development of public sector leaders in office, at least two spheres are important to consider here: What level of capacity

DOI: 10.4324/9781003205791-7

are required of schools and institutes of public administration and other organisations that train civil service leaders and public sector organisations to meet current leadership training challenges? How do public sector organisations themselves provide space, structure, and opportunity for practising integrative leadership and learning? How does training, learning, and development change when the challenge of the cross-sectoral systems approach and human-centeredness is taken seriously? These are the issues that will be discussed in this chapter.

### *7.1.2 Learning as a catalyst*

Schools and institutes of Public Administration constitute the global backbone of civil servants' leadership training and development. In organisational terms, public leadership training institutions are often closely affiliated to the government. The amount and level of formality of their comprehensive and integrated training strategies differ from country to country but in various ways, these institutions seek to serve the changing landscape of public administration in their respective countries (Virtanen & Tammeaid, 2020; de Hollanda et al., 2019; OECD, 2017). The important question here is, however, whether these institutions end up acting more as the guardians of established governmental procedures than equipping participants in their training programmes with the tools to face the complex and wicked issues they are increasingly likely to face in their day-to-day work. Have they taken as their lodestar the desire to develop leaders whose central ability is to take their organisations and networks into the new, multi-angled, adaptive space? Is supporting human-centred renewal and the idea of developing leadership meta-skills central in their work?

It seems that while such schools and institutes of public administration in different parts of the world have broadened their teaching methods to encompass team-based activities, their general approach suggests a continuing preference for one-way classroom training (de Hollanda et al., 2019; OECD, 2017). Encouraging learning and skills development is already widely noted to be a strategic choice for governments, and some countries (e.g., the UK, Canada, Australia, New Zealand, Singapore, the Netherlands, and Estonia) have renewed their thinking of civil service skills further in the direction of capability building (Virtanen & Tammeaid, 2020; de Hollanda et al., 2019; OECD, 2017). Indeed, the OECD has already highlighted the need to further develop the innovative capacities of these institutions (OECD, 2017). These trends can however be interpreted as the seeds of a meta-skills approach. Meta-skills, as such, do not appear in any of these surveys, which is understandable since we are talking about a novel way of understanding and developing public sector leadership.

Placing the human-centred leadership approach and meta-skilling at the foundation of public leadership development extends the demand to re-examine the assumptions of a public leader as an effective change-maker and the pedagogical assumptions of the trainer supporting leadership development. In their synthesising article about adult learners, Murtonen and Lehtinen (2020, p. 108) highlight how conceptions of oneself, learning, knowledge, the subject of learning, and teaching all affect teaching and learning processes. As discussed previously, in Chapter 5, instilling the ability to contextualise integrative thinking is central in both adulthood and professional learning (Kallio, 2020b). Adopting conceptions and beliefs fostering and impeding integrative learning ability is then key to impactful learning, accelerating growth and change.

This shift in perspective applies to beliefs concerning one's own learning skill and self-efficacy, detaching learning from certain places or times, seeing learning as an active state instead of merely the intake of knowledge, abandoning black-and-white conceptions of knowledge, valuing the multiplicity of types of knowledge and seeing knowledge formation as a process, as well as recognising the role of beliefs and the personal relevance of the subject of the learning and considering the role of teaching as supporting learning and understanding instead of simply delivering facts (Murtonen & Lehtinen, 2020). All of these 'shifts' benefit from the creation of collaborative learning environments, providing an important social support for learning.

Making and enabling these kinds of learning environments and learning processes is work of great importance and the primary task of trainers and training institutions. When the validity of information does not only stem from seeking to uncover 'facts' but also from the interrelationships that form the phenomenon and, furthermore, from our assumptions that largely create the world, we are able to discover (Cooperrider, 2017), whether it is important to ask whether the pedagogical assumptions of the trainers of public sector leaders follow this same approach. Do they support the formation of new knowledge and understanding as a social, culturally changing and time- and place-bound development process (Gergen, 2015; Stacey, 2010, pp. 118–138; Ståhle et al., 2020; Sparrer, 2007, pp. 1–6)? Instead of providing programmes with experts lecturing about different issues in a loosely related manner, the key to providing relevant educational services is the skilful design of collaborative, relational, and enabling learning processes. This also involves working on both joint and individual learning targets and building a firm connection between theory and practice (Järvelä et al., 2010). Here the capabilities to facilitate experiential learning and intertwined individual and collaborative reflection come to the fore, as does conducting integrative development processes starting not from knowledge but rather from engaging in an activity, then reflecting on and conceptualising the experience, and followed up by trying out and testing new skills and abilities (Maurer-Hankovszky & Szabó, 2002; Kolb, 1984; Kolb & Fry, 1975).

The traditional view of leadership training as it relates to public leadership still rests upon a structural or position-based view of power. Broadening out from that view is however crucial here as all forms of control are, ultimately, multi-directional. That also renders leadership a dynamic and relational phenomenon by nature. In human systems, echoing Bateson (1972), events proceed as circular chains of interaction, and the realities are shared, maintained, and transformed through nonlinear, iterative interaction, and dialogue (Gergen, 2015; Ståhle et al., 2020, p. 191; Godat, 2013; Wals & Schwarzin, 2012; Stacey, 2010, pp. 132–133; Paavola & Hakkarainen, 2005, p. 538; Watson, 2001). Using learning as a catalyst of change involves not only adding coaching, co-creation, and facilitation skills to training programmes but also creating awareness of the implications of the systems approach to training and learning as well as those thinking patterns in our minds that guide knowledge creation, learning, training, and renewal.

### *7.1.3 Dialogical and collaborative learning as change-making*

The link between societal change-making, i.e., the *raison d'être* of the public sector and the capabilities of the civil service *cadre* to meet this task in a manner compatible with current and future prosperity is, on the one hand, self-evident, yet on the other sometimes difficult to grasp. The challenge combines the large-scale mission and impact-oriented horizon with mundane everyday actions. Effective learning and change-making address both spheres simultaneously in an emergent manner (Toom & Husu, 2020, p. 147; Virtanen & Tammeaid, 2020, pp. 125–126; Darling et al., 2016; Calleja, 2014, pp. 117–119).

As with many other spheres of life, teaching and learning can be approached in very different ways. One recognisable approach is technical orientation (Nivala & Ryynänen, 2019), also referred to as the adaptive (Eriksson, 2014) or 'monological' approach (Paavola & Hakkarainen, 2005). Typically, this orientation is based on underlying, sometimes implicit, assumptions about an existing good or desirable direction distributed to others. In the public sector context, it seeks to train participants to fulfil predefined tasks and roles in a regulated way (Presseau et al., 2019; Kriznik et al., 2019). As a training approach, it is primarily directed at knowledge acquisition by individual learners and to adapting individual variety to a pre-set model or ideal. Characteristic of this is also the so-called 'up-down approach' and the bypassing of the contextuality and ambiguity of the surrounding realities. As an approach to training design, it quickly becomes apparent in seeking to plan and run programmes widely and in a standardised form. The dominant empirical-analytical trend across the scientific community has fortified this approach to learning and training and facilitated an educational planning culture seeking linear measurement and interventions suitable for multiplication (Presseau et al., 2019; Raelin, 2012; Johnson, 2008).

Recognition of what constitutes 'good' public leadership has fluctuated over time, as noted earlier in Section 3.4, but much of this debate has been personalised to focus on the characteristics of an individual (Wilson, 2013). This technically oriented approach is present in many historical definitions of what it is to be 'a good civil servant' focusing on honesty, irreproachableness, and probity. This Weberian approach, focusing on the personal qualities of individuals, remains a core element of the 'civil service ethos' in many countries (Dwivedi, 2007). Current challenges including an increasingly diversified and multidisciplinary public sector however require collaborative skills to a much greater extent than ever before. Being a talented individual of good repute can be understood at most as the starting point for public sector leadership capabilities and learning objectives in a complex world. Public sector leadership is about succeeding together over organisational and institutional fences. Puonti (2004) has described this challenge of learning to work together in a cross-sectoral manner, a shift from the (traditional) sequential collaboration of authorities to their parallel collaboration.

A dialogical orientation to training and learning seeks to build joint learning networks which are powerful in triggering learning in adulthood contexts (Murtonen & Lehtinen, 2020; Wals & Schwarzin, 2012; Paavola & Hakkarainen, 2005). Dialogic and collaborative training design highlights horizontal relationships between learners and between leaders and teachers. It relies on hermeneutics and emphasises the dynamic relationship between theory and practice and the central role of human growth, local adaptations, and agency. Seeking common purpose, meaningfulness, and betterment in terms of quality of life are characteristic of the dialogical approach to training (Berg & Karlsen, 2016; Raelin, 2012; Mezirow, 2000). *This dialogically oriented approach* to the civil service is likely to generate training that genuinely meets the developing needs of the participants and helps to address the issues they face at work. It does not only address individual needs but rather creates a human-centred culture within the public sector and in the tackling of common challenges. As a pedagogical approach, it generates transformative learning environments, where it is possible to discover new perspectives on life and action in the social dimension by looking at dilemmas as shared and negotiable experiences and finding ways to function from this new perspective (Ståhle et al., 2020, p. 192; Calleja, 2014; Mezirow, 2000). One weak point of the dialogical approach, however, concerns shifting from dialogue to practice. Dialogue brings up myriads of individual perspectives and does not seek conclusions (Isaacs, 1999, 2007). After careful listening and gaining an understanding of the issue at hand, a civil service leader usually must proceed from speech to strategic action (see also Grant & O'Connor, 2018).

*Critical-emancipatory approaches* to teaching and learning, like social pedagogy, fit well with the idea of the collective societal purpose of the public sector. The approach highlights the opportunities for civil service leaders to take the initiative in terms of promoting better welfare and progressive societal change. It supports self-reflection, the relinquishing of restrictive beliefs, and the creation of new opportunities for new kinds of participation and agency. The dark side of the emancipatory approach is the possibility that it is applied in a strongly political or ideological manner, which goes against the character of civil service. Where the emancipatory approach is associated with any type of identity politics, the approach faces the same pitfalls, in terms of bypassing complexity, as the technical approach outlined previously.

Raelin defines the *action-oriented approach* to training and learning as post-bureaucratic, deliberative, and as taking an alternative role by empowering others (Raelin, 2012). It is characterised by actively facilitating emancipatory dialogue, thus increasing understanding, enhancing collective wisdom, creativity, and dignity in a manner respecting both individuality and the collective. This type of collaborative and dialogical approach is intended to facilitate new kinds of exploration, decision-making, and the taking of collaborative action (Raelin, 2012). Paavola and Hakkarainen call for a "trialogical" approach here, i.e., learning as a process of knowledge creation which concentrates on mediated processes where common objects of activity are developed collaboratively (Murtonen & Lehtinen, 2020, pp. 111–113; Paavola & Hakkarainen, 2005). Nonaka and Takeuchi (1995) refer to the same kind of dynamics in their view on organisational knowledge creation. As an approach, it nurtures dynamic intersubjectivity that creates room for polyphonic future possibilities to emerge. Philosopher Martin Buber's work around reciprocity and connection lays an important foundation for the role of collaborative and opportunity-opening training approach. In addition to many other theories of social cohesion and community building, Buber emphasises that reciprocity and true connection can also be created between different people; it does not take support for the same football team or something alike (Morgan & Guilherme, 2010). Similarly, likeness does not directly build connection or community (Tammeaid, 2016). In a dialogical and collaborative relationship, act and consequences are dynamically nested and fortify the positive spiral. The possibility to create connected and development-oriented varied communities is an important task of training and learning in societies full of competing values and norms (Martin, 2019).

Looking at different approaches to training and learning leads us to ask important questions as learning and training designers: what kind of professional orientation are leaders trained for? How do they view the people they encounter—as a resource in terms of deployable assets in person-years or as human beings? What kind of information do they feel they need in their work? How do they define the phenomena they deal with at work? How do they choose their policies and methods? and What do they strive to achieve at the individual (personal), public administration (professional), and societal levels? These questions position the participants as subjects of a learning process while the answers to these questions lead the way to formulating learning objectives in a training or other development process accelerating the human-centred approach.

### *7.1.4 Problem and solutions-focused learning*

Awareness of one's own thinking and mindset is at the core of leadership development (Ciporen, 2010). The choice of working orientation determines to a large extent the results (Chiva & Habib, 2015; Cooperrider, 2017; Fredrickson, 2013). Freedom to choose and change one's work orientation is available in any profession and role and in any given operating environment. In organisations, work orientations are inherited by those who follow into a job or position so training processes are important, and from the pedagogical point, training should be designed to make that process as fruitful as possible. Shifting the perspective of training and learning to active contextual collaboration and the creation of learning environments, enabling individual and collective transformational learning, is one way to lead public sector leaders and organisations towards the discovery of new perspectives by questioning underlying purposes and principles. In the academic discussion of organisational learning, this has been dealt with in relation to triple-loop learning (Tosey et al., 2011; Argyris, 1991).

The opportunity-creating nature of learning processes is realised when learners can act in a situation where everyone involved has their intellect and abilities equally recognised and involved. It is essential here to avoid of presuppositions about what a person can know or understand based on their background and instead invest in their ability to delve into an issue together with others. The Solution-Focused approach to learning and development puts front and centre the renewal of relationships to issues and people simultaneously, i.e., renewing our spheres of thinking, relating, and action as parallel and interactional learning processes. That introduces a comprehensive and multidisciplinary view of abstract, social, and human phenomena—something characteristic of all systems-type approaches (Ståhle et al., 2020, p. 191)—instead of the prevailing compartmentalised and reductionist tendencies to make sense of the world around us. It also considers that learning is not only a cognitive phenomenon but a combination of different levels of interacting processes not reducible to each other (Kallio, 2020a, p. 3; Stacey, 2010, p. 158).

The difference between problem-focused and Solution-Focused learning facilitation can be seen in the ways in which the participants archive, change, and renew their ways of working (Bannik, 2006, pp. 1–25; Priest & Gass, 1997). Whereas in problem-focused facilitation, participants are assisted to help them know more about the problems faced to eliminate them, the Solution-Focused way of working seeks disengagement from problem-focused thinking, sustaining the problem, and is instead interested in identifying preferred outcomes and orientating towards new goal setting and resource activation, including the identification of strengths and new future possibilities (Grant et al., 2012; Grant, 2011). This approach to engaging in learning, transformation, and change-making makes the Solution-Focused approach effective in archiving real change beyond the training sessions. Solution-Focused facilitation of transformation and change processes seems to increase perceived goal attainability, self-efficacy, and commitment, generate action steps, and reduce the negative impact of problems (Neipp et al., 2016, 2021; Grant et al., 2012; Grant, 2011). While the problem-focused approach is more likely to elicit thoughts of self-regulation, the Solution-Focused approach seeks to strengthen usage of available tools and resources (Abdulla & Woods, 2020), as well as increase working in a more transdisciplinary way (Medina & Beyebach, 2014).

To make learning processes platforms of opportunity and renewal as well as incubators for meta-skills development, it is crucial that the trainers and facilitators gear their own thinking and facilitation style to the Solution-Focus, rather than the problem-focused approach. This includes adopting the Solution-Focused approach to viewing people as resourceful and learning the Solution-Focused interviewing skills applicable in all formal and informal training settings and in conducting co-operational and interactional group learning (Cloete, 2010; Lipchik & de Shazer, 2017; De Jong & Cronkright, 2011; Bannik, 2006). Solution-Focused facilitative questions focus on outcomes (e.g., hope, difference, benefit, and what is wanted), progress (e.g., instances, resources, small steps, options, and ratings), means (e.g., engagement, positivity, agency, resilience, confidence, energy, and resources), and perspectives (e.g., on possible *locations, relationships, language use and time*) (SF Question Tree in Brooker, 2020).

While the problem-focused approach seeks to know and describe problems, Solution-Focused interviewing and dialogue pay attention to the crucial link between language and action in curating human systems and as crucial elements of learning to think, learn, and transform (McKergow, 2011; Lang & McAdam, 2011; Cronen et al., 2009; Lang et al., 1990). An example of an action-oriented, dialogical, and cross-sectoral leadership training process conducted in a Solution-Focused way is thoroughly described in Virtanen and Tammeaid (2020, pp. 95–172).

## 7.2 Developing meta-skills

Public administration is inherently a human-centred system and the leadership meta-skills discussed in this book possess the ability to strengthen the contents of human-centredness. In Chapter 5, the organisational landscape of leadership meta-skills was outlined with the help of the interviews of 22 high-ranking civil service leaders working in the central government sector in Finland. We were interested in the respondents' insights into the development of meta-skills, and whether they felt they can be taught and, if so, how? The interviewees were unanimously positive in this respect—at least to some extent. Their notions of ongoing and desirable leadership and organisational shift within the government as well as an individual leader's opportunities to meta-skilfully orchestrate development towards cross-sectoral and people-oriented ways of working are presented in this section, considering the available scholarly knowledge in respect of relational, motivational, and intentional approaches, as well as reflecting on demands for training and development supporting capabilities for renewal.

### *7.2.1 Towards an enabling shift in leadership and training*

According to the interviewees, understanding the concept and value of meta-skills requires continuous training, awareness, and support. Changes within government and leadership culture tend to be long-term cultural processes but are, nevertheless important and necessary to invest in. The interviewees highlighted four things as being of fundamental importance in terms of public leadership training, with a view to developing meta-skilfulness in public sector leaders, namely, horizontal (i.e., cross-sectoral) training groups developing a shared culture within government, 'thought-shaking' and future-oriented contents, sufficient longevity instead of trying to change the world/mindset/government 'in two hours', and a focus on leading people and understanding citizen or service user demands. The fourth point, 'people focus-related', elicited a considerable number of comments in the interviews, because the development of human-oriented people skills in leading people depends primarily on having a personal interest in developing oneself.

The skills required to lead are primarily those that are used in coaching leadership, i.e., fostering psychological safety by deep listening, adoption of a dialogic and reflective stance as well as using encouragement and developing a positive feedback culture, learning to learn from failure, harnessing reframing and other thinking skills, shaping organisational culture by reforming practices, enhancing everyday learning, and using questions to spark insight in the other person (Ibarra, 2021; Törmänen et al., 2021; Berg & Karlsen, 2016; Schein, 2013; O'Connell et al., 2012; Green & Grant, 2003). The relational change this brings about in leadership was described by an interviewed Director General with a government agency affiliation and over 20 years of leadership experience from various government branches:

> *We will no longer say no, but we say under what conditions this is possible. A civil servant tends easily to say no, and then not much else. Where the organisational culture in build on fear of mistakes and seeking 100% certainty in decisions, then enabling is difficult. It takes courage and the giving up of the premise of security and the omnipotent ability to control [others/society].*

Most of the interviewees noted that various developments in the direction of a more human approach had taken place in the government leadership culture over the past 20 years, but there is still a long way to go. One Secretary-of-State interviewee with over 30 years of leadership experience from various government branches reflected on this ongoing process as follows:

> *It involves a whole transformation of leadership. As late as the 1980s, there was a generation that had gone to war as leaders and leadership was through chains of command. Today, such leadership would no longer be acceptable. Dialogue is*

> *a prerequisite for coaching or developmental leadership. The coaching approach does not work if the leader is not ready to drop his/her own authority out of the discussion and move forward on an equal footing. And the more leadership focuses on enabling, the more important this is. In practice, the dialogue skills of government administration leaders vary enormously, and currently these skills are not being thought to us anywhere. For me the best school in this has been international cooperation.*

Another Director General interviewee with ministerial affiliation and decades of leadership and other experience from government agencies and ministerial organisations of different government branches reflected on the same issue thus:

> *Moving from the strategic to the operational level and from there down to 'hands on' leadership skills and bringing this whole thing together in a credible way in a modern understanding of leadership, there is still a lot of work to be done. Also, Covid-19 has shown it. We have good conditions and the ability and also support from the top, but we are still on the way.*

On many occasions, public administration is often discussed in terms of preserving and ensuring continuity. However, as Acemoglu and Robinson note in their famous book *The Narrow Corridor* (Acemoglu & Robinson, 2020), a society needs both strong institutions and a strong civil society. To maintain the balance, the public sector and society must run at equal speeds (Acemoglu & Robinson, 2020). A Secretary-of-State interviewee with around 30 years of government leadership experience reflects the same issue thus:

> *All good leadership is proactive. And then there is this other stream: reactive running of administrative duties. In this process of leadership change has been going on for at least 20 years. A big part of that is that we as leaders should be proactive rather than reactive and take a critical look on how we have done things previously. If there is a belief that some things in government are forever and cannot ever be changed, then nothing will change.*

### 7.2.2 Motivation and intention at the centre of meta-skills development

The importance of how civil service training is conducted was underlined by many of the interviewees. For example, an interviewed Director General with ministerial affiliation and around 15 years of experience in both government agencies and ministerial organisations noted that

> *good education is conducted through living it together [immersion] and discussions.*

And another Director General interviewee with around 40 years of experience of both ministerial and government agency leadership reflected similarly:

> *However, the way of learning must be deep learning, in which these things become part of our own identity; one changes as a person, looks at the world differently than before when things become internalised. Therefore, the way of learning must build on the intrinsic motivation of the individual. And the enablers of learning [facilitators, trainers] then bring cognitive dissonance to it and take the group to the space of emergent learning. There we reach real dialogue, polyphony, tolerance to uncertainty and reflection. Via reflection, learning becomes, or does not become, a part of identity.*

Facilitation, planning, and conducting this type of learning process sets up the challenge of promoting pedagogic understanding and skills in schools and institutes of public administration and other institutions and trainers working with the public sector. Shifting mindsets from teacher-driven course production to dialogical and collaborative co-creation with the participants can, however, be a lengthy process but conscious skills development in conducting open-ended dialogical group processes in a solution-oriented way is what is required here. Giving up the certainty of conclusions and trust in ready-made models represents an important learning journey for educators themselves. Many trainers enjoy being in the spotlight and presenting their own knowledge. The impact of that choice should however be thoroughly scrutinised.

Developing further the argument by Deci and Ryan (2000), it can be said that external change pressure can be associated with poorer motivation and a lower level of change capacity than building on intrinsic motivation via strengthening the conditions supporting competence, autonomy, and relatedness. Although experts may have a profound knowledge of their field, self-generated arguments are more persuasive in behavioural change than arguments provided by others (Müller et al., 2017). This is particularly so if self-generation takes place in environments where it feels easy. This makes professional efforts to create a safe training atmosphere and stimulating learning environments even more important (Sharry, 2004).

Cognitive dissonance serves well as a platform for change, but it is important to bring it into training contexts in such a way that it takes into consideration the identities of the participants (Hinojosa et al., 2017). The Solution-Focused approach argues that paradigm shifts and new insights occur in a not-knowing-zone, a concept developed in practice and teaching experiences (Malinen, 2004). The not-knowing attitude implies gazing at even quite familiar issues with beginner's eyes, careful pre-judgement free listening, and seeing people as the experts in terms of their own lives and circumstances. It is, as Andersson defines it (see Malinen, 2004), about leaving one's own professional descriptions outside the room and inviting others into the collaborative relationship in the dialogical conversation. An important part of using any information or expertise is to take great care of one's own intentionality in providing any knowledge; whether it is for the purposes of food for thought or imposing a conviction, generalisation, or conclusion that might not be applicable and relevant in the context of the discussion partner. Conversations in mental not-knowing-space are worth organising, since they take us to the liminal space needed for new understanding to arise. They also widen our observation skills and touch us on an emotional level releasing energy and creating opportunities for change.

Training conducted in the manner described earlier promotes the deployment of personal agency to put the new learning into action (Neipp et al., 2016, 2021; Abdulla & Woods, 2020; Grant, 2011). Agency is referred to here as a critical function referring to the pursuit of the objectives participants have themselves set through insight, a willingness to participate in joint change efforts, and doing so in an experimental atmosphere. Agency in this view takes participants as active and resourceful agents of their own work role and profession (Martin, 2019; Bannik, 2006, pp. 6–12; Mussmann, 2006). A well-designed training process enables and accelerates that agency.

### *7.2.3 The relational core of organisations and leadership*

Another issue deserving of scrutiny is that of how trainers view public sector organisations. Do they see public sector organisations through mechanistic metaphors, as hierarchical compartmentalised implementation machineries or co-created human-centred learning systems (Lowe et al., 2020; Laloux, 2014; Reed, 2006)? And do they direct training for developing organisational and managerial thinking that understands the demands of organisations as social constructions (Cooperrider, 2017; Hersted & Gergen, 2013; Jensen Schleiter et al., 2015; McKergow, 2011; Stacey, 2010; Watson, 2001).

Echoing Morgan (2016), the images we have of organisations direct our perception and determine what we tend to see and what we tend to leave unseen. Changing metaphors serves as a generative tool for challenging taken-for-granted ways of seeing and as a vehicle to deal with the multidimensional complexity of organisations and their functions (Örtenblad et al., 2016; Morgan, 2016; Schenck, 2013). Many of the interviewees brought up the notion that leadership does not develop if it is not thought about regularly and as an own phenomenon. One Secretary-of-State interviewee with a long working life of ministerial leadership described choosing the socially constructed and interactional focus and its implications to training needs in the following way:

> *Really looking at how organisations function [in practice] is terribly important in order to develop the ability to form the framework for an organisation to function*

> *well. I argue, and this is not my idea, that very talented people may not accomplish anything in a bad organisation. In a well led and organised organisation output is quite different. Training should be directed to seeing what meta-skills mean in leading and creating an organisation. There must be some good routines (this is a bad word) so that basic things work at a sufficient level and reliably, with little effort to make space and time for important things. So, that the organisation is not a prisoner of things that fall on top and run head over heels, [instead] a kind of peace comes to the organisation.*

The referred Secretary of State continued:

> *and the other important thing is developing appreciative interaction that is the prerequisite of dialogue. It is very much dependent on the organisational culture. Here, by the way, it is not the job of the leader to say what that appreciative interaction is, but rather, to show by example what it is to him/her. Here, the leader should think about how he or she would like to be led in an expert organisation. And it is about surprisingly small things, about really listening to everyone, organising meetings and discussions in groups small enough to be able have a real discussion. If there are too many people, the information can be shared with them in other ways. And that the leader doesn't handle email or anything else at meetings; and begins meetings by listening to what the others have to say. That is the essence of putting things into practice. . . . Leaders need to learn this. And all this must be trained, so that thinking [of leadership] is directed towards it. And that we realise early enough that we are not doing the right things and creating trust needs to be taught. And that the leader lets the experts act or decide differently from what the leader would have thought or done. Of course, there must be some kind of framework, the rules of the game—not breaking the law—but when [appreciation and freedom] exist it allows for much greater creativity and trust. To some extent, this can probably be taught as can learning how good organisations work i.e., [bench learning] what kinds of practices they really have on a practical level.*

Table 5.1 in Chapter 5 provided practical ideas on how to develop meta-skilful public organisations based on the interviews with the high-ranking civil service leaders working in the Finnish central government. Training meta-skills provides a level of preparedness to be better able to handle the various challenges and situations leaders generally encounter in their work. As a training focus, it entails a shift from providing uniform procedures and models to nurturing the elaboration of actions and working forms and orchestrating future-driven collaborative change capabilities. One Director General interviewee with government agency affiliation and over 20 years of leadership experience from across various government branches described a succeeded mindset shift in the following way:

> *For someone like me who chats easily with others, it just happens that I talk about everything with colleagues and team members and therefore we learn together. For an introvert, it can be more difficult. And it occurred to me that it is important to understand that learning is done together. When you talk about what you have experienced and learned and apply those things in practice, you learn from that. You can also easily ignore learning and just follow the rule and what has always been done. I rather ask that if we have had this kind of a rule, instruction, or way of working, has it worked, has it delivered what it was supposed to deliver?*

According to current research on behaviour change interventions, people need the capability, motivation, and opportunity to change (Michie et al., 2011). Both leadership and leadership training processes with human-centred learning design possess great potential to provide a platform for these conditions to accelerate development. In a training context, this particularly applies to learning design that reaches out of the classroom and uses a wide variety of working methods of active collaborative learning starting from blended learning and storytelling to real-setting experiments and future-scouting (Murtonen & Lehtinen, 2020, pp. 111–113; Virtanen & Tammeaid, 2020, pp. 117–172; Laal, 2013; Laal et al., 2012; Laal & Laal, 2012; Tuominen & Kallio, 2020). Training institutions have an important role to play in inviting public sector leaders to (re)connect with the end users of their decisions and citizens in general. As with any other huge organisational complex, the government also tends to focus on fine tuning its internal procedures in terms of efficiency and smooth-running procedures. Human-centred renewal focuses on fulfilling the societal purposes of the existence of the public sector. This cannot, however, be done effectively without a living link to the world outside administration. Leaders are, due to the nature of their work, particularly exposed to the internal and operational functions of an organisation, as described in Chapter 1. Seeing and treating the end users and citizens as active agents in society is then an important feature of human-centred and enabling governance, while opening these windows represents both an important opportunity and duty for public sector leadership training.

The Theoretical Domains Framework summarises 33 psychological theories and identifies 14 domains or influences on behaviour (Cane et al., 2012). This framework advises us to pay attention to knowledge, skills, social/professional roles or identities, beliefs about capabilities, optimism and confidence, beliefs about consequences, reinforcement, intentions, goals, past experiences, attention, and decision processes, the environmental context and available resources, social influences, emotions, and behavioural regulation (Cane et al., 2012). Interestingly these are consistent with the emphasis and impact of Solution-Focused coaching and facilitation questions presented in Section 7.1.2 in terms of adopting a collaborative, interactional, and future-focused orientation to change-making. Solution-Focused questions provide a vehicle for capacity building and practical change-making (Virtanen & Tammeaid, 2020, pp. 120–126; De Jong & Kim Berg, 2013; Kim Berg & Szabó, 2005).

In an OECD survey on schools and institutes of Public Administration (OECD, 2017) there is a topical discussion about making use of digital learning possibilities within government. Digital learning works well as a form of blended learning (Cronje, 2021). It does not replace the value of live communication and live training but does provide opportunities for learning detached from time and place. The core question in developing leadership meta-skills is not however the venue—live or digital—but rather, the mindset and perception; not focusing on analysing problems or fighting against the old but directing the energy towards emergent opportunities and supporting the new.

### *7.2.4 Career development dynamics serving meta-skills development*

All the interviewees reflected on their own learning paths in the interviews, considering the deliberate choices they made in taking on new challenges and throwing themselves into new situations, new networks, new organisations, and new professional fields as the most powerful way of learning and developing meta-skills. As one Director interviewee with government agency affiliation and over 20 years of experience from different branches of government put it:

> *Promotion of all of these [meta-skills] takes place in such a way that I have led, done and gone into new roles. Then you can't cling to the old and it becomes clear that you depend on the skills of others and dialogically you yourself learn from your subordinates and partners.*

Taking care of one's own opportunities to learn and develop was considered crucial by the interviewees. A lot of it is learning and challenging oneself in everyday duties, walking onto 'weak ice', joining, and initiating joint projects with other organisations and starting bottom-up processes. One generally expressed opinion among these leaders was that a leadership role provides great opportunities for learning, but for learning to happen it is required that a leader opens themselves up to learning and develops the attitude of learning-to-learn. An omnipotent attitude kills the opportunity to both learn in our everyday work and in making use of organised learning opportunities. To best preserve the developing and learning-to-learn attitude, interviewees called for more structural learning mechanisms to enhance meta-skills and to identify them in recruitment and appointment procedures. Countries and administrative branches differ significantly in terms of the level and organisation of leadership rotation and job-switching mechanisms and in making use of the development opportunities it provides (Virtanen & Tammeaid, 2020, pp. 110–114). A few interviewees mentioned the Dutch rotation model as an example of a practice that supports the development of leaders through different types of postings, allowing top leaders to change to more consultative roles after periods in demanding leadership positions. In this way, these leaders, it is argued, are better able to 'preserve the sparkle' of development, refresh and 'go again' in a more sustainable way.

Furthermore, many of the interviewees noted that there is still a lot to do in terms of valuing meta-skills and leadership skills in relation to general recruitment, appointments, and qualification requirements. There may already have been a lot of talk about the importance of leadership capabilities, but the actual processes of filling positions still tend to emphasise more formal education and substantive skills. According to the interviewees, it is still common in some ministries that heads of units have been assigned 60% expert work and 40% managerial work. That is a structure that firmly keeps in place the compartmentalised public sector approach and thus the status quo. From the perspective of good public leadership and meta-skilfulness endorsing the valuing leadership and learning potential approach could provide public organisations with an important new dynamic. A Director General interviewee with ministerial affiliation and over 30 years of leadership experience from different ministries describes this in the following way:

> *And then there is this thing, a public leader's ability to lead learning in the organisation. And what is the learning curve of a public leader if the selection criteria are ability, skill and a proven civic citizenship, all of which are ex post. But I strongly state that we should evaluate the development curve. And in those situations where it can be done—within the framework of the law—always take the one who may not yet have all the skills required, but a good ability and interest to learn and develop. In general, these kinds of persons can have a great impact on the learning of the whole work community. Unfortunately, it is often the case that if the perfect ones are chosen and they freeze themselves into the positions of the state, their interest in the work will wane and this will, ultimately, have a terrible effect on the organisation.*

### *7.2.5 Measuring learning outcomes*

How then can we measure the outcomes of training and learning targeted at the development of leadership meta-skills? This is a tough question for those embedded in the traditional ways of looking at the public sector primarily in terms of efficiency and results. In that tradition, training is often dealt with in an instrumental manner, a multipliable standard 'piece of learning' that takes individual know-how in a defined issue from one level to another. This technical approach can also be found in purchasing leadership training or any other training within the government.

This approach is derived from the way in which the discipline of economics looks at organisations and their impacts. There is clearly a desire to measure return on investment and of time and money spent on training in economic terms and in terms of the scale impact of the investment. Deliberate efforts to increase the reach and impact of successful projects to benefit more people can be seen as a reasonable way to spend taxpayers' money. However, fitting these aspirations into training and learning approaches collides with the nonlinear logics of learning, human growth, and transformative development. That is also in general characteristic for systemic endeavours, where functional change essentials like building relationships, establishing shared purpose, and developing shared values do not translate well in terms of measurable metrics (Lowe et al., 2020). Trying to measure them in terms of impact frames can, paradoxically, lead to less rather than more understanding of the real impacts (Lowe & Wilson, 2017).

Most of the 22 interviewed high-ranking civil service leaders underlined the importance of the personal growth of a leader, as well as the need for time, space, and support for this life-long endeavour to become a better leader. Growth and developing new ways of thinking and working need safe spaces, transformative learning opportunities, and other niches protected from daily operational concerns (Moore et al., 2015). In general, learning and development can be witnessed by the participants themselves and to some extent also by other people. Real growth and development are set to follow some observable changes in terms of our ways of thinking, working, and acting but on an indefinite timeline in following processes of metacognition and reflection on self-directed and *ecosystemic* learning (Johnson, 2008; von Wright, 1992). Some effects can be seen in the short term, others can take years before emerging (Kallio, 2020b; Moore et al., 2015).

Systemic, dialogical, and collaborative training and development endeavours call for co-created evaluation and local meaning-giving of the results and scaling opportunities. Measuring systems' bound learning and training results in the return of an investment logic that does not always make sense (Murtonen & Lehtinen, 2020, pp. 111–116; Johnson, 2008; Cronbach, 2000). It easily leads to measuring technical details (presence, absence, cost, variable coat, satisfaction rating) instead of actual learning outcomes derived from learning and change targets. In living systems, learning and growth also produce so-called unbudgeted benefits, favourable or counter-productive ripple effects that easily remain undocumented and therefore unnoticed (Warwick et al., 2017). In this view, training and learning for public sector leaders is always a social intervention not applicable to handling the logics of performance data (Lowe & Wilson, 2017). Doing so may even disrupt systems change having a good start and lead to oversimplifications of the possibilities to scale a training 'product' without taking into consideration the essential conditions (knowhow, resources etc.) crucial to repeating any success (Virtanen & Tammeaid, 2020, pp. 158–170). This can be defined as separating thinking from its relational context (Fisher, 2021; Stacey, 2010). Bateson (2016, p. 83) has also highlighted the uselessness of context-free data, since it leaves out processes of interdependency crucial for understanding complexity around the phenomenon and drawing meaningful conclusions:

> *the problem with problem-solving is the idea that a solution is an endpoint. There are no endpoints in complex systems, only tendrils that diffuse and reorganise situations . . . compensations come in crooked streams and don't end up where you thought they would. DDT stopped insects briefly, then became problematic in countless other ways. Increasing the water resources of a city meets the needs of the people but increases the population potential. Treating symptoms, teaching to the test, gathering statistics . . . all of these forms of engagement have something in common . . . blindness to the complexity of the issue being addressed.*

Thanks to Kirkpatrick and his successors, professional evaluation of the impact of training is often done by trying to reach out to the co-created assessment of comparing intentions with results and, in that way, fortifying continuous improvement from the point of view of both participants and trainers (Kirkpatrick & Kayser Kirkpatrick, 2016; Kaufman & Keller, 1994). Kirkpatrick's idea of the return of expectations may not, however, be sufficient in a complex world, where training can and should serve as a window to wider horizons, beyond the initial expectations made in the context of a narrower or partial view of the given systemic entity. Positive developments towards measuring the progress made in learning to work together in a cross-sectoral way for the benefit of the end user have been made for example by the Centre for Public Impact (centreforpublicimpact.org) and local coordination agencies in Sweden (nnsfinsam.se/). CPI has done remarkable work on what they call the 'shared power principle' applied, for example, to modelling social care for children in a manner prioritising time and relationships with children and families (Frontline et al., 2020); designing the development and measurement of social learning (Lowe & Plimmer, 2019); and using storytelling to make, evaluate, and showcase what is happening in systems change (Snow et al., 2021). The Swedish coordination agencies work on matching employability efforts between different authorities and have worked towards producing a national model to verify progress in a way that is fitting to the governmental reporting culture but true to the same values that guide the work itself. To summarise, both experiences suggest the need to measure the results of the actual learning and change efforts first and foremost by the relevance felt by the end user and the effect on their experienced life quality, the perspective of the front-end officials in how they know that they are moving in the right direction in their work, how engaged they are in their work, and how easy they find choosing new relational ways of working as well as the percentage of actual cases solved by the new cross-sectoral way of working. Cost is an important measure in public services, but in this context only one important measure of economic sustainability considers historic costs and the predicted development of service needs. In addition, the anticipatory perspective of what should be in place that the present services would not be needed at all is an important issue to bear in mind in measuring, to ensure that measuring does not infer standing still but helps in opening new paths. Swedish coordination agencies have included this in their model of inquiry in the following way: 'Have the experiences from your collaboration led to the development of preventive measures?' Their national inquiry is addressed to all interest groups from end users, front line, and back-office professionals to unit managers and boards of directors. In the same inquiry, they are also interested in "[whether] the resourceful view regarding human possibilities is shared by everybody in the coordinated effort?"[1]

Both the CPI and the Swedish coordination agencies' approaches to measurement support the relational, motivational, and intentional essence of change-making in human systems, where learning is one critical element of a larger systems change and not meaningfully measurable as a separate entity. Or when done, the measuring model forces the measuring process into focusing on smaller and smaller standardised details in order to generate results in the traditional way (see, e.g., Taylor et al., 2020; Presseau et al., 2019). A valuable way to look at scaling change efforts here is to consider the concept of *scaling deep* developed in Canada and presented by Moore, Riddell, and Vocisano (Moore et al., 2015, p. 71). They argue that scaling the process of any social change "necessarily involve[s] changes to rules, resource flows, cultural beliefs and relationships in a social system at multiple spatial or institutional scales".

Scaling for impact thinking is too narrow and too much of a product-oriented approach to grasp the social system of beliefs, connections, and workflows in which the new ways of working are born and spread. The notion of *scaling deep* in the Moore, Riddell, and Vocisano model comes closest to the target of leadership training and development describing change-making in meaning, impacting cultural roots. This is done by reframing stories of change beliefs and norms, the mutual sharing of knowledge, investing in transformative learning processes and establishing communities of learning and practice. Undertaking large-scale systems change in society usually requires seeking alternative resources, building networks and partnerships, and broadening the frame of the viewing window. (Moore et al., 2015)

When the aspiration of the societal change-maker is to impact greater numbers of people or organisations, the effective strategy is *scaling out*, with replication followed by spreading the principles of adaptation and the co-generation of knowledge. Scaling out cannot be effectively done by transposing a standard way of proceeding with a standard change process omitting contextual and local knowledge factors. Where it is applicable to pursue changes in laws and regulations to achieve new policy developments, this is called *scaling up*. Mixing these three scaling strategies together is usually required to create a pathway to largescale or systemic impact, they argue (Moore et al., 2015).

An illustrative example of the alternative approach is evidenced by the technical and superficial culture of measuring outcomes in training institutions and purchasers' tendency to ask for evaluation forms to be filled in by the participants after separate lectures or other sub-sections of a training programme. This type of approach illustrates the existence of only a vague understanding of learning as a *process*, both in terms of knowledge generation and timely meaning terms. A well-designed learning process is always an entity which is not possible to be reduced to individual parts, either which can work or be evaluated on their own (Virtanen & Tammeaid, 2020, pp. 95–172; Cooperrider & McQuade, 2012; Cooperrider et al., 2008). Social learning and growth as a leader, professional, or human being are deep and multifaceted processes often entailing a lot of bewilderment, which is an important part of the process. Mechanical attempts to evaluate learning in the middle of the process can easily disturb the emerging process of deep learning, while regular dialogical evaluation of the learning experience serves not only as feedback but also as feed-forward to new spheres of thinking and action (Virtanen & Tammeaid, 2020, pp. 158–170; Carless, 2007).

According to a survey made by the OECD observatory of public sector innovation (OECD-OPSI, 2021), the individual-level challenges connected to future-orientation, anticipation, and innovation capability among government civil service leaders in Finland were linked first and foremost to the linear, engineering mindset as well as to a lack of alternative experience and open-mindedness, fear of failure, and a strong expert bias. In addition, procrastination, lack of knowledge, risk aversion, and rejection of change were also mentioned (OECD-OPSI, 2021). All these hindrances to the future-oriented renewal of public sector leadership can be addressed by training and development efforts designed to harness public sector leadership meta-skills and with training practices following meta-skills thinking and in line with putting meta-skills into action. As discussed earlier, this requires the promotion of three guiding principles in terms of conducting public sector leadership training and learning, i.e., the *relational view* of leadership, public sector functions, knowledge creation, and systems' change-making; the *motivational view* building on intrinsic motivation and contextual relevance; and the *intentional view* strengthening future-driven agency and co-creation.

## 7.3 Developing public organisations through learning

### *7.3.1 Leading with learning and strengths*

Apart from using schools and institutes of Public Administration and other training institutions, public sector organisations themselves can do a lot to develop a human-centred approach, both inside and outside the organisation. Issues of key importance here are to what extent the ideas behind the systems thinking and strengths revolution (Cooperrider, 2017; Hämäläinen et al., 2014; Dutton et al., 2010) have penetrated public organisations and to what extent they act as platforms of active learning and development.

In the socio-constructivist conception, learning in an organisational context implies a shared vision of the direction and organisational support for individual and group learning (Törmänen et al., 2021; Argyris, 1991, 1993; Argyris & Schon, 1978). In general, viewing an organisation from the perspective of functional processes that enable (or inhibit) learning and development, it is important to examine how an organisation emphasises learning in its operating culture and how meaning-giving to different things, terms, and events is happening in an organisation (Mezirow, 2000; Rosso et al., 2010; Argyris, 1991). Learning and development should be considered a positive and important holistic thing, not something extra or separate from everyday work and life (Caride, 2020; Elliot, 2020), indeed, as one Director-General interviewee with ministerial affiliation and over 20 years of leadership experience notes:

> *One key factor is that this is what the formal leaders and thought leaders think. Learning culture doesn't come from drawing a new kind of organisational chart for learning or assigning responsibility for it to someone else. It requires a long-term mindset, and that top management appreciates and encourages such thinking. Without this it withers away. And then in terms of meta-skills it is an important point in work* <u>*and*</u> *in other spheres of life: a diamond fine insight. To get new ideas and new innovations, even if we have a great learning organisation, is difficult if you don't get stimuli from outside, then you're deadlocked and that's not enough.*

Leadership style is composed of mundane, everyday micro-behaviours (Hämäläinen et al., 2014; Stacey, 2010; Kolb, 1984) in which the interactional choices of those in public administration leadership positions play an important role. Positive attitudes for individual and collective development require reciprocal encountering, a dialogical stance, and the social practices supporting them. According to the interviewees, these capabilities can be learned from many sources. A Director General interviewee with five years of ministerial affiliation and a vast experience from municipal public sector leadership tells it like this:

> *I consider non-professional learning to be very important, for example fiction is often much better reading than management guidebooks. I do that and could do more. Recently also built architecture and fine arts have brought me inspiration.*

In organisational life, ordinary social structures like meetings matter a lot (Kauffeld & Lehmann-Willenbrock, 2011; Bannik, 2006, pp. 134–140). Paying attention to the creation of an attuned and nourishing meeting culture is one of the everyday opportunities to reform public organisations through learning. Meetings serve two general purposes, the symbolic and the functional (Sandwith, 1992). While functional meaning meetings promote shared understanding and the progressing of issues on the table, symbolic meaning meetings define the organisational communication culture and promote the value systems which set the base for meaning making. An open and inclusive communication climate is essential to achieve a better work environment and a lot of that happens through functional communication in meetings (Bergman et al., 2016; Bannik, 2006, p. 135). One Director General interviewee with around 20 years of public sector leadership experience from both ministerial work and other branches of government reflected on the cultural challenges of government in the following way:

> *What I try to influence is that the ministry is an organisation based heavily on expert work. It is thought to be very hierarchical, but it is more bottom-up. What makes it challenging is that many experts don't see the whole and are very sensitive about their own expertise. In my own group, I make sure that this is not the case, I emphasise that we are not here to perform our expertise but to help the organisation achieve its goals. It's a different angle and has also brought the biggest schisms. People become very concerned if their expertise is in doubt. We have people who think the legislation is theirs.*

Even within complex and difficult large entities, leaders have opportunities to develop their own organisational units in line with collaborative learning and meta-skills thinking. The interviewees also noted that they had initiated a number of other practical ways to make learning and development a part of everyday work in their organisations or departments, including, for example, taking a fully mobile and interactive learning platform (Howspace) into use in the internal communications of the department, making sure that reflective learning is integrated into every process in the department, initiating a theme year around making things 'a bit simpler' in terms of internal processes, taking frequent field tours to different parts of the country, sending follow-up letters after tough negotiations, deliberately appointing persons who bring out-of-the-box thinking to the board, having regular cross-sectoral project reviews in the board meetings, starting talent programmes and systematic future forum work, and rotating heads of departments and the responsibility fields of the board members so that a more holistic understanding of and responsibility for issues can develop.

Adapting the strengths of the leader was also mentioned several times. Strengths and virtues offer great potential for growth and development

(Berg & Karlsen, 2016; Linley et al., 2010; Peterson & Seligman, 2004; Sheldon et al., 2002) see also Chapter 5) and this is how one Director General interviewee with ministerial affiliation and around 20 years of public sector leadership experience reflected on the issue:

> *First of all, I have to say that this matter of focusing on strengths rather than on weaknesses is the most important thing I adopted from the Renewing Public Sector training. For 20 years, we have discussed in all development discussions that you should try to develop where you are weak. If you're an introvert by birth, then it doesn't help for me simply to say that you have now to become an extrovert. Rather, we need instead to consider where those introvert abilities are most suitable and how to make the best use of them in the organisation. Since this realisation, I have used this approach as a load-bearing structure in all development discussions. In other words, I have completely abandoned the weak characteristics focus.*

A key dynamic in terms of adopting the strengths view and the dialogical stance as the backbone of leadership is widening the opportunities for success on the individual and group level, since through our assumptions and choice of method we largely determine what can become possible (Cooperrider, 2017; Dutton et al., 2010). The concept of meta-skills has been used to some extent in the psychological and coaching literature but thus far mainly from a problem-focused point of view linking meta-skills to individual features and to problematic mindsets that needed mending (e.g., Kegan & Lahey, 2009; Eigel, 2005). This use of the meta-skills concept follows in the long traditions of structuralist psychology and learning concentrating on individual competencies, taking an external predetermined—i.e., not interactional or collaborative—lens to human talent and analysing and defining hierarchical stages and taxonomies of development (e.g., Kegan & Lahey, 2009; Eigel, 2005; Fischer, 1980). It is however important to note here that the meta-skills conception presented in this book is rather based on a co-created and appreciative view of human collaboration, the usefulness of multifaceted human potential and of nourishing it for the benefit of the community, organisation, and the society (Berg & Karlsen, 2016; Cooperrider, 2017; Beverland et al., 2016; Fredrickson, 2013; Linley et al., 2010; Dutton et al., 2010; Biswas-Diener, 2009; Peterson & Seligman, 2004; Sheldon et al., 2002). This successfully grounds the idea of respecting the variety of collaborative strengths and their value in different circumstances, reaching out for strategic alliances between people with different strengths working together, as well as defining the leader's role in providing opportunities for development and growth for everyone from their own starting point (Annala et al., 2020; Linley, 2008; O'Reilly & Pfeffer, 2000; Godat, 2013). Moreover, Kallio (2020b) has highlighted the 'many-values logic' and brought up the pitfalls of mechanistic stage thinking, as well as the importance of adopting an interactive and integrative view on human wisdom (see also Tynjälä et al., 2020, pp. 167–170).

The strengths- and resource-based choices of leaders are fortified by combing them with coaching leadership, which portrays itself in integrating learning and development as part of the work and promoting the idea of the leader-employee partnership in learning (Berg & Karlsen, 2016; Schein, 2013; Goffee & Jones, 2000). Leaders who themselves receive coaching are more likely to be goal- and relationship-oriented and to provide more guidance than managers who do not receive such coaching (Berg & Karlsen, 2016). Moreover, they also tend to have more interest in learning, improving self-awareness, and a higher degree of personal development (Devine et al., 2013). One Director General interviewee with around 30 years of leadership experience from ministerial and government agency leadership talks about their role in terms of leadership coaching as follows:

> *I actively think about both my successes and failures and how for things have gone well or badly. I have used sparring help, so I have used coaches. There are ideas here that a coach can usefully provide. Personally, I have enjoyed this opportunity. And I've been actively working to evolve and it's just hugely important to all leaders. If the idea is there that you do not need anything, then you are totally lost.*

### *7.3.2 Opening doors to cross-sectoral policy planning*

Given their role, leaders have more opportunities than others to engage in change-making, so it is important that they act on this responsibility in terms of delivering action-oriented systems change (Hämäläinen et al., 2014; Williams, 2005). Leaders clearly play an important role in setting the organisational culture; they can 'go against the stream' where necessary and take action that leaves people, organisations, and the public sector in a better place (Tanskanen et al., 2019; Goffee & Jones, 2000). From a human-centred perspective, this applies to initiating emergent cross-cutting policy preparation and, by that means, broadening the scope and quality of possible policy choices. In the research literature, this function has been dealt with as *boundary spanning* requiring a different bridge-builder's skill set and social learning (Zingale & Higl, 2021; Van Meerkerk & Edelenbos, 2018; Carey et al., 2017).

Organisations differ a lot in the ways in which they react to active change-making. As described in the Finnish case study presented in Chapter 5.4, change-makers can find themselves in very lonely positions in an organisation. The interviewees highlighted the importance of cross-sectoral training, co-creation labs, and the increased use of cross-sectoral policy planning to ensure that changes to work processes respond to the needs of the 2020s. In situations where public sector organisations have been slow to adapt to new cross-sectoral ways of working, we have seen a stream of powerful learning and change-making networks and movements emerge, some international like One Team Government, others more country specific such as Change-Makers and Work2.0 in Finland.

Opportunities nevertheless abound in terms of adopting the human-centred, cross-sectoral approach and using it to shape the way in which the government and public sector organisations more generally organise their daily work. The conviction that these structures should enable target-oriented co-creation, not *vice versa* was portrayed by one Director General interviewee with government agency affiliation and over 20 years of leadership experience from different government branches like this:

> *And when we carried out this reform here, special attention was paid to the fact that structures must not hinder cooperation but, on the contrary, we should support the kind of structures that promote and encourage cooperation. And if only someone would shake this Government entity a little, then what could emerge in between, what kinds of new entities from different perspectives would emerge? But this basic organisation has hardly changed in recent decades. After all, the real idea of phenomenon-orientation would be both the strategic allocation of money and true co-creation.*

Another Director General with ministerial affiliation and around 20 years of leadership experience reflected the same challenge as follows:

> *It is important to go into partnerships and working groups that involve other ministries and sectors, so the perspective expands and there you can learn. And even if it happens such that you are left behind or ignored or criticised, it helps to grow and understand the whole. But how is this expansion being done in the basic preparatory work—which is what the officials are doing—this should, by means of leadership, be changed to be actual preparatory [policy planning] work; anyway, the same money we use here in the end and work is done for the same employer [the state]. It shouldn't matter in which ministry's budget allocation a thing is.*

One Director General with government agency affiliation and around 30 years of leadership experience described the desired changemaking thus:

> *It is important to gather a bunch of people around different phenomena, albeit a little forcibly. Then we would develop in practice through work stuff. And whenever it happens that there is a work thing to do with the colleagues you have met on joint trainings, it's nice and it takes you to a whole new level.*

Administrative pseudo-co-operation was brought up as a cautionary example here. As an interviewed Secretary of State with over 30 years of leadership experience from several government branches put it:

> *It is important that organisations collect observations and analyse them, here the level of maturity of the organisations concerned may however be very different. In this government entity, for financial and operational reasons, the cross-sectoral approach represents something of a challenge in terms of budget, functionality, and readiness. I do not see any change in the way the [policy]preparation has been made, even though the preparatory work has been formally brought under the prime minister's office. During this term of government, issues relating to our sector have been at the forefront of governmental business, but this has also brought about tensions that are difficult to deal with. Especially if drastic solutions are made quickly without multi-angled dialogue.*

Tackling complex social phenomena requires multifaceted thinking, the broad inclusion of different parties, and reaching out to include the construction of new solutions from a human-centred point of view. In this challenging undertaking, where boundary spanning is a necessity, leadership meta-skills are very much required. Paying attention to meta-skills increases leadership capabilities in 'boundary-spanning behaviour' which, according to Van Meerkerk and Edelenbos (2018), portrays itself in the facilitative style of project management, paying attention to empowerment and integrative participation, as well as resources mobilisation and creating space for the change from the executive side. When different people from various backgrounds collaborate meta-skilfully, the conditions for emergent learning triggering new solutions (Tynjälä et al., 2020, pp. 162–164) are in place. Unlocking the potential held in the different parts of the system is not done simply by seeking uniformity but rather by creating the conditions for succeeding with different people and different viewpoints and aiming for results that are better than the separate elements involved. One Director General interviewee with government agency affiliation and around 30 years of leadership experience envisioned a good future like this:

> *if the Ministry of Finance were to aim for shared performance targets and leadership agreements across the administrative branches that would create joint efforts across government towards a new societal purpose and these six meta-skills would be needed in many ways and on many levels to help us succeed in that shift.*

## 7.4 Synthesis—learning as an integral part of human-centred leadership development

In this chapter, we have discussed the role of learning in reforming public leadership and public organisations. When we focus on gearing public sector functions to better address the real needs of end users in a cross-sectoral manner, this deliberate paradigm shift in the way leadership training and learning are enabled, both inside and outside public sector organisations, requires support. Leadership development has increasingly become something that is accomplished together in dialogue with other people by solving common societal, institutional, and organisational challenges.

The six public sector leadership meta-skills presented in this book provide a practical concept for accelerating the cultural shift in public organisations and institutions. Highlighting meta-skills fortifies collaboration and co-creation, recognising the multiple voices within public organisations, the government, and society. It also improves the public administration's capabilities to renew its ways of working at pace with emerging societal phenomena, enabling it to deliver on the needs-based public services agenda.

Through theoretical, conceptual, and empirical scrutiny we can see that the job orientation of 'a homo novicius publicae' is

- *future driven*—with 'what do we want to create in terms of the mission and purpose?' being the key question in mind.
- *daring to trust* in emergence instead of insidious planning—creating individual and joint agency.
- *context sensitive* instead of seeking one-size-fits-all solutions—utilising a variety of viewpoints and people instead of looking for rigorous consensus or uniformity.
- *possesses the mindset focusing on opportunities and enabling* instead of on problems and constraints—i.e., resource-, strengths- and solution-oriented.
- *human-centred* instead of decision-maker centred—i.e., opens gates for everyday creativity and nonlinear spaces of opportunity.
- and finally *understands that legitimacy is built socially and change happens through interaction*—i.e., creating inclusion and systems' change by means of these choices.

Leadership training and learning need updating, both by public leaders themselves and by the institutions that enable learning. It also requires the development of pedagogical skills and mindsets supporting a systems view of change. Learning is an important catalyst for human-centred societal change if it is conducted in a collaborative and co-creational manner; it builds on intrinsic motivation and strengths while bearing the citizen and end-purpose of the work in mind. Succeeding in this task requires an understanding that the tools of public leadership in the 2020s stem from the promotion of cross-sectoral co-operation, enabling agency, and the taking of skilful action for bridgebuilding between different angles of entry.

Investing in the development of leadership meta-skills equips public sector leaders with the ability to carry out human-centred government reforms and public service initiatives based on citizen's demands. This change in leadership approach is characterised by being future-driven, collaborative, and relational in the design of transformational processes while lowering the threshold for boundary crossing. It is about taking an active view of the world and of leadership instead of a problem-focused and passive structure-bound stand.

Public sector leaders need different meta-skills in different leadership positions during their career. Moreover, as organisations, institutions, and governance networks evolve, new competencies are required and old ones must be discarded. Therefore, it is crucial to maintain constant learning as an essential component of public sector careers from the beginning to the end and to ask what kinds of meta-skills strengthen boundary-spanning capacities in different situations as well as triggering the emergence of new solutions for the benefit of the citizen. Human learning then is a key component of change-making, both at the individual level and at the societal level.

## Note

1. Information obtained by interviewing Jonas Wells from NNS and South Dalecarlia Coordination Agency, Spring 2021.

## References

Abdulla, A., & Woods, R. (2020). Obstacles vs. resources—comparing the effects of a problem-focused, solution-focused and combined approach on perceived goal attainability and commitment. *International Journal of Applied Positive Psychology, 6*(2), 175–194. https://doi.org/10.1007/s41042-020-00044-6

Acemoglu, D., & Robinson, J. A. (2020). *The narrow corridor: States, societies, and the fate of liberty*. Penguin Random House.

Annala, M., Leppänen, J., Mertsola, S., & Sabel, C. F. (2020). *Humble government: How to realize ambitious reforms prudently*. Government's Analysis, Assessments, and Research Activities. https://tietokayttoon.fi/documents/1927382/2158283/Humble+Government.pdf/

Argyris, C. (1991, May–June). Teaching smart people how to learn. *Harvard Business Review*, 99–109. https://hbr.org/1991/05/teaching-smart-people-how-to-learn

Argyris, C. (1993). *Knowledge for action: A guide to overcoming barriers to organizational change*. Jossey-Bass Publishers.

Argyris, C., & Schon, D. (1978). *Organizational learning: A theory of action perspective*. Addison-Wesley Publishing Co.

Bannik, F. (2006). *1001 solution-focused questions: Handbook for solution-focused interviewing*. Norton.

Bateson, G. (1972). *Steps to an ecology of mind*. Ballantine Books.

Bateson, N. (2016). Knowledge & complexity. *Cybernetics and Human Knowing, 23*(3), 81–84. www.ingentaconnect.com/content/imp/chk/2016/00000023/00000003

Berg, M. E., & Karlsen, J. T. (2016). A study of coaching leadership style practice in projects. *Management Research Review, 39*(9), 1122–1142. https://doi.org/10.1108/MRR-07-2015-0157

Bergman, C., Dellve, L., & Skagert, K. (2016). Exploring communication processes in workplace meetings: A mixed methods study in a Swedish healthcare organization. *Work, 54*(3), 533–541. https://doi.org/10.3233/WOR-162366

Beverland, M. B., Micheli, P., & Farrelly, F. J. (2016). Resourceful sensemaking: Overcoming barriers between: Marketing and design in NPD. *Journal of Product Innovation Management, 33*(5), 628–648. https://doi.org/10.1111/jpim.12313

Biswas-Diener, R. (2009). Average to A+: Realizing strengths in yourself and others, by A. Linley. *The Journal of Positive Psychology, 4*(5), 423–425. https://doi.org/10.1080/17439760902992480

Brooker, J. (2020). *Jump now! Tackle messy challenges better with solution focus collaboration.* Book Printing.

Calleja, C. (2014). Jack Mezirow's conceptualisation of adult transformative learning: A review. *Journal of Adult and Continuing Education, 20*(1). https://doi.org/10.7227/JACE.20.1.8

Cane, J., O'Connor, D., & Michie, S. (2012). Validation of the theoretical domains framework for use in behaviour change and implementation research. *Implementation Science*, 7, 37. https://doi.org/10.1186/1748-5908-7-37

Carey, G., Landvogt, K., & Corrie, T. (2017). Working the Spaces in between: A case study practice of a boundary-spanning model to help facilitate cross-sectoral policy work. *Australian Journal of Public Administration*, 77(3), 500–509. https://doi.org/10.1111/1467-8500.12300

Caride, J. A. (2020). To educate and educate ourselves in time, pedagogically and socially. *Revista española de Pedagogía, 78*(277), 395–413. https://doi.org/10.22550/REP78-3-2020-03

Carless, D. (2007). Learning-oriented assessment: Conceptual bases and practical implications. *Journal of Innovations in Education and Teaching International, 44*(1), 57–66. https://doi.org/10.1080/14703290601081332

Chiva, R., & Habib, J. (2015). A framework for organizational learning: Zero, adaptive and generative learning. *Journal of Management & Organization, 21*(3), 1–19. https://doi.org/10.1017/jmo.2014.88

Ciporen, R. (2010). The role of personally transformative learning in leadership development: A case study, *Journal of Leadership & Organization Studies, 17*(2), 177–191. https://doi.org/10.1177/1548051810368544

Cloete, S. (2010). Team tease: An SF approach to team motivation. *The InterAction, 2*(2), 88–101. www.ingentaconnect.com/contentone/sfct/inter/2010/00000002/00000002/art00007

Cooperrider, D. (2017). The gift of new eyes: Personal reflections after 30 years of appreciative inquiry in organizational life. *Research in Organizational Change and Development, 25*, 81–142. Emerald Publishing Limited. https://doi.org/10.1108/S0897-301620170000025003

Cooperrider, D., & McQuade, M. (2012). The positive arc of systemic strengths: How appreciative inquiry and sustainable designing can bring out the best in human systems. *Journal of Corporate Citizenship, 46*. https://doi.org/10.9774/GLEAF.4700.2012.su.00006

Cooperrider, D., Whitney, D., & Stavros, J. M. (2008). *Appreciative inquiry handbook for leaders of change.* Crown Custom Publishing.

Cronbach, L. J. (2000). Course improvement through evaluation. In D. L. Stufflebeam, G. F. Madaus, & T. Kellaghan (Eds.), *Evaluation models: Evaluation in education and human services* (p. 49). Springer. https://doi.org/10.1007/0-306-47559-6_14

Cronen, E. C., Lang, P., & Lang, S. (2009). Circular questions and coordinated management of meaning theory. *Human Systems: The Journal of Therapy, Consultation &*

*Training*, *20*(1), 7–34. www.humansystemsjournal.eu/library/volume-20–2010/issue-20-1-2

Cronje, J. (2021). A decision framework for blended learning in the COVID-19 pandemic. *Academia Letters*, Article 275. https://doi.org/10.20935/AL275

Darling, M. J., Gruber, H., Smith, J. S., & Stiles, J. E. M. (2016). Emergent learning: A framework for whole-system strategy, learning, and adaptation. *The Foundation Review*, *8*(1). https://doi.org/10.9707/1944–5660.1284

Deci, E. L., & Ryan, R. M. (2000). The "what" and "why" of goal pursuits: Human needs and the self-determination of behavior. *Psychological Inquiry*, *11*(4), 227–268. https://doi.org/10.1207/S15327965PLI1104_01

De Hollanda, P. P. T., Cardoso, S. A. A., Fernandes, C. C. C., & Rosa, C. H. A. (2019). Schools of government: A comparative study. *Revista do Serviço Público Brasília*, *70*(Especial), 15–33. https://revista.enap.gov.br/index.php/RSP/issue/view/219

De Jong, P., & Cronkright, A. (2011). Learning solution-focused interviewing skills: BSW student voices. *Journal of Teaching in Social Work*, *31*(1), 21–37. https://doi.org/abs/10.1080/08841233.2011.539131

De Jong, P., & Kim Berg, I. (2013). *Interviewing for solutions*. Books/Cole.

Devine, M., Meyers, R., & Houssemand, C. (2013). How can coaching make a positive impact within educational settings? *Procedia—Social and Behavioral Sciences*, *93*, 1382–1389. https://doi.org/10.1016/j.sbspro.2013.10.048

Dutton, J., Morgan Roberts, L., & Bednar, J. (2010). Pathways for positive identity construction at work: Four types of positive identity and the building of social resources. *Academy of Management Review*, *35*(2), 265–293. https://doi.org/10.5465/AMR.2010.48463334

Dwivedi, O. P. (2007). On administrative reforms: Musings. *Indian Journal of Public Administration*, *53*(3). https://doi.org/10.1177/0019556120070302

Eigel, K. M., & Kuhnert, K. W. (2005). Authentic development: Leadership development level and executive effectiveness. In W. L. Gardner, B. J. Avolio, & F. O. Walumbwa (Eds.), *Authentic leadership theory and practice: Origins, effects and development monographs in leadership and management* (Vol. 3, pp. 357–385). Emerald. https://citeseerx.ist.psu.edu/viewdoc/download?doi=10.1.1.535.9048&rep=rep1&type=pdf

Elliot, I. C. (2020). Organisational learning and change in a public sector context. *Teaching Public Administration*, *38*(3), 270–283. https://doi.org/10.1177/0144739420903783

Eriksson, L. (2014). The understandings of social pedagogy from northern European perspectives. *Journal of Social Work*, *14*(2), 165–182. https://doi.org/10.1177/1468017313477325

Fischer, K. W. (1980). Learning and problem solving as the development of organized behavior. *Journal of Structural Learning*, *6*, 253–267. https://psycnet.apa.org/record/1997-72114-001

Fisher, W. P. (2021). Bateson and Wright on number and quantity: How to not separate thinking from its relational context. *Symmetry*, *13*, 1415. https://doi.org/10.3390/sym13081415

Fredrickson, B. L. (2013). Chapter one—positive emotions broaden and build. *Advances in Experimental Social Psychology*, *47*, 1–53. https://doi.org/10.1016/B978-0-12-407236-7.00001-2

Frontline, CPI, & Buurtzorg. (2020). *A blueprint for children's social care*. www.centreforpublicimpact.org/partnering-for-learning/a-blueprint-for-children-s-social-care

Gergen, K. J. (2015). *An invitation to social construction*. Sage. https://dx.doi.org/10.4135/9781473921276

Gershenson, C. (2014). Requisite variety, autopoiesis, and self-organization. *Kybernetes, 44*(6–7). https://doi.org/10.1108/K-01-2015-0001

Godat, D. (2013). Solution focused leadership—The other side of the elephant: Four distinctions between SFL and SF coaching. *InterAction, 5*(2), 20–34. www.ingentaconnect.com/content/sfct/inter/2013/00000005/00000002/art00003

Goffee, R., & Jones, G. (2000, September–October). Why should anyone be led by you? *Harvard Business Review*. https://hbr.org/2000/09/why-should-anyone-be-led-by-you

Grant, A. M. (2011). The solution-focused inventory: A tripartite taxonomy for teaching, measuring and conceptualising solution-focused approaches to coaching. *The Coaching Psychologist*, 7(2). Semantic Scholar Corpus ID: 28591093.

Grant, A. M., Cavanagh, M., Kleitman, S., Spence, G., Lakota, M., & Yu, N. (2012). Development and validation of the solution-focused inventory. *The Journal of Positive Psychology*, 7(4), 334–348. https://doi.org/10.1080/17439760.2012.697184

Grant, A. M., & O'Connor, A. (2018). Broadening and building solution-focused coaching: Feeling good is not enough. *Coaching: An International Journal of Theory, Research and Practice, 11*(2), 165–185. https://doi.org/10.1080/17521882.2018.1489868

Green, J., & Grant, A. M. (2003). *Solution-focused coaching: Managing people in a complex world*. Pearson.

Hämäläinen, R. P., Jones, R., & Saarinen, E. (2014). *Being better Gulliford: Living with systems intelligence*. Aalto University Publications.

Hersted, L., & Gergen, K. J. (2013). *Relational leading: Practices for dialogically based collaboration*. Taos Institute Publications.

Hinojosa, A. S., Gardner, W. L., Walker, H. J., Cogliser, C., & Gullifor, D (2017). A review of cognitive dissonance theory in management research: Opportunities for further development. *Journal of Management, 43*(1), 170–199. https://doi.org/10.1177/0149206316668236

Ibarra, H. (2021). Five leadership skills for the future. *Leader to Leader, 100*, 14–17. https://doi.org/10.1002/ltl.20557

Isaacs, W. N. (1999). *Dialogue and the art of thinking together*. Currency.

Isaacs, W. N. (2007). Toward an action theory of dialogue. *International Journal of Public Administration, 24*(7–8), 709–748. https://doi.org/10.1081/PAD-100104771

Jensen Schleiter, A., Secchi, D., & Wiben Jensen, T. (2015). *Emotional dynamics, distributed cognition and strategy-as-practice: The case of tension and commitment in a business meeting*. Conference paper Egos. www.researchgate.net/publication/283687972

Johnson, E. S. (2008). Ecological systems and complexity theory: Toward an alternative model of accountability in education. *Complicity: An International Journal of Complexity and Education, 5*(1), 1–10. https://doi.org/10.29173/cmplct8777

Järvelä, S., Volet, S., & Järvenoja, H. (2010). Research on motivation in collaborative learning: Moving beyond the cognitive—situative divide and combining individual and social processes. *Educational Psychologist, 45*(1),15–27. https://doi.org/10.1080/00461520903433539

Kallio, E. K. (2020a). Introduction. In E. K. Kallio (Ed.), *Development of adult learning: Interdisciplinary perspectives on cognitive development and adult learning* (pp. 1–6). Routledge. https://doi.org/10.4324/9781315187464

Kallio, E. K. (2020b). From multiperspective to contextual integrative thinking in adulthood: Considerations on theorisation of adult thinking and its place as a component of wisdom. In E. K. Kallio (Ed.), *Development of adult learning: Interdisciplinary perspectives on cognitive development and adult learning* (pp. 9–32). Routledge. https://doi.org/10.4324/9781315187464

Kauffeld, S., & Lehmann-Willenbrock, N. (2011). Meetings matter: Effects of team meetings on team and organizational success. *Small Group Research, 43*(2),130–158. https://doi.org/10.1177/1046496411429599

Kaufman, R., & Keller, J. M. (1994). Levels of evaluation: Beyond Kirkpatrick. *Human Resource Development Quarterly, 5*(4), 371–380. https://doi.org/10.1002/hrdq.3920050408

Kegan, R., & Lahey, L. (2009). *Immunity to change: How to overcome it and unlock potential in yourself and your organization.* Harvard Business School Press.

Kim Berg, I., & Szabó, P. (2005). *Brief coaching for lasting solutions.* W. W. Norton.

Kirkpatrick, J. D., & Kayser Kirkpatrick, W. (2016). *Kirkpatrick's four levels of training.* Association for Talent Development.

Kolb, D. A. (1984). *Experiential learning experience as a source of learning and development.* Prentice Hall. www.researchgate.net/publication/235701029_Experiential_Learning_Experience_As_The_Source_Of_Learning_And_Development

Kolb, D. A., & Fry, R. (1975). Towards an applied theory of experiential learning. In C. Cooper (Ed.), *Theories of group processes.* John Wiley & Sons. www.researchgate.net/profile/David-Kolb-2/publication/238759143_Toward_an_Applied_Theory_of_Experiential_Learning/links/57d2aea608ae5f03b48cbdd0/Toward-an-Applied-Theory-of-Experiential-Learning.pdf

Kriznik, N. M., Lamé, G., & Dixon-Woods, M (2019). Challenges in making standardisation work in healthcare: Lessons from a qualitative interview study of line-labelling policy in a UK region. *BMJ Open, 9*(11). http://dx.doi.org/10.1136/bmjopen-2019-031771

Laal, M. (2013). Collaborative learning; elements. *Procedia—Social and Behavioral Sciences, 83*, 814–818. https://doi.org/10.1016/j.sbspro.2013.06.153

Laal, M., & Laal, M. (2012). Collaborative learning: What is it? *Procedia—Social and Behavioral Sciences, 31*, 491–495. https://doi.org/10.1016/j.sbspro.2011.12.092

Laal, M., Laal, M., & Kermanshahi, Z. K. (2012). 21st century learning; learning in collaboration. *Procedia—Social and Behavioral Sciences, 47*, 1696–1701. https://doi.org/10.1016/j.sbspro.2012.06.885

Laloux, F. (2014). *Reinventing organizations: A guide to creating organizations inspired by the next stage of human consciousness.* Nelson Parker.

Lang, P., & McAdam, E. (2011). Stories giving account and systemic descriptions. Perspectives and positions in conversations, feeding and fanning the winds of creative imagination. Reprint in *Human Systems, 22*(1), 351–382. http://www.humansystemsjournal.eu/library/volume-22-2011-1/Tribute-to-KCC

Lang, P., Little, M., & Cronen, V. (1990). The systemic professional domains of action and the question of neutrality. *Human Systems: The Journal of Systemic Consultation and Management, 1*(1). www.humansystemsjournal.eu/library/volume-1-1990

Linley, P. A. (2008). *Average to A+: Realising strengths in yourself and others.* CAPP Press.

Linley, P. A., Nielsen, K. M., Gillett, R., & Biswas-Diener, R. (2010). Using signature strengths in pursuit of goals: Effects on goal progress, need satisfaction, and well-being, and implications for coaching psychologists. *International Coaching Psychology Review, 5*(1), 6–15. Corpus ID: 157060133.

Lipchik, E., & de Shazer, S. (2017). The purposeful interview. *Journal of Systemic Therapies, 36*(2). https://doi.org/10.1521/jsyt.2017.36.2.54

Lowe, T., French, M., Hawkins, M., Hesselgreaves, H., & Wilson, R. (2020). New development: Responding to complexity in public services—the human learning systems approach. *Public Money & Management, 41*(7). https://doi.org/10.1080/09540962.2020.1832738

Lowe, T., & Plimmer, D. (2019). Exploring the new world: Practical insights for funding, commissioning and managing in complexity. *Collaborate*. www.collaboratecic.com/exploring-the-new-world-practical-insights-for-funding-commissioning-and-managing-in-complexity-20a0c53b89aa

Lowe, T., & Wilson, R. (2017). Playing the game of outcomes-based performance management. is gamesmanship inevitable? Evidence from theory and practice. *Social Policy and Administration, 51*(7), 981–1001. https://doi.org/10.1111/spol.12205

Malinen, T. (2004). Interview: The wisdom of not knowing? A conversation with Harlene Anderson. *Journal of Systemic Therapies, 23*(2), 68–77. https://doi.org/10.1521/jsyt.23.2.68.36646

Martin, J. (2019). Rom Harré on personal agency. In B. Allesøe Christensen (Ed.), *The second cognitive revolution: A tribute to Rom Harré* (pp. 35–42). https://doi.org/10.1007/978-3-030-26680-6_4

Maurer-Hankovszky, K., & Szabó, P. (2002). Elemente lösungsorientierter Didaktik. *Lernende Organisation, 9*, 29–32. Available in English as, Elements of Solution-focused Training Methodology. www.solutionsurfers.ro/articles/

McKergow, M. (2011). Language, complexity and narrative emergence: Lessons from solution focused practice. In A. Tait & K. A. Richardson (Eds.), *Moving forward with complexity* (pp. 309–327). Emergent Publications. ISBN 978-0984216598. Academia.edu/1029239

Medina, A., & Beyebach, M. (2014). The impact of solution-focused training on professionals' beliefs, practices and burnout of child protection workers in Tenerife Island. *Child Care in Practice, 20*(1), 7–36. https://doi.org/10.1080/13575279.2013.847058

Mezirow, J. (2000). Learning to think like an adult: Core concepts of transformation theory. In J. Mezirow (Ed.), *Learning as transformation. Critical perspectives on a theory in progress* (pp. 3–33). Jossey-Bass Publishers. ISBN: ISBN-0-7879-4845-4

Michie, S., van Stralen, M. M., & West, R. (2011). The behaviour change wheel: A new method for characterising and designing behaviour change interventions. *Implementation Science, 6*, article number 42. https://doi.org/10.1186/1748-5908-6-42

Moore, M. L., Riddell, D., & Vocisano, D. (2015). Scaling out, scaling up, scaling deep: Strategies of non-profits in advancing systemic social innovation. *The Journal of Corporate Citizenship, 58*, 68–84. https://doi.org/10.9774/GLEAF.4700.2015.ju.00009

Morgan, G. (2016). Commentary: Beyond Morgan's eight metaphors. *Human Relations, 69*(4), 1029–1042. https://doi.org/10.1177/0018726715624497

Morgan, J. W., & Guilherme, A. (2010). I and thou: The educational lessons of Martin Buber's dialogue with the conflicts of his times. *Educational Philosophy and Theory, 44*(9). https://doi.org/10.1111/j.1469-5812.2010.00681.x

Müller, B. C. N., van Someren, D. H., Gloudemans, R. T. M., van Leeuwen, M. L., & Greifeneder, R. (2017). Helping made easy: Ease of argument generation enhances intentions to help. *Social Psychology, 48*(2). https://doi.org/10.1027/1864-9335/a000293

Murtonen, M., & Lehtinen, E. (2020). Adult learners and theories of learning. In E. K. Kallio (Ed.), *Development of adult learning: Interdisciplinary perspectives on cognitive development and adult learning* (pp. 97–122). Routledge. https://doi.org/10.4324/9781315187464-7

Mussmann, C. (2006). Solution-focused leadership: The range between theory and practical application. In G. Lueger & H. P. Korn (Eds.), *Solution-focused management* (pp. 99–101). Rainer Hampp Verlag.

Neipp, M.-C., Beyebach, M., Nuñez, R. M., & Martínez-González, M.-C. (2016). The effect of solution-focused versus problem-focused questions: A replication. *Journal of Marital and Family Therapy, 42* (3), 525–535. https://doi.org/10.1111/jmft.12140

Neipp, M. C., Beyebach, M., Sanchez-Prada, A., Delgado, Á., & del Carmen, M. (2021). Solution-focused versus problem-focused questions: Differential effects of miracles, exceptions and scales. *Journal of Family Therapy, 43*(4), 728–747. https://doi.org/10.1111/1467-6427.12345

Nivala, E., & Ryynänen, S. (2019). *Sosiaalipedagogiikka [Social pedagogy]*. Gaudeamus. ISBN: 9789523450134.

Nonaka, I., & Takeuchi, H. (1995). *The knowledge-creating company: How Japanese companies create the dynamics of innovation*. Oxford University Press.

O'Connell, B., Palmer, S., & Williams, H. (2012). *Solution focused coaching in practice*. Routledge.

OECD. (2017). *Public governance reviews, national schools of government: Building civil service capacity*. OECD. https://doi.org/10.1787/22190414

OECD-OPSI. (2021, September 1). *Towards an anticipatory innovation governance system in Finland findings from the intermediate assessment report*. https://oecd-opsi.org/wp-content/uploads/2021/09/Anticipatory-Innovation-Governance-in-Finland.pdf

O'Reilly, C. A., & Pfeffer, J. (2000). *Hidden value: How great companies achieve extraordinary results with ordinary people*. Harvard Business School Press. www.researchgate.net/publication/40942719

Paavola, S., & Hakkarainen, K. (2005). The knowledge creation metaphor—an emergent epistemological approach to learning. *Science & Education, 14*, 535–557. https://doi.org/10.1007/s11191-004-5157-0

Peterson, C., & Seligman, M. E. P. (2004). *Character strengths and virtues: A handbook and classification*. American Psychological Association, Oxford University Press.

Presseau, J., McCleary, N., Lorencatto, F., Patey, A. M., Grimshaw, J. M., & Francis, J. J. (2019). Action, actor, context, target, time (AACTT): A framework for specifying behaviour. *Implementation Science, 14*(102). https://doi.org/10.1186/s13012-019-0951-x

Priest, S., & Gass, M. (1997, May 1). An examination of "problem-solving" versus "solution-focused" facilitation styles in a corporate setting. *Journal of Experiential Education*. https://doi.org/10.1177/105382599702000106

Puonti, A. (2004). *Learning to work together: Collaboration between authorities in economic-crime investigation* [Dissertation, University of Helsinki, Faculty of Education, Department of Education]. http://urn.fi/URN:ISBN:952-10-1702-3

Raelin, J. A. (2012). The manager as facilitator of dialogue. *Organization, 20*(6), 818–839. https://doi.org/10.1177/1350508412455085

Reed, G. E. (2006, May–June). Leadership and systems thinking. *Defense AT&L Magazine*. Defense Acquisition University. www.academia.edu/8874138/Leadership_and_Systems_Thinking

Rosso, B. D., Dekas, K. H., & Wrzesniewski, A. (2010). On the meaning of work: A theoretical integration and review. *Research in Organizational Behavior, 30*, 91–127. https://doi.org/10.1016/j.riob.2010.09.001

Sandwith, P. (1992). Better meetings for better communication. *Training & Development, 46*(1). Gale Academic OneFile. www.link.gale.com/apps/doc/A12082513/AONE?u=anon~d2c5756&sid=googleScholar&xid=5f52f993

Schein, E. H. (2013). *Humble inquiry: The gentle art of asking instead of telling*. Berrett-Koehler.

Schenck, K. (2013). So what's a meta for? *InterAction, 5*(2), 35–53. www.ingentaconnect.com/content/sfct/inter/2013/00000005/00000002/art00004

Sharry, J. (2004). *Solution-focused groupwork*. Sage.

Sheldon, K. M., Kasser, T., Smith, K., & Share, T. (2002). Personal goals and psychological growth: Testing an intervention to enhance goal attainment and personality integration. *Journal of Personality, 70*(1). https://doi.org/10.1111/1467-6494.00176

Snow, T., Murikumthara, D., Dusseldorp, D., Fyfe, R., Wolff, L., & McCracken, J. (2021). *Storytelling for systems change: Insights from the field*. Centre for Public Impact, Dusseldorp Forum, Hands Up Mallee. www.centreforpublicimpact.org/partnering-for-learning/storytelling-for-systems-change

Sparrer, I. (2007). *Miracle, solution and system: Solution-focused systemic structural constellations for therapy and organisational change*. Solutions Books. ISBN 9780954974954.

Stacey, R. D. (2010). *Complexity and organizational reality: Uncertainty and the need to rethink management after the collapse of investment capitalism*. Routledge.

Ståhle, P., Mononen, L., Tynjälä, P., & Kallio, E. K. (2020). Systems thinking and adult cognitive development. In E. K. Kallio (Ed.), *Development of adult learning: Interdisciplinary perspectives on cognitive development and adult learning* (pp. 191–207). Routledge. https://doi.org/10.4324/9781315187464-12

Tammeaid, M. (2016). Photography—a powerful tool in solution focused use. *InterAction, 4*(2). www.ingentaconnect.com/content/sfct/inter/2012/00000004/00000002/art00005

Tanskanen, J., Mäkelä, L., & Viitala, R. (2019). Linking managerial coaching and leader—member exchange on work engagement and performance. *Journal of Happiness Studies, 20*, 1217–1240. https://doi.org/10.1007/s10902-018-9996-9

Taylor, S., Calvo-Amodio, J., & Well, J. (2020). A method for measuring systems thinking learning. *School Systems, 8*(2). https://doi.org/10.3390/systems8020011

Toom, A., & Husu, J. (2020). Tacit knowledge and knowing at the core of individual and collective expertise and professional action. In E. K. Kallio (Ed.), *Development of adult learning: Interdisciplinary perspectives on cognitive development and adult learning* (pp. 191–207). Routledge. http://dx.doi.org/10.4324/9781315187464-9

Tosey, P., Visser, M., & Saunders, M. N. K. (2011). The origins and conceptualizations of "triple-loop" learning: A critical review. *Management Learning, 43*(3), 291–307. https://doi.org/10.1177/1350507611426239

Tuominen, M., & Kallio, E. K. (2020). Logical contradiction, contrary opposites, and epistemological relativism: Critical philosophical reflections on the psychological models of adult cognitive development. In E. K. Kallio (Ed.), *Development of adult learning: Interdisciplinary perspectives on cognitive development and adult learning* (pp. 208–229). Routledge. https://doi.org/10.4324/9781315187464-13

Tynjälä, P., Kallio, E. K., & Heikkinen, H. L. T. (2020). Professional expertise, integrative thinking, wisdom, and phronesis. In E. K. Kallio (Ed.), *Development of adult learning: Interdisciplinary perspectives on cognitive development and adult learning* (pp. 156–174). Routledge. https://doi.org/10.4324/9781315187464-10

Törmänen, J., Hämäläinen, R. P., & Saarinen, E. (2021). Perceived systems intelligence and performance in organizations. In *The learning organization*. Emerald Publishing Limited. https://doi.org/10.1108/TLO-04-2021-0045

Ungar, M. (2021). Modelling multisystemic resilience: Connecting biological, psychological, social, and ecological adaptation in contexts of adversity. In M. Ungar (Ed.),

*Multisystemic resilience: Adaptation and transformation in contexts of change* (pp. 6–34). Oxford University Press.

Van Meerkerk, I., & Edelenbos, J. (2018). Facilitating conditions for boundary-spanning behaviour in governance networks. *Public Management Review, 20*(4), 503–524. https://doi.org/10.1080/14719037.2017.1302248

Virtanen, P., & Tammeaid, M. (2020). *Developing public sector leadership: New rationale, best practices and tools*. Springer. https://doi.org/10.1007/978-3-030-42311-7

von Wright, J. (1992). Reflections on reflection. *Learning and Instruction, 2*(1), 59–68. https://doi.org/10.1016/0959-4752(92)90005-7

Wals, A. E. J., & Schwarzin, L. (2012). Fostering organizational sustainability through dialogical interaction. *The Learning Organization, 19*(1), 11–27. https://doi.org/10.1108/09696471211190338

Warwick, R. J., Palmer, A., & McCray, J. (2017). Action learning: Ripples within and beyond the set. *Leadership in Health Services, 30*(2), 138–147. https://doi.org/10.1108/LHS-10-2016-0049

Watson, T. J. (2001). Beyond managism: Negotiated narratives and critical management education in practice. *British Journal of Management, 12*(4), 385–396. https://doi.org/10.1111/1467-8551.00216

Williams, G. (2005). Geoffrey Vickers: Philosopher of responsibility. *Systems Research and Behavioral Science, 22*(4), 291–298. https://doi.org/10.1002/sres.693

Wilson, S. (2013). *Thinking differently about leadership: A critical history of the form and formation of leadership studies* [Doctoral thesis, Victoria University of Wellington]. www.researchgate.net/publication/265208344

Zingale, N. C., & Higl, A. (2021). Case study analysis of hermeneutic boundary spanning during policy change and transition. *Administration & Society, 53*(6), 872–906. https://doi.org/10.1177/0095399720976529

Örtenblad, A., Putnam, L. L., & Trehan, K. (2016). Beyond Morgan's eight metaphors: Adding to and developing organization theory. *Human Relations, 69*(4), 875–889. https://doi.org/10.1177/0018726715623999

# 8 The essence of public leadership builds upon human-centredness

## 8.1 The evolution of human-centred organisational behaviour

Intuitively, it would be an oversimplification to suggest that human-centredness has been historically absent from the theories and practice of leadership. Leadership theory has always engaged with the topic of human-centredness due to the simple fact that leadership is about leading people. It should however be noted that the emphasis on the human aspects varies considerably between different theoretical schools of leadership. The same goes for the idea of putting greater emphasis on customers, clients, and—as far as public services are concerned—service users and citizens.

Commenting on Douglas McGregor's seminal work, *The Human Side of Enterprise* (McGregor, 1960), Bennis (2006, pp. xv–xvi) gives McGregor credit for encapsulating "a timely idea in such a striking wording that the idea quickly penetrates the general consciousness". The book, published in 1960, was the only book he ever wrote. Bennis (2006, p. xvi) makes a substantial point in making explicit his views about the value of McGregor's work. In what follows, we will present Bennis' propositions and comment on them from the perspective and context of this book.

First, there is the question of participation by all involved. From the perspective of public leadership, this proposition is as valid from the employee's/service staff's point of view as it is from that of the service users/citizens. The legitimacy of public institutions relates to how they succeed in this participation challenge. Second, there is the resolution between individual needs and public institutions' goals and how this happens. Interpersonal dialogue and relationships between public leadership, service staff/employees, and service users represent the key nexus in applying this consolidation. The question of underutilised potential is also a key point here. In McGregor's treatise on employees, he often reminds his readers about this and conveys the idea that, under specific conditions, employees can raise their professional and intellectual capacity and potential. We believe that this view holds also from the perspective of public service users if they can feel that the use of public services generates value for them. Third, there is the concept of

DOI: 10.4324/9781003205791-8

influence that relates to openness, mutual commitment, respect, working through differences, and joint agenda setting—and not to coercion, evasion, or avoidance. Fourth, there is the question of human growth as an ultimate landmark for the betterment of society. From the perspective of public leadership, human growth generates individually and most of all, collectively, in the context of trust, feedback, learning, and authentic human relationships.

The propositions put forward by Bennis (2006, pp. xv–xvii) and elaborated here are seemingly simple arguments. From the perspective of public leadership, perhaps the most important question behind them rests on the idea of what public leaders value and how they act. Furthermore, these propositions relate to the question over public leaders' assumptions about the most appropriate and useful ways to lead and manage people. From the perspective of this book, these propositions presented by Bennis (2006) based on the inspiration provided by McGregor's seminal book are today still valid, even though the world conceived in McGregor's book has changed dramatically (e.g., the digitalisation, globalisation, climate change and its implications for the traditional economic growth model, the collapse of the traditional social contract around work, the succession of various quality management doctrines and philosophies, the emergence of the service society, the rise of religious fundamentalism).

Considering the nature of public leadership development trajectories over the past century, the transformative evolution of public leadership towards human-centredness has been a gradual, not a cataclysmic, change process, deriving its origins and sources from various public leadership traditions and practice modes that relate, first, to the overall evolution of leadership as a science and practice over a century (addressing the role of employees and human motivation); second, to the drive for quality, related to public sector quality and the improvement in public service delivery beginning in the early 1970s (underlining the role of citizens and service users as well as the evolution of accountability ideology and mechanisms focusing on horizontal accountability measures and practices); and, finally, on the public management paradigms of the late 20th century (particularly New Public Management (NPM) and New Public Governance (NPG), which gradually and eventually strengthened the people-focused leadership and service user participation principles as key elements of public leadership theory and practice.

In the context of this book, public leadership human-centredness concerns four agencies. First, it relates to the leadership function two-dimensionally—both top-level civil servants at ministerial and government agency level public institutions and public managers between top-level civil servants and front line working at the interface between public services and service users. Second, human-centredness is incorporated into organisational life at all levels of organising. This brings in the human-centred picture with public employees working at different public administration layers and branches. For them, the human-centred way of doing things comes alive in patterns of how people are treated and how organisational cultures value the principles, for example, of dignity, thankfulness, and respect for others. The question thus emerges, what constitutes leadership and who exercises it? Metaphorically, whereas, for example, in a monastic life the abbot is all-powerful, modern public institutions take a different route to leadership by sharing responsibilities, trusting each other, and strengthening self-direction. Third, public service delivery is the context in which public authorities and public service staff encounter service users. From a human-centred point of view, accountabilities that concern the performance outcomes for service staff fundamentally relate to how public services add value to the lives and service demands of the public service users. This setting changes the interface between service authorities and service users, which has traditionally been viewed as a paternalistic relationship. Fourth, human-centredness is also reflected in wider, constituency-related agency, to include civil society. The message that public services embody, embrace, and value human values and principles extends the legitimacy of the public sector, public administration, public institutions, and public service.

## 8.2 The evolution of human-centred public leadership

In this book, our intention has been to describe how public leadership is positioned at the complex interface between the policy planning, policy implementation level, and public service delivery. Through this process, we have learned that our book underlines the observation that the bottom-up approach is a big part of this human-centred public leadership. This section summarises the main rationale and arguments put forward in the previous chapters. First, public leadership human-centredness comes with a two-dimensional approach, combining organisational (leadership of people) and service user perspectives further reframing the context of leadership in public institutions. Putting together these two dimensions, public leadership appears to have genuine potential, given its unique practice which differs significantly from leadership perspectives that have occupied other societal sectors and particularly that approach to leadership associated with the private (business) and non-governmental sectors of society. In public institutions and organisations, this development gained influence from the 1960s onwards from multiple leadership theories and streams, for example through the service mentality principles that were emphasised by the servant leadership and humanistic leadership traditions.

Second, the general evolution of public leadership paradigms echoing the status of given public management systems has been a lengthy and non-linear one. If we take an even longer time perspective beyond that of the 1960s, we can see the parallel development contents more clearly between public leadership practice and the development of general leadership theories, trends, and paradigms (see more on changes in theories and paradigms, e.g., Shafritz & Hyde, 2019; Bryer, 2021). From the public management paradigm's and public leadership perspective, the 1990s turned out to be a turning point in this development with the emergence of New Public Management (NPM) and a general shift towards the neo-Weberian government model (which emphasised the rule of law as important and as the basic constitution of public actions). New Public Management (NPM) and New Public Governance (NPG) emerged as the main public leadership management paradigms and thus as landmarks for the public leadership profession—i.e., these paradigmatic changes have not only framed the practice of public leadership, but they have also strengthened public leaders' discipline base as an autonomous leadership style and practice.

Today, public leadership increasingly encompasses the meta-level determinants that create the conditions for human-centredness. These determinants include trust, cooperation, the exchange of ideas, giving voice, and doing things better together. Public services—i.e., the borderline between the state/public domain and the citizens as constituency—has been moderated and re-framed extensively in most of the OECD countries since the emergence of New Public Management (NPM) as the central public management approach at the beginning of the 1990s. This has generated upheavals in service user involvement and participation opportunities, to performance metrics, and to multiple accountability practices—of which, horizontal accountability seems to be the most interesting when considering human-centred principles in public service. To obtain a more detailed view of the development of human-centredness, based on leadership scholarship, public leadership merits more practice-oriented translational research (answering the fundamental questions of what the human-centred way is to practice leadership, what forms it takes, how it is experienced etc.). Eventually, this development process would also benefit people in leadership positions in public institutions, in that they would gain a broader understanding of their everyday work.

Third, recent years have seen a rapid increase in studies focusing on systemic change and the complex nature of public administration. These studies have highlighted the importance of holistic thinking. Researchers and practitioners are familiar with the difficulties emerging when societal problems have been addressed following the prevailing administrative logic. Wicked problems obey neither the limits set by public administration nor those of scientific disciplines. As organisational boundaries are blurring and many services are produced in ecosystems consisting of many actors, there is a need to develop public leadership skills that help leaders to navigate in these multi-actor environments. New skills are also critical to strengthen societal resilience which materialises as a multisystemic phenomenon, including numerous actors and various subsystems. There is clearly then a need for a complexity-informed interpretation of the societal resilience and public leaders' role in contributing to its development because societal resilience is an emergent pattern that arises out of the multiplicity of interactions.

Fourth, increasing human-centredness in public organisations requires us to approach public leadership as a shared endeavour of public organisations, shifting the perspective from law and rule-based restrictions towards co-created learning and solution-building. From the perspective of leading people, this administrative shift brings about a new culture that appreciates the flourishing of people in organisations. In practical terms, this kind of interactional leadership seeks to make the best use of everybody's strengths and capacities providing space for human growth and purpose-driven change-making. This change also helps to deliver another change: in the context of government decision-making and policy planning, this requires using existing organisational structures and resources in a new way—by attracting people to co-create something new together. Succeeding in these crucial leadership undertakings requires meta-skills that portray themselves among public leaders in terms of interaction generating a new impetus in their everyday organisational and cross-sectoral environments. Paying attention to the meta-skills that promote cross-contextual cooperation and renewal is crucial then to succeed in building public institutions and organisations that develop in parallel with the betterment of the society which, in turn, creates public administration structures and services that are more resilient during periods of sudden and predictable changes and capable of anticipating future developments. Adopting and developing leadership meta-skills enables successful boundary-crossing between public institutions and over the interfaces between the public sector and other sectors of society. In public service delivery, however, there is still a long way to go in terms of taking service users along as the co-creators of service experiences and leading the multitude of different available services in a service-user-oriented and needs-based way. Leadership meta-skills pave the way for different service users and interest groups to see and build common goals and become better at learning how to better serve people. In government policy planning, which normally takes place at quite a distance from the average citizen, human-centredness means keeping the impacts of policy choices and their effects on ordinary people in mind during all phases of the decision-making process, assuring multi-angled phenomena-based scrutiny of the issues being addressed rather than a narrow sectoral view and opening the possibilities for direct interaction and dialogue. In building readiness for this type of boundary-crossing collaboration among the public leaders, the importance of meta-skills cannot be bypassed.

Fifth, the primary focus of public sector reform has been on improving, streamlining, and reinventing public administrations, institutions, and organisations. Reform, for example, promises the effective use of public resources, better services, or more inclusiveness in terms of public service implementation. Reforms differ in their ambition levels. Tame reforms are characterised by the low level of uncertainty, and managing them is facilitated by the fact that uncertainties in the process are detached from the people engaging in the process. Wicked reforms, in contrast, are associated with deep uncertainty and competing values, which means that where there are no solutions which are either simply true or false, we instead must rely on better or worse. A human approach to public reform addresses reform as an epistemic process through which reformers frame the operational environment, identify actors, and define norms and ideals. It is often emphasised that reform induces value conflicts which cannot be 'solved' but can only be coped with. Coping can be supported through sensemaking, embracing diversity, and responsive interactions.

Sixth, public leadership approached in a human-centred way postulates re-thinking the pedagogic assumptions of leadership training, as well as re-examining assumptions on effective organisation and change-making. Human-centredness starts from the coherence of viewing public leadership as an approach which appreciates human strengths and enables human agency, rather than supporting a structural or position-based view of power while understanding change-making as relational, motivational, and intentional learning process of human systems. Reforming public leadership through learning builds participation and trust and unlocks the potential of public institutions and organisations. It highlights that legitimacy both in organisations and in society more generally is built socially and through dialogue and that change happens through interaction. When these determinants are shared by both leadership trainers and leaders, human-centredness has a good opportunity to establish itself within public organisations and in collaborations with civil society and service users. Shifting the perspective of training and learning towards a transformative contextual collaboration and co-created knowledge building accelerates both individual and organisational renewal. It is also a prerequisite for the porousness that allows citizens and service end users to better approach the scene and forums of public policy making. Training, learning, and developing meta-skills as part of public sector leadership capacity-building provide a way to renew public sector leadership and public sector institutions in an energising and human way. Investing in leadership meta-skills strengthens boundary-spanning capacities and emergent learning triggering new solutions for the benefit of society.

## 8.3 Human-centredness in public leadership: a generic causal-chain model

Theories of management are useful when they enable leaders to understand, explain, and even predict various phenomena. Good theories help leaders to frame and put scattered observations into context. They also increase leaders' ability to identify emergent issues which may have significant consequences. However, it is always wise to critically assess the premises and ideas behind these given theories. Otherwise, there is a risk that bad management theories destroy good management practices (Ghoshal, 2005). To avoid a naive approach to the promises and pitfalls of public leadership, we believe that defining human-centredness requires a careful blend of theory, conceptual dimensions, ambition to learn from human-centredness and realism to put it into practice. This 'careful blend' of conceptual ideas derives its origins from a generic causal-chain model of leadership, a model advocated by Van Wart (2017, pp. 34–38), who has been a seminal authority in the scholarly academic leadership literature for decades. What follows in this penultimate section is a blend of contextual and analytical framing grounded on Van Wart's (2017) thinking and supplemented by amended ideas originating from Vedung (1997) and Pawson and Tilley (1997). The public leadership human-centred contextual and analytical frame of reference is presented in Table 8.1.

*Table 8.1* Public leadership as a human-centred approach.

| *LEADERSHIP MECHANISM:* *Leadership style factors* | *LEADERSHIP CONTEXT: Contingency factors* | *LEADERSHIP OUTCOME: Outcome and performance goal factors* |
|---|---|---|
| *Focus of leadership:*<br>Meta-skillfullness, employee, service user, and citizen focus.<br>*Behavioural variables related to public leaders:*<br>**Follower sphere:** Supportive, delegative, goal attainment oriented, inspirational, collaborative, self-direction strengthening.<br>**Service user & citizen sphere:** Transparency and participation-oriented, horizontally accountable.<br>*Motivational aspects:*<br>Betterment of society as a general objective, enhancing strong public institutions in society.<br>Betterment in terms of the well-being of employees and citizens. | *Ideal conditions (as intervening variables):*<br>Collaboration network among leader peers for navigating in complex society.<br>Strengthened organisational resilience in public institutions.<br>Broad view of society's public landscape.<br>Structural rotation within and between branches of government and other societal sectors.<br>*Strategies for success:*<br>Action-oriented organisational values.<br>Putting into practice public leadership meta-skills.<br>The abandonment of the risk-aversive public sector mentality.<br>Future leadership career perspective based on learning.<br>Adaptivity to societally complex structures.<br>Understanding of service user service needs. | *Intended desired outcomes:*<br>Improved organisational goal attainment and self-direction.<br>Employee strength deployment and prospective career-thinking.<br>Service user involvement service delivery and satisfaction.<br>*Unintended positive outcomes:*<br>The building of societal responsiveness in public organisations.<br>Strengthened organisational cultures.<br>*Unintended negative outcomes:*<br>Management difficulties of participation expectations.<br>Possible loss of organisational vision.<br>Organisational competence myopias.<br>Naming and shaming mentality in public institutions.<br>*Displacement effects:*<br>The twisted societal image of public institutions.<br>Social media harassment.<br>Failure demand in delivering public services.<br>*Deadweight effects:*<br>The attribution of leadership to government and public sector reforms. |

According to Van Wart (2017, p. 34), "theories of leadership come in all shapes, sizes and formats", which brings about the need to scrutinise, in some detail, the level and nature of human-centredness as it relates to public leadership by addressing the distinct factors that relate to leadership. In the conceptual model created by Van Wart (2017, pp. 34–36), these factors come in three forms: behavioural variables, contingency factors, and performance factors, which are defined as follows. *Behavioural variables* make explicit how leaders 'behave' when they 'do' leadership, i.e., how they act with relation to their followers, peers, colleagues, and superiors (often politicians, elected through processes of representative democracy). These variables define a leadership style that determines what leadership is as everyday practice in public institutions and organisations. Van Wart (2017, pp. 53–54) suggests that there are ten basic leadership styles (partly overlapping) to choose from in practising leadership in public organisations (e.g., Laissez-faire, directive, supportive, participative, delegative, achievement-oriented, inspirational, strategic, collaborative, and a combination of styles). *Contingency factors*, then, are of two types: ideal conditions and strategies for success. Ideal conditions—or intervening variables—predominantly justify the selected leadership mode (i.e., what leadership style to choose to deploy the most effective 'way to do' mechanism and to optimise the desired leadership/organisational outcome). Other factors—those which regulate the strength and quality of leadership actions are labelled as strategies for success or as moderating variables. *Performance goal factors* make explicit the intended effects of public leadership and public organisations (i.e., specific desired outcomes) and can be measured, for instance, from the perspective of public organisations (e.g., organisational efficiency and effectiveness, the adaptivity of organisational culture, organisational resilience) and from the perspective of public leadership practice (e.g., superior/stakeholder/employee satisfaction, the attribution of leadership activities with organisational goal attainment).

In Table 8.1, Van Wart's (2017) criteria have been amended with the ideas provided by Vedung (1997) and Pawson and Tilley (1997). Vedung offers not only a comprehensive set of rationale for programme evaluation but also insights related to goal attainment. For Vedung, public policy goals should be viewed two-dimensionally by making a distinction between intended and unintended effects. As intended goals are positive at the outset (e.g., highlighting the idea of societal betterment), unintended effects can be positive or negative. This means that public actions can also generate negative effects (e.g., publicly supported entrepreneur and employment programmes can trigger malfunctions in the local market economy and cause problems for businesses that are not supported by public funding, causing higher levels of unemployment for certain groups of people). Therefore, it is important to look not only at the gross-outcome effects of public actions but also to explore the negative effects (e.g., the displacement effects which means that the goal attainment of public policies may have caused effects that have shifted to some other sectors in society) and deadweight effects of public actions (i.e., those effects that have taken place regardless of public actions and the activities implemented). Vedung's idea for the typology of multiple effects is important because it makes explicit the possible attribution problems that are incorporated in public actions and in the practice of public leadership in this case. Pawson and Tilley (1997) contribute not only to the academic discussion of public policy and programme evaluation theory and practice but also, at the time, to the emergent discussion of scientific realism. In a nutshell, their main idea is to think—in assessing the value and merit of public actions—about the relation between the public mechanism (i.e., public leadership in the context of this book), the context in which the public action takes place (contingency factors using the vocabulary of Van Wart, 2017) and societal, organisational, and public policy-related outcomes. Pawson's and Tilley's point is that all these conceptual entities are perquisites for understanding the value of public action to society. Bearing in mind the blend of Van Wart's (2017), Vedung's (1997), and Pawson and Tilley's (1997) ideas, Table 8.1 presents a cluster of factors affecting the human-centredness of public leadership practice as an analytical and conceptual summary that has been put forward throughout the chapters of this book.

## 8.4 Synthesis: public leadership as a catalyst for human-centredness in society

This book has dealt with the issue of human-centredness in public leadership. The approach adopted has been two-dimensional. It has considered, first, the leadership of people understood as leading public organisations and their employees. Second, human-centredness has dealt with bringing in service users and citizens through multiple ways of co-creation (public services) and creating de-liberalisation for people to participate in public decision-making. We hope that this practice has scalability potential—to go beyond public sector civil servant leaders and managers towards the political leadership, as well as extending towards other societal sectors, namely, the private and non-governmental sectors of society.

At the end of this book, several questions remain unanswered. First, is public leadership human-centredness a properly defined concept, an empirically tested theory, or just an abstract construct? We would answer, none of these and all of them, depending on the perspective and audience. First and foremost, human-centredness in public leadership is lived practice reaching beyond all governance levels (local, regional, national, supranational) and crossing *sui generis* national borders. Perhaps it is so, that public leaders, public service staff, service users, and academics have treated human-centredness as so self-evident that has not been discussed in detail as extensively as the topic merits. Human-centredness is—from this perspective—an invisible hand of leadership value and practice that has emerged over time across the 20th century.

Second, depending on the nature of human-centredness and considering the variety of public sector systems globally, is it reasonable to believe that human-centredness is applicable to all potential public management systems in existence, even those grounded in different historical and cultural traditions? This is a multivalent question, and it can be answered with both a yes and a no. Human-centredness exist in different administrative and public management systems, but it can be deployed both positively and negatively. Positive deployment refers, for example, to trusting in people and contributing to societal betterment, while the negative way to use it relates to harassing people, oppression, the everyday banalities of evil acts and all sorts of administrative evils, something which has been addressed extensively in the research literatures on administrative science and philosophy (e.g., Adams, 2011; Arendt, 1963; Balfour et al., 2020).

Third, remembering that we set sail with this book by quoting Professor William Foote Whyte (1959, pp. 25–26) and his book, *Man and Organization*, we would like to close the book by quoting Foote Whyte's book once again. He argues (Foote Whyte, 1959, pp. 25–26): "Let me now return to our philosophical question of free will versus determinism. Are men merely pawns of the environmental forces I have been describing? Or can men exert some control over their fates in organizations?" We think this is a very reasonable question and the only relevant landmark question for public institutions, public organisations, and public leaders to survive, to grow, and to reach the next level.

## References

Adams, G. B. (2011). The problem of administrative evil in a culture of technical rationality. *Public Integrity*, *13*(3), 275–286. https://doi.org/10.2753/PIN1099-9922130307

Arendt, H. (1963). *Eichmann in Jerusalem: A report on the banality of evil*. Viking Press.

Balfour, D. L., Adams, G. B., & Nickels, A. E. (2020). *Unmasking administrative evil* (5th ed.). Routledge.

Bennis, W. (2006). Foreword to the twenty-fifth anniversary printing. In Joel Cutcher-Gershenfield (Ed.), *The human side of the enterprise* (Annotated ed., pp. xv–xx). McGraw-Hill.

Bryer, T. A. (Ed.). (2021). *Handbook of theories of public administration and management*. Edward Elgar.

Foote Whyte, W. (1959). *Man and organization: Three problems in human relations in industry*. Richard D. Irwin, Inc.

Ghoshal, S. (2005). Bad management theories are destroying good management practices. *Academy of Management Learning and Education*, *4*(1), 75–91.

McGregor, D. (1960). *The human side of enterprise*. McGraw-Hill.

Pawson, R., & Tilley, N. (1997). *Realistic evaluation*. Sage.

Shafritz, J. M., & Hyde, A. C. (2019). *Classics of public administration* (8th ed.). Cengage Learning.

Van Wart, M. (2017). *Leadership in public organizations: An introduction*. Routledge.

Vedung, E. (1997). *Public policy and program evaluation*. Routledge.

# Index

Note: Page numbers followed by 'n' indicate a note on the corresponding page.